WADERS

WADERS

ANDREW MOTION

McSWEENEY'S
POETRY SERIES

McSWEENEY'S

SAN FRANCISCO

McSweeney's and colophon are registered trademarks of McSweeney's,
an independent, nonprofit publisher in San Francisco.

Edited by Jesse Nathan

Cover art by Karlotta Freier

ISBN: 978-1-95211-987-3

Printed in Canada

2 4 6 8 10 9 7 5 3 1

www.mcsweeneys.net

For Kyeong-Soo

CONTENTS

1

EVENING TRAFFIC

He stopped dead in heavy evening traffic,
leaving his truck unlocked at the roadside
and weaving his way between raindrops
into the cavernous bed store adjacent.

I thought before the lights changed
he looked in that instance like a man
from ancient history frozen in a glacier,
but then I only glanced up for a moment.

In truth he was trying out a new mattress,
seizing the chance to stretch flat on his back
with both hands clasped behind his head
and drumming his heels if I'm not mistaken.

*

I continued to the end of South Ann
then pulled over by the harbor wall
near the building site of the new hotel.

A US Navy destroyer had tied up there,
a sleek beast with both its gun turrets
shrouded in sheets of grey mackintosh.

There was no sign of any crew on deck
but I swear I smelled cigarette smoke,
just a delicate thread or two lingering.

I suppose they must have passed my way,
passed through the girls waiting I mean,
and been invited by them and continued.

*

I lay down later on my own bed to sleep,
but ever since the autumn cold arrived
and those hefty leaves fell from the vine
that sprawls in summer along my fence,

an extremely bright light that shines
all night above the parking lot opposite
and the empty cars glittering like waves
also sends its blaze across my ceiling.

What the hell. I put on my eyeshade
as if composing myself for a night flight
and drop down fast beneath the harbor
to stay there among its darkling rocks.

When I look upward I see schools of fish
in one mind while they change direction,
and sunlight in a dimpled ring as if hands
were washing there, or reaching through.

CHINCOTEAGUE

Walking in Chincoteague among the reeds
stitching thin air and sunlight into shade
I thought of Tabitha the seamstress dead,
Saint Peter at her bedside calling out
Get up!—which led me suddenly to you
on winter evenings from the time before,
hunched in a cone of yellow light, one hand
poising your needle like a trophy saved
from chaos that might any moment now
descend again, the other with a thread
you lifted to your pouting lips and kissed
to dampen and make sharp enough to pierce
the needle's eye before you pulled it tight
and cut the thread in two.

AMONG THE OTHERS

1.

Starlings
    if not God's finger
    dragged through the skin of the world.

God's breath and flag.

The smoke from God's skidding wheels
    in droops
         and puffs
    and plumes.

Starlings if not
      the sweat of air
    as it wrestles to stop God
    breaking through.

2.

Sparking up in their wisteria sleeping quarters
    fireflies are no match
      for the enormous night falling.

Think of them instead as a treasure hoard
    walled up centuries ago
      and now reflecting something of the lamp
a thief has hoisted in astonishment.

3.

When the meteor struck
   this cormorant skimmed away unscathed
      hugging the ocean surface
   then dozing on a rock for thirty million years.

Or he dived
   and dried in a pose of crucifixion.

Human questions will die down soon enough.

In the permanent frost of his brain
   that has always been perfectly clear.

Meanwhile
   no singing.

PANGOLIN

Even David Attenborough has grown older
since I saw him last, his right eye droops
and that famous squaring of the shoulders,
before reminding us how deeply in the soup

we are, is a good deal more wearily done.
But no wonder. He's seriously ancient now
and as for the poor world—both the sun
unfiltered, and the bulging oceans show

how little, or how much, etcetera. The thing
I keep remembering is how a pangolin,
before the poachers strip it bare and bring
those sliding scales (they're only keratin!)

to market, will circle nose to tail as though
insisting purely on itself might be a trick
that saves its life—when we already know
for it and for ourselves there's no such luck.

FOG IN NASKEAG HARBOR

for David Yezzi and Sarah Harrison Smith

When we had done our business with the lobster man,
choosing our dinner from dozens of creatures packed
in a fiberglass tank in his garage, their pincers bound
in thick rubber bands and mouths foamily sputtering,
spattered crimson undercoats the color of pure fury
curdling into fury proper when they were hoisted out
through suffocating air, in spasm now, legs spindling –
when we had done our business with the lobster man
he cast a glance at the still tall cloudless evening sky
and said with the authority of God there would be fog
so thick by morning we would not be able to make out
our hands were we to raise them in front of our faces.

*

Come dawn the next day we saw our own hands alright
but from the bedroom window overlooking the harbor
nothing except a few raindrop-seeds stuck to the glass
although we had never heard rain fall, and beyond them
a fog so thick there was no telling except by good sense
whether we were anchored and still held fast to our point
of granite overlooking the bracken-slope and shoreline,
or already far out to sea and drifting as the current chose
in which case we might strike any moment on the rocks
of Smuttynose or Mahoney or Deer Isle and be drowned.

By eight o'clock another miracle, when fog became mist
and vanished, leaving mother-of-pearl distilled in swathes
of crushed shell that pass for sand this far north in Maine,
exposing the bracken with its Mowgli fronds bent double
under their load of dew, and the bulbous fir tree festooned
with votive oars and life jackets, and wigs of brassy weed
which had slithered down to hide the expressions on rocks,
and the long harbor where one small island after another
gleamed briefly behind gauze then floated through as itself,
and the blocky fishing boats where at last the lobster men,
one of them our lobster man, arrived with the first real sun
to climb aboard then turn their engines and their music on
before heading out to sea with cloud still the only horizon.

THE CATCH

Tangier Island, Chesapeake Bay

Set out early
harbor dock slop
then waves full whack
through painter holes.

West Ridge to port
Uppards to starboard
that stand of pines
clean knocked down.

Valuable uprights
along with gravestones
bones return there
rolled in surf.

Violet marshes
courtship nests
a baseball diamond
ghostly drowned.

*

Who saw this spray
as a willow branch
its feathery swag
more seeding grass.

Who lived from the start
among arrowheads
worshipped in old ways
lay with tornadoes.

Now precious little
and language a sandpiper
peep peep peep
prints last no time.

                    *

Ravenous waves
run for deep water
fiberglass booming
reliable enough.

But think of death
sometimes desire it
flat earth edges
withering away.

Flow becoming
everything becoming
not a blade left
not a grain of sand.

Still gorse in bloom
last of its kind
and wind hissing through
annihilation.

*

Open the brain lid
glimpse the idea
big sky and waves
flicker like snow.

A long way home
with the island gone
sea hawks free
to fish dead center.

This hull meanwhile
crazy with sand grains
worked-in hairs
serving its purpose.

All aboard crab-catch
burned match eyes
blue arms poised
definitely feisty.

*

But think of home
love-cry ascending
touch still dragging
heart by the root.

Envisage the world
as wind across water
where galaxies swim
in the plainest surface.

*

Spray beads shake
their dots of sky
all fall down
damned to pieces.

White roofs now
sleek as leaves
a flood extending
the hungry stream.

Face in the window
that feathery too
the eye delighting
a lifetime longer.

The mind still sounding
one green hill
though belonging knows
what follows after.

HARDLY A DAY

Despair of Life, the Means of living shows
—Virgil, *The Aeneid*, Book 2, line 476,
translated by John Dryden

1.

All time indeterminate now
so this might be late or early
and hardly a day in itself.

Call it infernal nevertheless
with my first move a descent
into air thick with lamentation.

I mean tension in the clock
as it works toward sunrise
and fear becomes natural law.

*

Sparrows in the tree opposite
are ghosts from hollow graves
where green leaves denote death.

Dawn chorus also a madhouse,
given this scandalous deep hush
and human replies anonymous.

Forget even courtesies of touch
its delicious extended sentence
and bracing diamond textures.

*

Which reminds me to make clear
after speaking droplets of spittle
will stay airborne eight seconds.

Long enough anyone might think
to question what does and does not
remain subject to our attention.

If I mention my old man's hands
with their liver spots and arthritis
is that worth the risk of expression.

*

Interest does inflate a little
in the novelty of insults inflicted
e.g. cuticles cracked with washing,

or specs fogged with breath
funneled behind the face mask
and if oniony never that good.

Not to mention regions destitute
where the homicide rate holds up
that being too important to fail.

*

There is still noticing however.
There is the shining eye-machine
in the stalled remnants of life.

Impatient I might be elsewhere
but still favor neglected things
and continue democratic in that

littleness being one form of life
on the bleak shore. Or otherwise
inclined to seek the silent floods.

2.

Midday purgatorial stroll allowed
and today's high tide a black cut-out
the harbor at this time exactly fills.

Matching forms and the cormorant
also adaptive in its timely practice
vanishing then bobbing up well fed.

An angel too it goes without saying
there is one skims the glassy wastes
inviting me on shores unknown to lie.

*

Which leaves things where exactly.
Not a real heaven-sandal
trampling the water mouth,

more likely a lavender yoga nut
head-standing by the dry dock
her world knowingly upside down.

While current in the deep down
never knows what odd beauty
or obstacle might strike it next.

*

The port of entry long since gone
hands pressing for free passage
reefed sails and wonderful land.

Now it is wind over the harbor
where gusts worry at hastily torn
dull troughs and avid gleams.

Meaning in point of fact waves
lap-lapping to amuse themselves
while higher levels bide their time.

*

Fresh out of sympathy cards
things are that bad but easier
than life with no horizon line.

Although most it is true persist
who never did master their iCal
and here remain watchful enough.

Except to be honest why bother
every damn thing is wiped off
in the re-sale eventually all of it.

3.

Evening falling well that is still
reliable although no bird tonight
presumes to launch its flight.

The heavenly host instead rises
from fiery beds to speak to me
but I would say that wouldn't I.

Fireflies that is courteous lights
albeit mad dogs in their fashion
frisky through the dusk advance.

*

Call it paradise lost or more like
paradise impossible when claws
scrabble to rip my skylight open.

Also that dry note like cobwebs
coughed into the boiler's throat
on the dot as darkness settles in.

Until hello as usual the future
meets me with low intelligence
in the first two inches of gin.

*

Occasionally an ocean breeze
stinking of fish could be worse
just think of Gorilla Gang turf.

I might also mention there are
green peppers frying in the pan
and notice one losing it to gold.

But come on! That might well be
enough to contemplate in one day
before shutting down entirely.

*

Avernus which means bird-less
a sulfur lake in all probability
although not here so far as I know.

Here birds doze on black water
or blindly scavenge steered by
piratical scouring of the Earth.

Here my cat sits in the holly bush
with her mouth already wide open
to snaffle wings as they unfold.

*

My country gods I left behind
my soft approaches also
and my dreams that fly the day.

What hope remains my death
must give and that is not
to exaggerate in the slightest.

Meanwhile I fatten myself up
on forms without their bodies
and if feathers and dust so be it.

2

WADERS

1.

In days that follow, when the summer brings
slow afternoons with nothing left to do,
I take what used to be your garden chair
and park it underneath the wayward ash
elbowing forward where the garden swerves
to hide the house from view. In secret then
I conjure up the notebook I have found
among your bedside things and open it.
Blank pages. Thoughts you never had. Or had
but could not bring yourself to say. Should I
imagine them or write my own instead?
I close my eyes and scrutinize the white
that also lies inside me while the ash
rattles its pale green keys above my head.

2.

The milk float with its thin mosquito whine
straining through larch and elder from the lane,
the nervous bottles in their metal basket
intent on music but without a tune,
the milkman in his doctor's grubby coat
and sailor's rakish dark blue canvas cap,
are all invisible, imagined/dreamed
beyond my curtains in the early light,
along with tissue footprints in the frost,
our rinsed-out empties, and the rolled-up note
exchanged for bottles with their silver tops
the blue tits have already broken through
to sip the stiffened plugs of cream before
we come downstairs and bring our order in.

3.

To think the world is endless, prodigal,
to part the hedgerow-leaves and see the eggs
like planets in a crowded galaxy,
to hear my mother's voice advising me
the mother-bird herself will never mind
if I take only one and leave the rest,
means nothing more than showing interest.
As does the careful slow walk home, the ritual
of pinpricks through both ends, the steady breath
that blows the yolk and albumen clean out
but keeps the pretty shell intact, the nest
of crumpled paper in the cedar drawer,
the darkness falling then, the hush, and me
bringing the weight of my warm mind to bear.

4.

Before our time they used my room to store
apples collected from those crooked trees
now wading waist deep at the garden end
in frilly white-capped waves of cow parsley,
and laid them out in rows not touching quite.
I guess all this because the floorboards show
wherever they had missed one as it turned
to mush that sank a stain into the wood.
My bed stands over them and when at night
my eyes grow used to darkness they appear:
the Coxes, Bramleys, Blenheim Oranges
whose names alone can fill the empty air
with branches weighted down by next year's crop
that turn its scent half-cloying and half-sweet.

5.

I try my father's waders on for size
then take, with him encouraging, his rod
and wading stick, his canvas bag, his cap
rigid beneath its crown of favorite flies,
and step into the river. From the bank
he says I look like him. As for myself
I only think of how to stand upright
with water hardening one second round
my ankles, and the next uprooting me
as though I have no purchase on the world.
My father shouts, Don't fight it. I obey.
I let the deluge settle round my heart
then lay me on my back to carry me
round the long sweep beyond my father's sight.

6.

That roofless kennel where the nettles shake
their fine-haired leaves and tiny tight green buds.
That almost-buried path of blood-red bricks
where ivy scrawls across its own designs.
That ruined square of cracked disrupted blocks
where once a summer house turned round and stared.
These were the former glories of the house
although I like their fall and brokenness
much more than grieving for a time I missed.
As also I like walking with the ghosts
that wander through the garden everywhere –
the mother and her son whose footsteps leave
no prints beside us in the grass as though
our selves are all the company we keep.

ON HER BLINDNESS

Too faint for you the ghost-print on the glass
left by the owl that thought your kitchen light
was moonshine and would surely let him pass
in one piece through the house from night to night.

THE RING

Soon my father will lose his wedding ring
but before that happens we take the path
along the cliff edge past the sign that says
Danger: Keep Back because the waves below
have undermined it, and the next big storm
will be enough to bring the whole face down.

I know this but I can't help looking down
and noticing how each wave throws a ring
of primrose foam that's nothing like a storm
round fallen rocks forming a sort of path
for someone who might find themselves below
which no one ever would, my father says.

It's much too dangerous, my father says,
new rockfalls any time might tumble down
and injure them, and while the sea below
looks calm, a quickly rising tide would ring
and terrify them, devastate their path,
then drown them just as surely as a storm.

I hear him out about the calm and storm
and fall in line with everything he says,
continuing along the cliff-top path
until it leads us in a zigzag down
onto the seashore where a wormy ring
of sand recalls the tunneling below.

My father says the North Sea is below
freezing almost, thanks to a recent storm,
and so he eases off his wedding ring
because the cold is bound to shrink, he says,
his fingers, and his ring would then slip down
and vanish like the dangerous cliff path.

He turns around to see once more the path,
the dizzy fall, the rocks, the waves below.
He thinks his only choice is to set down
on one stone of the many that the storm
has carried from the North Sea bed, which says
a lot about the power of storms, his ring.

It slides down out of sight as though the storm
has also switched his path to run below.
This neither of us says. He never finds his ring.

IN THE FAMILY

1.

Like accelerated Proust
(just scenes, no thinking),
or like too-fast drinking,
my old mind lays waste

habits of logical progression,
and instead accidently slips
or decides to leap
from now-Andrew-Motion

into a previous I
via the apparently ample supply
of scenes reminding me
that I saw you die

even during those pretty times
when death
might either have been saving breath
or losing its true aim.

That day in the greenhouse, e.g.,
when I stepped up close
to discover how you chose
in the seedling tray

which young green shoots
to keep and encourage
and which sickly ones to scotch,
but also felt the weight

during that sensitive decision
of your bare thumb
turning further and further down
with tremendous precision

into the dark earth,
which then duly swallowed
the tail of frail white roots
before the rest of you followed.

2.

Only this morning
we scuffled again:
my brother, myself,
on Mersea Island,

crouched in the lee
of a derelict pill box,
that line of defense
deflecting the wind.

The North Sea fumed
in its ravenous bed;
decoy gulls
hung stiff in the wind.

But nothing stopped
the moment of truth,
and to beat the cold
my brother adopted

a thick tweed cap.
Top of the morning
he mouthed to waves
which included me,

then hoisted his cap
before fitting it back
with his face aghast
and starting for France.

3.

At the bend of the stairs
I turned my gaze
to the gravel outside,
where a red-faced man

stood with the fruit
he had stopped to steal
from our apple tree,
then back to the fly

on the windowpane
I had just this minute
squashed with my thumb
and discovered its guts

had the same dull gray
as the coils that oozed
from a firework I liked
called Vesuvius,

while my father agreed
in the kitchen below—
ignoring the fact
I might overhear—

with my mother cooking
he thought that now
I had reached the age
worth listening to.

FINDS AT BURTON AGNES

Remember that dusty hike we took
in the late days of our uncoupling
before place and history buckled?

Now the pigeon we heard clapping
ironically enough in the oak wood,
the hills poising like the North Sea

frozen, even the windcheaters tied
around our waists in flying tackles,
have lost their shine in comparison

to what lay nearby and beneath us
unknown to anyone. We thought
we were the subject and were wrong.

*

Small chalk drum 5,000 years old,
criss-crossed by straps or star-rays
and the fields between these filled

with spirals, triangles, a butterfly
which might be an hourglass.
To beautify is everything we know

and not enough. So think instead
of winding round a cord and that
unspooled again becoming how

the mind keeps track, a standard
measurement. In which case why
inter it here beside these children

like their toy? I'd say to listen for
reverberations of its stone and get
the accurate dimension of eternity.

*

Three children that is: two nose to
nose, one—the eldest—draped over,
their bones scumbled together now,

and the skull of that shepherding one
smashed open by the weight of earth,
transformed into a cup beside the drum.

Above their chalk bed drifting mist
flourishes as we continue briefly on,
deep green oaks and hills dissolving

in their summer stranglehold, our own
children, children we will never have,
following behind in perfect silence.

THE TRUTH IS

You never look back when you walk away,
and hard as I might stare at your bowed head
telling myself it shows you want to stay,

the truth is that it may not or it may,
because for reasons always left unsaid
you never look back when you walk away.

Is it your pride in holding me at bay,
or kindness shielding me from truths I dread,
telling myself it shows you want to stay?

Or is it proof of a profound dismay
you cannot bear to show me, so instead
you never look back when you walk away?

I doubt that, frankly, and I have to say
I'd rather spare you grief and be misled,
telling myself it shows you want to stay.

One thing is clear at least: another day
ends with me hopeful but dispirited.
You never look back when you walk away.
I tell myself it shows you want to stay.

THE BEE TREE

American linden alias American lime,
the family Basswood, *tilia americana*,
a handsome and deciduous street tree

with rugged bark in elephantine ridges
and russet twigs adopting green until,
when flowering, it amplifies with bees

that, as they tune their soporific song
and load their golden panniers, reveal
the tree knew what its name was all along.

*

Breezy with insouciant twitches
the example below my room
is playing the part of Summer,
flouncing her new feather boa

catching the eye of her paramour,
me, glued in the frame of my window
to see if a rival appears and is caught
in the black satin net of her shadow.

*

Loving a thing
(I know) is when
a becomes the.

The tree in view
I know is what
I love to see.

                        *

One night and then for a week after
a young gray heron with no idea
of the right and wrong place to live
takes up residence in the branches.

Only occasional passers-by below
pay any attention; mostly they see
a heavy white shit-trail and assume
it was sparrows making a bivouac.

Eventually I will realize my duty here
is to understand reality as it appears,
and see the puzzle is not what goes
where. The problem is one of scale.

                        *

In one account
the gods of Earth
cascaded down
on silken threads

and came to rest
in leaves of trees.
I witnessed them
in what became

a final blaze
of sun today—
a razor sheen,
here, then gone.

I want no more.
The life of things
will never speak
in any tongue.

*

Wearing a bright orange hi-vis jacket,
the leaf-blower dismisses fallen leaves
from left to right along the sidewalk,

while the wind with no color or form
orders them back in the other direction
to settle beneath the tree once more.

*

First thing and last thing
at this time of year,
a skein of Canada geese fly
over my roof and the tree

squeezing their rubber horns.
It is what I expect to hear
but the tree looks up amazed,
her dark fountain frozen.

So much extravagant move-
ment and all of it chosen!
In the aftermath a breeze
kicks off a different scene,

but the most branches do
is to stir very sluggishly,
as spars of flotsam will
in the weak hands of the sea.

*

This late in Autumn
she wears a contraption
made of gold leaf,
but even such glamor
is never enough
to keep her from harm.

The faintest breath
of disheveling air
and she's poor again,
a shivering waif
whose one ambition
remains to be warm.

*

As the tree points her bare arms
like a sinner appealing
to heaven

she makes her final count:
four pumpkin-brown leaves
and a fifth distressed green.

Beauty now depends on relation,
with her head unbowed
and these rags her crown.

*

Like my love when she takes off her ring
and lays it on the nightstand beside our bed,
the tree places her last leaf on the sidewalk
and stands completely naked wanting to play.

*

In one interruption
a buzz saw echoes
from Domino Sugars
across the harbor:

maybe the sound
of a sugar tree sliced
into saleable logs—
that mechanical whizz

and saccharine crash.
But this is a thought
I keep to myself
and the tree never has.

*

When Winter ends
I plunge my hand
inside the tree
and neighbors think
I'm about to snatch
a dove from a hat.

It's not like that.
I'm testing heat
and degrees of dark
to see if they match

the kind of box
I have in mind.

*

How are you today
is the question arising
from the street below
but only *today* carries.

How am I today,
which is not yesterday,
and still less tomorrow,
although not separate.

I wish it were otherwise.
I wish I could snap free
from the long link chain
of time's old fuckery.

To live without guilt,
sure, but also to quench
hope with its curled tongue
slavering to become.

Give me the green tree
again. Give me the word
now rising through shade
that finishes in sun.

3

ESSEX CLAY

1.

The intact frost of early morning
   and a blade of ice
    drawn from the tap in the stable yard.

The village as they drive through
   half asleep under twisting chimneys.

The church   Victorian Doomsday
   moored to the hilltop
   with its pretty flotilla of graves.

The weathervane cockerel's gold and flying eye.

The lane
   straightening beside water meadows
   its thatch of bare chestnuts
    shattered with daylight.

Gravel in the ford
   washed by the brimming stream
   the Blackwater
and pebbles magnified   tawny   beach colors
   with that other river   the river of shining tar
   shivering below.

Last night's snow dust
    in suddenly wide-open plowed fields.

Flints like hip bones and knee bones.

Clay clods supporting
    miniature drift-triangles on their windward side.

His mother beside him
    yellow hair trapped and placid in a hairnet
clean cream jodhpurs   red collar   black riding jacket
    stock like a bandage
    gold pin
        adorned with the mask of a fox.

*

He is seventeen   confident   opinionated
    and definitely at odds
    on this subject at least.

He does not approve.

But when he glances into the footwell
and sees his mother's narrow feet
    fluffy sheepskin slippers
    peddling by turns at the brake
        accelerator   clutch
    he is silent.

He cannot bring himself
   to make that scene again.

                    *

In the car park of the White Hart
   also the bus stop
he condescends   tips his head a little
   kisses his mother goodbye
a skim of skin
         is enough
but catches still in close-up her hairnet
    a black cobweb   tougher of course
   and feels it
      scratch
         the tip of his nose.

Then he is busily out in the wind buttoning his overcoat
   the ankle-length   topsoil brown   soldier's greatcoat
   the British Warm
         borrowed from his father without permission
   stolen more like
which makes him   he thinks   beside his holdall
   soldierly after a fashion.

                    *

Exactly as his mother grinds the Hillman into gear
    the silhouette of his bus
        bulges over the hilltop beyond the White Hart.

He flinches away
    to discover his mother's face is already no longer her face
        but an after-image
    hovering a little way behind her
as she guns the engine   and wriggles into the traffic flow.

Her exhaust plume rapidly fades into the specter of a specter.

Dark petrol dribbles escaping the pipe
    might well be a trail of breadcrumbs
        dot-dot-dot all the way home.

And the bus
    the snow-filthy bulk of it
            amazingly
        stops
when all he does is hoist his arm.

                        *

From the front seat on the top deck
    smearing window-fug
        with the whiskery coat sleeve that makes an O
    fringed with delicate scratch marks
he can pretend the world is simply a cabbage field
    creased with snow.

And there is no one the entire journey
　　even to notice　　let alone ridicule
　　either the relief or the alarm of solitude he reveals
by leaning his head against the glass
　　on the trembling chill
　　　　and pretending he is asleep.

Although despite appearances
　　he is still watching in fact
　　the shadow of the bus shrink
　　　　where it meets a burst of heavy snow
　　then elongate as the snow weakens

while he also imagines
　　clay six feet deep
　　the malevolent pasty glue
　　　　the ash smears and ocher
　　waiting with all the time in the world
　　to sculpt its lead around gumboots and plow blades
to rear and obliterate whatever it can

until an hour has gone ·
　　and the bus flusters into Sawbridgeworth
　　　　where its shadow abruptly
　　concertinas in through the window and sinks down
　　among the other shadows already assembled
　　　　and is absorbed.

*

Clambering out
    holdall thumping the door
        he forgets himself the instant he sets eyes on her.

Juliet.

Her face and playful love-name coinciding.

Her black hair   black
    not a black enough word.

Her red mouth.

Her skin white   but mainly full
    ripeness.

Her eyes liquid pouring
    straight into him
    her eyes glittering and
        completely ignoring her mother
    which he should not
so he shakes her mother's hand.

Headscarf   specs   face-fuzz powder
    how was your journey
            her space-voice dustily tinkling far elsewhere
    with Juliet continually here-and-now.

*

His cheek brush-collides with her cheek
 and he smells   peppermint
  should have thought of that.

Never mind.

Just find the car and
 but
 wait
 front seat or back.

Back.

Then ok hunch forward laying one forearm flat
  on pale green clammy plastic
 apparently all relaxed like
 despite Juliet's black hair a swelling wave
trapped inside her collar.

And breathe
 is the cliché
 he cannot resist.

And keep
 breathing.

Until they set off and shops   shop fronts   shoppers
     distract him
and the heater cranks up
     and mist solidifies into dribbles on the windscreen
     and Juliet
     summons him
simply by wriggling her hand
     inside this wave of black to set it free
          so it flood-slithers
over the shoulders of her coat onto his hand
     which jolts in the electric shock.

                              *

Afternoon already somehow
and despite the cold
     clouds and snow shoveling in west from Siberia
          he and Juliet leave her house for a walk.

He spares a thought for his mother   wondering
     will she be home already
     defeated
          she would say that
     defeated by cold.

But the thought vanishes
    when they step from the lee of the house
    and ice puffs immediately slit his eyes
confronting a dead prairie sprinkled with snow stones
       his greatcoat not so ridiculous now
no more at least than Juliet's white fur hat
    and Doctor Zhivago number
    fur blustering at collar and wrists
    while she butts into the wind
      one blue vein pulsing in her porcelain neck.

*

Down the long narrow headland they go
snowflakes sugary on winter wheat dithering beside them.

Jesus though it is laughable this cold
    laughable and
    gets the better of him
    rotating him
veering back the way they came
    only to find Juliet
      akimbo in his way.

His eyes
    blur in the windswept peering.

His heart
    starfish
    touches all four walls
        ceiling and floor
    of his rubbery chest cave.

His hand
    animaly inside her coat
    scalds on astounding radiator heat
        when he touches bare skin
    between the waist of her jeans and her jersey.

And her mouth
her mouth gasps into his ear
    the blaze of his own name.

                    *

But first the party   they did give their word
and Juliet
despite his flagrant stare
    to show how much he would rather not
despite her own luxurious deep mermaid curl
in the wave of an armchair
    left hand   square-tipped fingers
      tightening round her bare ankle
    and the little vein mesh there
    the blood delta
      pale lavender
Juliet is determined they should keep it.

*

So he collects and removes himself
as ordered into the soft-lit
    oak-paneled spare room
        with its cosily low ceiling.

He takes time
    shaking out creases
    from his brand-new white shirt
        with risky jabot collar
    his father would not be seen dead in.

He sounds
with all he dare of his weight
    the nervous springs in the high bed.

He begins to imagine later
    or will it be her room.

*

But a knock interrupts him
    the polite wood-knuckle sort.

Juliet   he thinks
has she   what
        is she
    here now already.

Then the door creaks and not Juliet
    Juliet's mother
        stares in.
His smile stiffens.
He asks himself   has she spied in his head
    and seen their plan laid bare.

But no.

Spying would not explain why
    she is pinching her nose
        dimpling the eiderdown with her fingertips
            the silver blue eiderdown
    stitched into lumpy waves
to occupy herself with the pattern she makes.

*

A grown woman she is obviously
    with her whole face crying
        like suffocation.

A face doing its best to look up
    still crying
        then methodical   for a moment at least

his father
has called
on the telephone
and his mother.

*

But now it is his turn to interrupt
    his turn
        to take pity and
    with the inspiration of dread
with a mind-burst like a sapling instantly becoming a tree
    tell her   he knows already
            what she is about to say.

Adding to himself at least
    he has expected this
        all his life
and is Juliet   where
            waiting
        or not any more
            how could she be waiting
or him
        how could he still be waiting
                not after this.

*

In the pause following he sneaks
    a look into the future   thinking
        he can beat facts at their own game.

He sees his mother on a high pillow bank
    yellow hair no
    shaved hair no   brush-bristles
        no longer summery fair.

Succulent bruise red green gray
maturing into a dead color already
    moleskin.

  Beautiful thinness
  bloating into a big belly
    a flagon
  pumped with drugs through a murky tube
    darting into the crook of her elbow.

Eyes dusty   eyes shut   eyes
    for three years
    he cannot yet
        count exactly cannot
        bring himself to that horizon
    eyes sunk into eye sockets unconscious
        three years despite oxygen tank chipped silver
treasure salvaged from a wreck.

*

Grief
  too little a word no spring lock inside it.

Grief
  primed to snap back to its opposite
  the second her eyes open again.

                    *

In the next moment
  which he understands at once
    is the beginning of continual afterward

which is silence arriving
  as Juliet's mother runs out of herself
    and leaves him be

he pulls back the curtain
  and watches the moon shimmy
    over a neat fold in her cloud-sheet.

He sees her decide
  it is time to change her orbit
    and swing closer to Earth.

She whispers to him
  in a white voice like ice hardening on glass
    she has taken over the duties of the sun.

That her bright light will now shine by day
    as well as by night.

And he accepts this
    believing the moon in sympathy
        will rest her entire mass
    against the shell of his chest and be
      weightless.

                        *

Injury is the word that occurs first   injury
    then accident
    when he goes to the party after all
        it is what his father thinks best.

Injury when Juliet's mother
spins away in a red-flare exhaust-ghost snow-flap
        relieved
            he understands.

Accident when he passes into a stranger's house
he thinks might not exist
    except as a stack of crammed and shining rooms
      bolted together with very loud music.

Although when it comes to the sitting-room dance floor
edged with a Stonehenge sideboard
　　which will never be the same
　　　　after that cigarette-end gouging a ruby furrow
words fail him.

He tries under the space-trip disco-ball spangles
　　scattering trashy light.

And again in the profound heat and rock-thrash
　　clamping shadows and flesh together.

He must tell everyone
　　he has this new distinction
　　　　at the top of his lungs if necessary.

Listen　　listen
　　his mother is dying　　probably
　　even as he stands here
　　　　his mother is dying.

But the room　　　the entire house
　　decides this is not important
　　　　and music drowns it.

*

Juliet will not have it either
he must be cheerful
　　he must be occupied
　　　　he must be　　taken out of himself.

So in the run-up to midnight after someone has dimmed the lights
    in the maze of a slow song
    she lays her long bare arms on his shoulders
        allowing him to breathe
the sleepy vanilla scent in the crease of her elbows
    linking her fingers behind his neck
    resting her head on his forehead
        her black hair
            her skin sealed to his skin
    as if her thoughts could flood him
with the perfect blank of superior happiness.

                        *

It is embarrassing or
        shameful
    when they slither into the deep cracked back seat
    of her mother's Rover
because at midnight sharp she has come to collect them
and he discovers after a mile or two
    Juliet is no longer noticeable to him.

Not really
    noticeable.

Not compared to the silence
    as witch trees weave their way home into a tunnel.

Not compared to doubly darkened air
    sharpening pin-prick foxy eyes
        in the fuel gauge and speedometer.

Not compared to Juliet's mother
    sparking a cigarette
        then milling open her window
    and the quick night traces
still outdone by blurry smoke whiff.

Not compared
    now he turns his head and ignores Juliet entirely
    to the lane behind them
        the underworld mouth
    where taillights flare gravel under narrowing branches
    and a wreckage wake of his mother's possessions

    her riding jacket   her red collar
    her hairnet   her sheepskin slippers
    her stock   her gold pin with the fox mask
    her black velvet hard hat

her whole wardrobe of everything in fact

not much for a life

vanishes along with the moment he sees it
    the glutinous pasty clay
        that stretches and grabs.

2.

After forty years Juliet emails him
    can they meet.

He reads her message again   and again
    counts.

Forty years
since their first   last
    lamplight sweating on oak panels
    and the moon intriguing a leaded window.

Four zero
since her not   slithering black hair
    creamy bare shoulders
        big soft wide not
mouth.

                        *

St. Pancras station   the Booking Office Bar her idea
where he arrives early like a fool
      giddy a bit
            thanks to the head-back stare
                  at the barrel vault roof
and sunset's lilacs and charcoals
      staining the many-colored glass.

Or are they ghosts of the steam age?

At any rate he expects to kill time
      inspecting John Betjeman
      coming or going or both
            in his flapping bronze mac
      trainspotting the Eurostar
flyblown chisel-face of the future.

                              *

But Juliet is before him.

It must be Juliet surely
      trailing in one hand her overnight wheelie bag
      the other
clamped to a mobile
      husband probably
            in Paris or wherever.

And why not
    except his disappointment exists
    and is frankly
with his tail and whatever else tucked between his legs
    scandalous even to him.

Also why not   Juliet is wearing dark glasses.

Very big   black-framed
    curved
    very dark dark glasses
    masking her face
        as far as possible.

But that is all he has time for.

Bye   she says
her first word
    to the phone naturally
Bye
    as her wheels trundle to a halt
and he imagines himself replying
when in fact he is silent
    and staring.

*

Not her hand
    smuggling the mobile into the slit
    of a navy overcoat pocket.

Not the beautiful black bob
    gray at the roots.

Not the mouth   again not the mouth
    thinned under its lipstick twirl
    think of the millions of breaths
        the words
            smoking over her lips
                think of feet wearing a threshold.

He is staring at scars on her face.

Scars dicing into her lips
    little hairline fractures
    glaze cracks
        fissures and faults
not faults
    scars.

What happened.

These are his first words
    after forty years.

What happened.

*

Juliet's hair shakes
blooms in a bridling pony-toss
    then soothes
and fits neatly again.

Therefore
    he pretends he has seen nothing
    and with a bluff enthusiasm
        which for all she knows
    is now his natural everyday manner
    steers her into the bar of the Booking
Office
and round to a
        bloody miracle
    empty corner table
without another word spoken.

*

In their background
    departure times and destinations
        deploy watery echoes.

In their immediate vicinity
    high-gloss woodwork   new olde
England
horse-brasses
    and everyone taking a breather.

He follows suit.
He orders house white
    and the waitress who understands speed is the essence
    rattles it down
        in a seriously nervous silver ice bucket.

*

Grief he remembers
the strange contentment of living in suffering
without the possibility
of such unhappiness
in whatever remained of life.

Grief even providing
a peculiar pleasure sometimes
like the buzz a mind feels
when a tongue
slides over a painful tooth.

Grief whispering he might be content
to live in a mirror-bright shining steel universe
that could never be altered.

*

Juliet meanwhile
    eases her dark glasses
    a fraction along her nose
        and rests them on a pale skin-ridge
the main scar there
    to hide it.

She has no time to waste
    and without the least flourish or sidestep
    delivers a boiled-down recitative
namely   her life since last they met
    and parted.

    Au pair   marriage
    two children   girls
    living in   freelance
    films   documentaries mostly.

                    *

He shuffles his glass on the tabletop
    creased apparently
    with ghostly cloth wipes
and cannot prevent himself
    still looking
    when he thinks she is not looking.

Hair sweetly hooked behind one ear.
Jittery ear stud on its plump little flesh cushion.

White throat   very white throat
   swelling when she swallows
   in the shadowy collar V
     of her expensive black silk shirt.

Surprising   forgotten
   blunt-tipped   almost square-ended fingers
   nails painted   milky suns
     rising from the cuticle.

*

Then it is his turn he thinks
   but that is not what she came for.

She stalls him.

She slips off her dark glasses
   and shows him her white face
     naked.

*

If she told him a wildcat
   launching out of a pine forest
if she told him a lightning strike
   a firework
     an alleyway bottle-lunge

if she told him a particularly sharp idea
　　an idea like a star bursting
　　the most brilliant idea imaginable
had shattered out of her brain
　　through her left cheek
　　engulfed her left eye
and scorched her mouth

he would believe her.

But　　a company car
　　the M40 late at night
　　darkness　　rain
　　and roly-poly down the embankment
outside High Wycombe

High
　　Wycombe

which Juliet offers
　　without him asking
he cannot accept
　　and must.

*

No sooner
    the wet tarmac rubber smear
    the barrier can-opened
        the mud gouge   the grass rip
the steaming hush and maniacal dashboard electrics
than his mother again
    in the seamless flash footage
        he cannot avoid quoting by heart.

Head shaved gingery bare
    tiger-slash operation scar
eyes pulpy   bruise-mashed
oxygen   tank   tube   mask
        oxygen itself
pressing a skeletal finger to pursed lips

    sssssssssssshhhhhhhh.

                *

Which Juliet has no time for
insisting the point is not
    only her accident   the point is
after that she lay unconscious three days.

Midwinter fields   no footprint
        among flint bones
            and bristly Essex clay lumps
no shadow
        only the seething snow surface
            opening
        and closing its lacy arms.

Unconscious Juliet continues
        then awake but not
awake-awake   not
herself.

More like a radio dial twiddling
picking on day one
        a French signal
        and her voice speaking French only
on day two
        her voice in English
        with a French accent
on day three normal
        her everyday voice
        beaming back to her
            from the spangling gas-warps
        of infinite deep brain space.

*

A waitress at the table adjacent
    clears cutlery like glittery fish in a handful.

He meanwhile
    sponges up what he hears.

He wrings out Juliet's language
    and squeezes it into his own language
    storing it
        along with the car wreck
    the rain the rain the rain   the headlights
    stubbed in embankment plow.

Although
    as the debris
    the confetti windscreen glass
        the smashed boxer's face fender
            the car radio
    churning its excitable jabber regardless
        and   in the midst of it all
Juliet's silence
    her scarred face   her unconsciousness

as the combined tangle of this groans
creaks
scrapes
sinks
settles
and enters his consciousness
he reminds himself
    Juliet is not his punishment.

Not if he chooses.

                    *

At which point
    she arrives at the point
    that brought her here in the first place.

She tells him   at last and suddenly
    she can remember nothing
    of her life before the accident.

She explains
    having forgotten everything herself
her sister remembered
        she knew him once.

She asks him what passed   please
    between them.

She is in his hands
she says.

*

Whereupon he straightens to meet Juliet's eye
meaning
      he enters her eye and drops
    down through liquid green-flecked chestnut brown
      into the dead center.

Which is prepared to believe him
albeit a cat look
    I know you   do I know you
      remind me.

And he deliberates.
weighing her featherweight weight.

He deliberates
    then lets her go.

He lets her life go
    and Juliet in their time remaining
      barefaced   dressed in her wounds
        leans forward
to catch what he has to say.

ACKNOWLEDGMENTS

Warm thanks to Jesse Nathan, and my gratitude also to
Amanda Uhle and the rest of the team at McSweeney's.
Poems in this book have previously appeared in the
following: *The American Scholar; Beltway Poetry Quarterly;
Fusion; Hopkins Review; Interim; Liberties; The New Yorker;
The New York Review of Books;* and *Times Literary Supplement.*
"Essex Clay" is a condensed version of the poem first
published by Faber and Faber in the UK in 2018.

ABOUT THE AUTHOR

ANDREW MOTION was born in London, England, in 1952 and worked for many years as a freelance writer and publisher before becoming Professor of Creative Writing at the University of East Anglia and then Royal Holloway College, University of London. His poetry has received the Dylan Thomas Prize, the Ted Hughes Award, and the Wilfred Owen Poetry Award, and from 1999–2009 he was the UK Poet Laureate. During this time he co-founded the Poetry Archive (poetryarchive.org), and in 2009 he was knighted for his services to poetry. In 2015 he moved to the United States, and now teaches in the Writing Seminars program at Johns Hopkins University. He lives in Baltimore.

Subtle Energy Work

Meditative Exercises for Healing, Self-Care, and Inner Balance

Dr. Synthia Andrews, ND

Foreword by Dannion Brinkley

NEW
PAGE

This edition first published in 2022 by New Page Books, an imprint of

Red Wheel/Weiser, LLC
With offices at:
65 Parker Street, Suite 7
Newburyport, MA 01950
www.redwheelweiser.com

ISBN: 978-1-63748-008-3

Library of Congress Cataloging-in-Publication Data available upon request.

Cover design by Leah Kent
Interior images in Chapter Three by Jeff Smolen with input from Johanna Sayre
Interior by Debby Dutton
Typeset in Sabon LT and Avenir LT

Printed in the United States of America
IBI

10   9   8   7   6   5   4   3   2   1

This book is dedicated to the three wise and great-hearted women who are my guiding stars. My aunts, Sandra Clark and Patsy Kalla, and my longtime friend, Johanna Sayre.

Contents

The circumstances of your life do not describe and cannot constrain the greatness of your soul.

—Synthia Andrews

Foreword

Every month, I receive eight or nine books by new authors to review. Eleven years ago, my wife Kathryn brought me the draft for the first edition of this book, *The Path of Energy*, along with several others to consider for endorsement. When I read the book, I was astounded. In it, Synthia details the many ways in which we are subtle energy. She provides a framework to understand subtle energy along with exercises to discover how this energy works. Anyone who isn't sure that subtle energy is real just has to try the exercises to learn the truth for themselves.

I love this book. I have loved it from the very beginning. I kept the original on my nightstand, carried it around with me, and later installed it on my phone. When I travel, I take it on the plane. Then if I'm stressed or out of alignment, I browse the book and do some exercises to reorganize myself and realign to the right path. In this book, Synthia has written a masterpiece.

Subtle energy is who we are. Understanding who we are and how to fully use our abilities is what this book is about. It's a guide to the mastering of self. Today, even science is looking at the subtlest of reality. We are learning that subtle energy is quantum and quantum is subtle energy. Scientists have created robots only an atom thick and nanoparticle machines that fit on the tip of a needle—no longer just the head of the needle, but the tip. And then there is you, a beautifully designed, living, cocreative, spiritual being. The exercises in this book reinforce that you, along with everyone else, are greater than all the nanomachines science has created. You are the ultimate nano-machine.

This book is about connection. It's a gift in this time of worldwide divide and disconnection from our true self. Understand that the discord and disconnection of today are not an accident. They're a planned part of the evolutionary times we're in. Now, more than ever, we need to engage the subtle beauty of who we are and restore the vitally important connection with self. This book offers a gateway to that reconnection, a gateway back to self.

We all want to be somebody. What Synthia has done in writing this step-by-step guide is help you understand that you are, already, somebody. The exercises prove and reinforce how great a somebody you are, a somebody who makes a difference in the lives of others and the world around you. This book supports you in operating and working from your true self.

The energy laws within help you interact in this refined level of nature. While the laws of nature can open your awareness, it's the nature of those laws that assist you in accessing higher consciousness. To use this book to its fullest, you need to set a goal higher than simply becoming an adept or an Empath. This book teaches a language anyone can grasp; it's basic. Your success depends on your motivation, on the reason you want to sense, understand, and use subtle energy. The panoramic life review we undergo when we leave this plane is never about what we do, but the motivation of why we do it. Without intent, without proper motivation and a will to achieve, much of what you learn and master in this book can work against you. That's because knowing better is not good enough. Being better is the only way now.

What is being better? Since I died, went to the other side, and came back not once but three times, people often ask what the purpose is of coming here to Earth, to this plane of existence. I'll tell you. Our job here is to practice being God. You think I'm having fun? Sit down and write all the things you consider God to be—compassionate, loving, caring, all knowing, protective, everything—and then ask yourself how many times a day you get to practice being one of those things. The answer is all day, every day, you get to practice all of these qualities. All day, every day, you get to practice being God. And that's our job. That's why we're here.

The truth of death is that it doesn't exist. We never leave heaven. This 3-D reality is an apparition. We manifest our consciousness here, accepting the illusion that we are separate, helpless, and lonely. We take on these limited illusions in order to practice being God. When you practice being God, you uplift more than yourself; you uplift every level of consciousness. This book will improve your ability to feel frequency and subtle energy. However, that is just the beginning. What's next is to feel the frequencies and harmonics of the evolution underway and participate in raising consciousness.

If you have ever wanted to empower yourself and be able to uplift others, this book is for you. Synthia has a splendid way of explaining subtle energy. But remember that life is not a science, it is an art. If you bring your heart to mastering these exercises, you will have the motivation and intent to succeed, and your success will bring you one step closer to being the somebody you truly are.

I love you,

—Dannion Brinkley, international and *New York Times* bestselling author, *www.lightstreamers.com*

Acknowledgments

Thank you to Michael Pye, acquisition editor at Red Wheel Weiser, for believing in this book and lobbying for this second edition. A big thank you to Jeff Smolen for the hours spent on the meditation illustrations that readers have asked for, and Johanna Sayre for the original drawings.

A huge and heartfelt thank you to Dannion Brinkley for writing the foreword to this edition. His instant understanding of my intent and ability to take the meditations so far beyond this book is an inspiration. My conversations with Dannion made all the difference in aligning me to the work ahead. So, thank you Dannion and Kathryn for your continued support and encouragement. And thank you to everyone who has kindly endorsed this book. Your support is so very much appreciated.

Thanks to Johanna Sayre, whose open-hearted conversations are always instructive. Thank you to the many teachers and mentors who inspired me through the years, especially Louisa Poole, Iona Marsaa Teegarden, founder of Jin Shin Do Bodymind Acupressure, Richard Kastl, Barbara Marciniak, who wrote the foreword to the first edition of this book, my husband Colin Andrews, and my children Erin and Adriel. It is through the greatness of others that we see ourselves most clearly.

Thank you to my agent John White and the staff at New Page Books and Red Wheel/Weiser. Last but not least, thank you to my clients and patients, who leave me speechless with their greatness of spirit.

Introduction

Two years ago, a scrappy Appaloosa mare came to live at our small farm. She was short, only fifteen hands, and held her jaw in a tight knot of disapproval. Her coloring was strawberry roan with white spots that looked as though someone splattered white paint over her, earning her the name Pebbles. There was wild in her eyes.

Pebbles did not know how to trust. She leapt through doorways, anticipating danger. She stood at the back of her stall and watched everything with a hypervigilance that didn't allow her to relax. She was afraid and managed her fear through intimidating behaviors. She nipped at hands, threatened to kick, and flattened her ears when approached. When she was ridden, she was a bundle of nerves, jumping at the gentlest of commands.

I expected that, like every other horse I'd brought home, she would relax as she learned that she was safe. However, none of the methods I used to provide safety helped. She refused to hook up and acted persecuted by the practices of natural horsemanship. I knew she had not been mistreated at her last home, even though she acted as though she had. Despite her threatening behavior, however, she wasn't a mean horse. She threatened, but she never actually bit or kicked anyone. Her preference was to run away, and if she couldn't run, she controlled her space by scaring people.

It took a while for me to realize that she was overly sensitive; she had no boundaries or protection against the stimulation around her. She perceived a normal talking voice as shouting. A gentle leg squeeze when being ridden felt to her like being kicked. It didn't matter how soft I was, the signals themselves instilled anxiety. It was as though we were speaking different languages.

My friend Tiokasin Ghosthorse is fond of saying, "We can't wake up with the same language that put us to sleep." He explains that our language shapes more than our thoughts; it shapes our ability to think. I believed I understood what he meant, that language structures how we frame reality, but Pebbles showed me his true meaning. She showed me that language itself is coded with emotional truama. It didn't matter how gentle I was. The words, signals, and ways of communicating were coded for her with fear from past trauma. The trauma she experienced was not intentional; she was loved, just misunderstood.

Pebbles and I were lucky. We found a gifted trainer, Kristen Eliot, who gave us a new language, a new way to communicate with each other that relied heavily on energy awareness. From using this language, Pebbles no longer has wild in her eyes. Her jaw is relaxed, and I can't remember the last time she nipped at anyone. She engages our activities with trust.

When looking at the polarized conditions of today, laced with division, fear, and righteousness, I think that perhaps, like Pebbles, we need a new language. The one we're using is coded with too much trauma. Our words no longer communicate; they direct us into corners for battle. This is a pivotal time in history. We're facing unprecedented, worldwide challenges. Old ways will not take us forward. We have to step outside of the box.

The social and environmental chaos we're experiencing is a reflection of changing energy patterns. Frequencies are shifting, causing disruption as the old crumbles. Ancient prophecy calls this a time of purification, a cleansing of outmoded ways via pestilence, pandemics, social divide, economic disruption, and Earth changes. This may well be an evolutionary leap since prophecies also claim the purification is the birthing of enlightenment.

Whether enlightenment is delivered dead or alive is entirely up to us. How each of us acts, what each of us brings to the table during this transitional period is creating the quality of the future. If we remain attached to the frequency of fear and division, we will present the worst of who we are as the best we have to offer and create it.

We need a language of the heart, one of transformation that everyone can speak and understand. I suspect this language is energy awareness. Every person, in every nation, every animal, every plant, Earth itself communicates through energy. We are born understanding this language; we are wired to negotiate the energy terrain of transformation. In the process of socialization, we've simply forgotten how. This book offers support in remembering.

We're not born with an owner's manual, and this book isn't trying to be one. Each person experiences subtle energy in their own way as their instincts direct. This book is meant to provide suggestions for helping to wake up a sluggish system. It's meant to help open energy perceptions and use the principles of energy to create better life conditions. It supports people to confidently develop their own almanac of energy awareness. In a time when deception abounds, we must learn to trust our own perceptions.

In a holographic universe, the whole evolves together. Every one of us is part of the transformation underway. We are all being challenged to grow. Each of us holds a piece of the puzzle, and to move forward we need to put all the pieces together. We are born for this time. Let's awaken and take this leap into greater awareness delighting in the mystery of life.

It is my greatest pleasure in offering this material and my greatest hope that you find it helpful. As Dannion says in his foreword, what's missing in this book is the intent and heart the reader brings. Bring all of yourself, bring your heart, and enjoy!

How This Book Works

Part I (Chapters 1–4) consists of thirteen meditations to activate and move energy. They're the heart of the book and include instructions with simple descriptions, benefits, and uses. Instructions are basic, easy to follow and understand, and encourage individual discovery. Part I also explores principles of subtle energy, explains how to activate the energy meditations, provides simple guidelines, and offers a troubleshooting guide to pinpoint difficulty.

Part II (Chapters 5–9) puts personal experience into a larger context. Anyone having difficulty understanding the meditations might want to read this section first. For others, this section will be old hat and skipping it is the best thing to do. This section describes energetic anatomy, explores the relationship between energy and emotions, assists in translating energy information, stimulates intuition, and examines the role of attitudes and beliefs in creating human experience.

Part III (Chapters 10–21) provides hands-on exercises for everyday use. The more you experience and practice moving energy, the more useful this section will be. It covers basics such as how to ground and center, create protection, clear space, manifest your dreams, vision your life, and build intimate relationships. It also helps develop higher awareness through expanded perception, remote sensing, channeling your higher self, and more. This section provides suggestions when the possibilities seem overwhelming. The recipes are suggestions only—examples of what is possible. Use them as is or modify as desired. They are only meant to inspire. The recipes are based on the thirteen meditations, but feel free to substitute your own inspiration.

Appendix A provides a brief description of how the meditations came into being and were originally used. Most are original, although some are modifications of traditional patterns with a new twist.

Appendix B is a resource guide with a list of books, websites, and resources for further study into energy reality.

Part 1

Transformation and the Art of Moving Energy

This book provides tools to activate our energy body. The thirteen energy meditations help us awaken inner resources and abilities. Old patterns are cleared so new solutions can emerge. Letting go of the old isn't always easy, especially in today's uncertainty. The activations/meditations strengthen our connection to our authentic self. They promote alignment with Spirit, allowing us to live fully in the present moment.

Everything we need we already have; these energy meditations help us access our inner abilities.

Chapter 1

The Terrain

Energy, Matter, and Awareness

Einstein's groundbreaking equation $E=mc^2$ (energy equals matter times the speed of light squared) explains that energy and matter are the same substance separated only by their rate of vibration. Energy and matter live in a perpetual dance of transformation: energy entrained in matter, matter released back to energy. This dance creates the world we know—all we see, feel, hear, taste, touch, sense, and measure with our technology. The body-mind is the instrument through which we experience and explore this world.

The body-mind is equipped with all the senses and extensions of the senses needed to fully engage the universe. Every experience we have, we're biologically wired for. Think about it: You can't experience anything you're not designed to experience. You can't physically see frequencies of light outside the design of your eyes; you can't physically hear frequencies outside the design of your ears. So if you're having spiritual experiences—visions, telepathy, talking to people who have passed over—it's because you're designed to.

We are designed with extensions of our everyday senses that engage multiple levels of reality. These are our energy senses. Most of the time, we ignore the information they provide.

We are capable of so much more than we allow ourselves to experience. We have been civilized right out of our senses!

The Adventure

Astrophysicists who discovered dark energy and dark matter have determined that these mysterious forces, which can be neither seen nor measured, are the scaffolding on which all matter in the universe is organized.[1] Mystics agree: matter is organized into form by energy templates, and the energy side of Einstein's famous equation is the creative part of the dance.

Interacting with the energy side of the spectrum is what we call subtle-energy awareness. As chapter 6 explains, energy organizes matter through frequency templates. Everything we know exists along a spectrum of electromagnetic frequency. Science can measure the signature frequency of thoughts, attitudes, emotions, and beliefs that impact our energy and create life conditions. It is said that to change our world, we must first change our mind. But what comes first, changing our mind or changing our energy?

Interacting in the realm of subtle energy is natural. We do it all the time. It's part of the automatic functions of our subconscious mind. However, we don't have to leave this interaction to our subconscious programming. The energy that holds our body in form is accessible. Our body-mind is equipped with everything we need to consciously interact and create our reality. We've just forgotten how. The energy activations in this book are meant to wake up our memory. No more theory is necessary—no philosophy, historical perspective, warnings on what might go wrong, or directions on the "right experience" are needed.

We can remember only through experience. Each of us is different. Your experience is yours. No matter what anyone else has to say, including me, only you know what's true for you. These meditations are maps. Change and adjust them as you chart your own territory. However, if the world of energy feels completely unfamiliar, refer to Part II for energy anatomy, terms, and principles.

The following energy keys form the foundation of the meditations. You may agree with them or not; it won't affect the power of the work. Ultimately what we believe determines our experience; however, your beliefs don't have to match mine for these meditations to be effective. If, as you read, your inner truth is validated, it will make your commitment to the practice stronger. If your belief is challenged, it can make your desire to explore and discover stronger. If your reaction is incredulity and ridicule, you probably won't try the meditations.

Energy Keys: Quick Access Summary

E=mc²
Energy and matter are the same stuff; the only difference is the rate at which they vibrate. Light is the first order of measurable matter stepped down from pure energy.

Like light, subtle energy is both a particle (matter) and a wave (energy).
Subtle energy has palpable substance and is also experienced as flow.

Energy and matter express along an electromagnetic continuum.
What we call subtle energy is a frequency with a vibration and wavelength that exist outside of the range of our current technology.

Energy can be neither created nor destroyed.
Energy and matter are in continual exchange. Influencing one impacts the other.

Energy waves are carriers of information.
In nature and technology, information is coded on carrier waves as vibration.

Everything in the material world has an energy template.
The human template holds a record of a person's individual karma, constitution, and life plan. Awareness can access this template.

All ancient cultures engaged subtle energy.
Every culture has a concept of subtle energy and name for it. Here are a few: Life-force, prana, chi, ki, pneuma, mana, ruan, ka, orgone, biofield, Life-field, and Factor-X.

Key functions of vital energy are to:
- organize matter into form.
- unify by providing the interconnecting web of life.
- nourish and sustain life.
- encode and transmit information.
- be a vehicle for consciousness.

Energy flows through matter in an organized manner.
Energy flows into, through, and around matter in an organized fashion and can be interacted with and influenced.

Energy structures are universal.
Plants, animals, humans, Earth, all have them. These structures can be interacted with to improve health, balance, and harmony.

The nature of energy is to move.
Moving energy nourishes and sustains life with information and vitality. Stagnating energy causes illness, emotional disturbance, pain, disillusionment, fear, and any number of ailments.

There is no such thing as negative energy.
Energy is neutral. It can be held in patterns that produce "negative" effects, be directed by someone with harmful intent, flow backward, or become stagnant and produce limitation. However, when the pattern is broken, the energy released is simply energy.

Each of us is responsible for our own space.
No one else created it; no one else can change it.

Energy flows where the mind goes.
Where you put your attention is where your energy flows.

Awareness is intentional attention.
When the intention of the heart directs the attention of the mind, magic happens.

We are the sum total of our choices.
Although born to specific circumstances, how we respond and what we do are choices.

To change our life, we must first change our mind.
This requires two things: awareness and discipline.

We are spiritual beings having a human experience.
We have access with our soul and spirit to spiritual realms. We're biologically wired for the experience, and our body-mind is the instrument we have to traverse these realms.

Guidance comes in myriad forms.
Everyone receives guidance differently. Every way is right.

Only love is real.
Love is the glue that holds the universe together, and unconditional love is the most powerful and transformative force possible.

High frequency is not necessarily more spiritual than low frequency.
High frequency creates complex patterns; low frequency creates simple patterns. Both are connected to spirit. Getting stuck in one or the other is where problems arise.

Perception is influenced by expectation.
To receive truthful energy information, we must silence our bias and expectation, observe with non-judgment, and let love be our guide.

Awareness is medicine.
Change is a reflection of awareness.

You are never alone.
We live in a spiritual universe and are connected to all other sentient beings. Support is always available.

Chapter 2

The Tools

The Keys to Awareness

The meditations in this book activate patterns of energy flow in the body that stimulate specific states of awareness. Energy is dynamic and interactive. It flows along precise pathways (meridians), is gathered and transformed in identifiable centers (chakras), and radiates through the energetic biofield (aura). Energy, as vibration, streams through these structures creating an ever-changing mosaic of geometric patterns. Each pattern represents a specific response to an individual event. Most of the time, the patterns are fluid, changing with our perceptions, thoughts, and emotions. When we become locked in one point of view, the patterns become more solid. How we manage our energy reflects the quality of our being, and the quality of our being attracts our life.

Activating the energy flows in these meditations can be life changing.

Activating Energy

The body-mind is our vehicle for exploring the sea of energy we live within. How our internal energy flows between energy structures is determined by our thoughts, attitudes, beliefs, and emotions. Energy activations shift the configuration of our energy, freeing the mind from limiting patterns and enhancing our energy sensitivity.

Let's imagine the energy pathways in our body as highways with exit ramps and subsidiary roads. The energy travels on different routes for different reasons. For example, consider how your energy might flow during a disaster. You might mobilize meridian energy along the kidney and bladder meridians to give you a boost of physical strength. At the same time, a surge of energy might activate your Root Chakra, stimulating survival instincts, and Third Eye Chakra, activating higher perception, while your aura coalesces into a protective shield. As much vital life-force as possible is directed into configuring your energy flow to ensure survival. If you could freeze-frame your energy picture at this moment, you would see a very precise pattern of activation.

Now let's look at a different event. Consider getting married. In this case, your energy might mobilize along the heart meridian as you access your Spirit. Your Second Chakra of creative sexual energy and passion might be filled, along with your Heart and Crown Chakras. Your aura might glow with the frequency of love. Freeze-framing this pattern reveals an entirely different activation from the previous example and invites an entirely different level of awareness.

Every thought impacts energy flow. Repetitive thoughts create solid configurations of energy that are difficult to shift. Since energy creates reality, using the same patterns creates the same outcomes. Many people are stuck in survival patterns even when there's no threat. By seeing every situation as threatening, the same configuration is activated and the same life conditions are attracted.

Being stuck in a pattern causes missed opportunities. The meditations in this book help shift firmly lodged, reactive patterns to allow more creative options.

Meditation

Meditation is the practice of quieting the mind and becoming free of the incessant noise of surface thoughts that maintain a continuous cycle of reviewing the past and anticipating the future. In this state, it's easy to lose awareness of the present. In meditation, free of our background chatter, we can more easily access our deeper wisdom in the present moment.

The point of power is always in the present moment. We can't change the past, and the future unfolds according to the decisions of today. Experiencing the present is a full-body awareness that engages all the senses. It intensifies focus and stimulates awareness. Quieting the mind involves letting go of habitual thoughts and freeing our attention. With a quiet mind, awake to our body, we can access deeper states of awareness.

The key to meditation is the breath. Paying attention to the breath brings attention more deeply into the body and promotes inner stillness. Slowing the breath changes brain waves, allowing better access to the subconscious mind. In this state of awareness, we can assess the flow and vitality of our life-force. The free attention gained in meditation connects to our true self.

Different brain-wave states promote specific levels of awareness. Very simply, beta waves are the highest in frequency and govern the everyday awareness and mental function. As the mind quiets, it moves into deeper, lower-frequency states of alpha, theta, and delta brain waves. Alpha states enhance creativity and the ability to visualize. Theta states enhance deep meditation and intuition. Although delta states are mostly related to sleep, in meditation they can produce detached awareness and provide the greatest gateway to the divine intelligence. High and low frequency are both connected to Spirit; low frequencies allow us to move more deeply into the contact.

Visualization

Visualization is the creation of images in the mind's eye. Visualization uses the focus produced in meditation as a canvas. We can use this canvas to create images that reflect our intentions and desires; as well, we can use it to sit in receptivity, inviting images to form as a direct, intuitive communication. Visualization uses the focus of meditation and the power of the imagination to create. Since the body responds to our mind, the images we see influence our physiology. Visualization is used by successful people in all fields, including athletes, CEOs, and scientists to increase creativity and performance.

The meditations in this book rely on visualization to activate energy flow. Meditation focuses the mind, and visualization activates the energy flow. Our body provides the feedback to know whether or not we're successfully moving energy. What we feel, sense, and experience becomes our guideposts on the journey.

Experiencing Energy

The first step in developing energy awareness is paying attention to the body. The energy that flows into, through, and around us is converted into body events such as muscle tension, breathing patterns, emotions, gut feelings, sensations, thoughts, memory associations, and a multitude of other communications (see Chapter 9). Body awareness is the first step toward energy awareness.

Through the body, distinct sensations indicate energy flow. There's no right or wrong sensation. Some people feel a vibration or "quickening." Others describe a feeling of softening or opening. Either may be accompanied by the sensation of warmth and flow, as though warm water, honey, or lava is pouring through the body. For some, the body seems to expand and become more sensitive. People experience "rushes," electric tingling, warmth, pressure, magnetism, electric shocks, and an assortment of other sensations. Some see flashes of light or undergo changes in awareness.

Feeling energy is different for everyone. We may have only one of these sensations, all of them, or none of them. As we engage this practice we discover our personal energy language. By taking note of our sensations, perhaps cataloging them in a journal, we begin to recognize shifts in energy and what they mean.

Attention and Discipline

Experiencing the world from an energy perspective can be elusive. We're probing for something very subtle while much of our past training was focused on the obvious. In addition, our bodies may not be highly tuned. How many times have you been told to relax when you thought you were?

Being disciplined in paying attention to and interacting with the information from our body-mind opens the door to energy awareness. Discipline requires maintaining a fraction of our awareness on our body at all times. This is part of what is meant by "being present"—in other words, being in our body for the events that are taking place.

Get in the practice of taking inventory. Right at this moment, what muscles are tense? Where are you relaxed? What do you feel, other than simply "better," when you release a muscle tension? How deeply are you breathing? How much resistance and how much flow are present? Can you feel flow? What is that like for you?

There are no right or wrong experiences, no need to change a thing, just notice. Then ask, what are you responding to that's creating this condition? Maybe it's past conditioning, or maybe a present influence, or maybe a future desire. Nothing to change, just notice.

Authenticity

Energy awareness is developed using the combined tools of meditation, visualization, and discipline. Through observing how our energy responds to the outer world of events and relationships and the inner world of thoughts, beliefs, attitudes, and emotions, we make conscious the choices that shape our life. With meditation, we tune into our deeper beliefs, where they come from, and whether they serve our authentic self. By paying attention to energy flow, we observe how our beliefs direct our choices and create the circumstances of our life. Visualization activates our creative abilities and consciously connects our intentions to our authenticity. In this way, our world begins to reflect the core of who we are.

Shifting Frequency

The meditations/activations in this book shift frequency. Through different activations we can experience these different frequencies and the mind-states that accompany them. Being able to shift frequency is both the goal of energy awareness and the best tool we have to access it, so the better we are at shifting frequency, the better we will be at sensing energy.

As we become more proficient, we are able to feel the fine vibrations of specific frequencies. In the meantime, the best way to shift frequency is to change emotional states. Heightened frequency can be experienced using self-transcendent emotions. These are emotions that lift us above everyday concerns about our own lives to those that encompass the larger whole.[1] Transcendent emotions include elevation, compassion, unconditional love, awe, wonder, admiration, and gratitude. The energy flow created through these emotions activates the best of who we are.

We can shift into a self-transcendent emotion by remembering a time when we felt that emotion. Immediately on remembering, the emotion begins to shift our frequency. The more we can embody the memory, the more we will shift. How did the muscles feel, the heart, the stomach? What thoughts accompanied these feelings? If we can immerse all of our senses in feeling the transcendent emotion, we will shift our energy.

A process to shift uses the principles of neuroplasticity. Lauryn Maloney-Gepfert (*nfiheals.com*) refers to this as see, say, and do. In our version of this process, feel the self-transcendent emotion and visualize yourself in a situation where you are deep into the emotion. At the same time, use your voice to further direct you to the upliftment of that emotion. This can be a chant, a prayer, an affirmation, or the name of a guru. Finally, as you're doing this, perform an action such as placing a hand over a chakra, such as your heart. Doing this will promote a shift.

Whenever shifting frequency is discussed in upcoming chapters, remember the transcendent emotions and this process.

Chapter 3

Patterns of Light

Thirteen Energy Meditations

The energy meditations in this chapter activate specific energy flows for different aspects of awareness. They're divided into three types: Foundations, Explorations in Light, and Master Activations.

The *Foundations* (meditations one through four) open the energy body and provide the basis for the rest of the meditations. They activate the primary human energy structures of the aura, chakras, Hara-line, meridians, and Energy Template in relation to the larger universe.

The second group, *Explorations in Light* (meditations five through ten), open patterns of energy that shift perception. Working with them welcomes conscious cocreation of life circumstances and experiences.

The last group, *Master Activations* (meditations eleven through thirteen), accelerate individual and planetary growth. They function in a larger capacity than personal development, opening doorways into universal consciousness.

The final meditation, *Dancing with the Elements,* is not an activation; it's a moving exercise to integrate your energy senses. It's in honor of Louisa Poole, my first energy teacher.

If you're experienced with meditation, visualization, and moving energy, you probably want to jump right in and explore the patterns. However, if this is new to you, here are some guidelines for getting started. If you have a hard time visualizing the meditations because you don't know the energy structures being referred to, start with Part II of this book for a basic construct.

Prepare a quiet, comfortable space.
It's helpful to practice in a quiet, comfortable location, free from interruption. When you're proficient, you'll be able to shift your energy

patterns anywhere, anytime. In fact, to use the meditations as a tool of awareness requires you to access them as needed in any situation.

Open sessions with the first meditation, the Spiral Pillar of Light, and keep it active during the session.
This creates a sacred space and establishes an intention aligned with unconditional love. It also keeps your own energy contained so that your attention remains focused.

Breathing helps energy move along the intended pathways.
Conscious breathing uses the diaphragm to breathe deeply into the lower abdomen. Use your inhalation to build energy and your exhalation to disperse energy. Vision the pathway you wish to activate being filled with your breath when you inhale. Vision your breath as light. You might find the light changes colors to activate different aspects of a meditation.

You can practice the patterns in any order.
The first four meditations are arranged to complement each other and become the foundation of the rest. If you're just starting out, you may find it useful to practice them first. However, the meditations can be used in any order. The order in this book is not the order in which they were developed, so don't limit your exploration.

Trust yourself. If the flow seems wrong for you, change it.
Use your body to feel or sense the rightness of any particular pattern. If it doesn't feel right, explore it and find out how it wants to be for you. The practice is interactive. Energy has consciousness and, as you work with it, you'll create patterns that match specific needs in your life.

Activation of these energy patterns can be done in a split second.
At first, you may need to use the directions to activate the patterns. With practice, you'll be able to activate the pattern by simply visualizing the pathway. Later, you'll only need to think of the name of the pattern, or feel the need for one and it will activate automatically.

Keep a journal of your experiences.
At the end of a meditation session, record what you felt, saw, sensed, and experienced. Make a library of energy experiences to guide your practice. This book is not an authority; each of us has access to our own creative inspiration. A journal is a record of your journey for charting and navigating your path; it's your library of energy information.

Pay attention to communications from guidance.
Communications may take the form of dreams, synchronicity, strong intuitions, a sense of knowing, abrupt new thoughts, unusual feelings, and body sensations, and also more direct means such as telepathy, clairaudience, clairvoyance, or visitations. Do not discard any inspiration: Spirit speaks to each of us uniquely and personally.
Enjoy yourself! Joy is the point.

The Foundations

Spiral Pillar of Light

(Adapted from a meditation of author/channel Barbara Marciniak.)

Keyword: Centering

Description: This meditation activates the boundaries of the aura, creating a powerful circle of safety and healing. The pattern pulls energy in spirals from the heavens to the center of the Earth, creating a pillar of living light. This is the center of the storm: the winds are howling all around; within this space are calm and peace. It is sacred space, a place to go for connection, protection, renewal, and resolve. It is unconditional love.

Benefits:
- Strengthens boundaries and promotes centering.
- Harmonizes the aura and supports spiritual alignment.
- Enhances inner strength and resolve.
- Promotes calmness, inner peace, balance, clarity, and focus.
- Provides protection from unwanted influences.

Use to:
- Create sacred space.
- Cleanse rooms, buildings, gardens, and so on.
- Enhance focus and clarity.
- Establish balance when feeling off-center, overwhelmed, or in shock.
- Establish safety and protection.
- Maintain your boundaries during chaos, conflict, or draining situations.
- Contain and transform your own destructive projections.

Flow Pattern:
Visualize yourself standing on Earth.

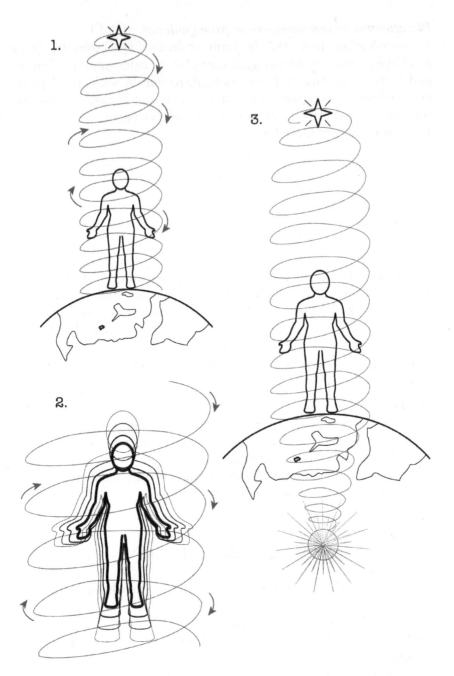

Spiral Pillar of Light

Breathe in and imagine a cascading spiral of light descending from your Source, your Star in the sky, flowing into, through, and around you to Earth.

Visualize this energy filling and enveloping you in safety and healing.

See the Spiral reinforcing the edge of your aura, strengthening your boundary with pulsating light.

Radiate your energy outward to meet the circumference of light.

This is your space; fully inhabit it and fill it with light from your Star.

Invite spiritual guidance.

Breathe, noticing your feelings, sensations, emotions, and thoughts.

Imagine the energy in the Spiral Pillar flowing downward to connect with Earth's core.

The Spiral Pillar is your personal cone of power and protection. Expand your inner strength and calmness with peace, focus, and clarity.

Variations:

- Eliminate the spiral; see the energy as a straight pillar. Does one feel more comfortable? Does one have more energy, strength, or flow? What is activated in you with each?
- Change the color of light to one that magnifies the emotion you are radiating.
- When feeling internal negativity, activate the spiral pillar to avoid projecting your emotions onto others or hooking into their energy field and draining them.
- Let your projections of fear, pain, or anger extend to the Spiral Pillar and be absorbed, then returned as loving self-acceptance and understanding.

Earth and Sky

Keyword: Grounding

Description: The Earth and Sky meditation opens the Hara-line, the channel of energy that runs up the vertical core of your body. This meditation establishes your place as the bridge between Heaven and Earth; the point of exchange between energy and matter. When you become the fulcrum between polarities, you are in a position of power, able to move in any direction. It's the difference between reacting and responding; here you are free to respond with balance and confidence.

Benefits:
- Promotes grounding and centering.
- Strengthens the Hara-line.
- Integrates material and spiritual polarities.
- Balances masculine and feminine principles.
- Facilitates inner balance between polar or conflicting concepts/ideas.
- Promotes wholeness.

Use to:
- Bring ideas and concepts into physical form.
- Create inner strength: physical, spiritual, mental, emotional.
- Promote balance between conflicting life demands.
- Maintain a grounded approach to life circumstances.
- Integrate conflicting desires and beliefs in decision-making.
- Reduce stress and manage anxiety.

Flow Pattern:
Sit or stand. Take a few deep breaths, and calm your mind and body. Bring your awareness to the core of your body.

Connect with the channel running between your perineum and the top of your head through the center of your body. This is the Inner Central Channel, also called the Hara-line. It connects your star in the sky to the center of the Earth and vice versa.

Step 1: *Connect Sky to Base Chakra, see figure 1 in the Earth and Sky illustration.* Inhale. Imagine drawing light from your Star in through your Crown Chakra at the top of your head, down through your Hara-line and into your Base Chakra at your sacrum, filling your body with freedom, space, and light. Be free.

Step 2: *Connect Sky to Earth, see figure 2 in the Earth and Sky illustration.* Exhale and send energy downward through your body, out of your Base Chakra, sending roots deep into the Earth. Feel the solidity, stability, and safety of Earth. See yourself safe.

Step 3: *Raising Earth Energy, see figure 3 in the Earth and Sky illustration.* Inhale and imagine pulling Earthlight up into your body through your Base Chakra, bringing the stability and safety of Earth into your Hara-line. Feel yourself strong, safe, and flexible.

Step 4: *Connect Earth to Sky, see figure 4 in the Earth and Sky illustration.* Exhale, sending Earth energy out through the top of your head, sending branches into the sky, and sending the strength of Earth into the heavens.

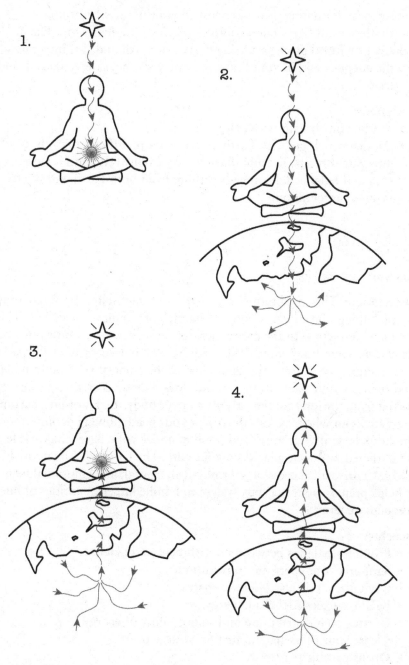

Earth and Sky

Repeat this alternating flow of energy in your natural breathing
   rhythm: send Earth energy into sky; bring sky energy into Earth.
Take your natural place as a bridge between Earth and sky. Integrate
   the energies within your body, becoming strong, safe, balanced, and
   free.

Variations:
- Infuse your breath with color.
- Notice which polarity, Earth or sky, is more difficult for you to
  integrate. Breathe in from that polarity exclusively until it feels
  easy and balanced. Resume breathing from both Earth and sky to
  promote integration.

Circle of Life

Keyword: Energizing

Description: This meditation activates your meridians by circulating
energy along the Great Central Channel of Chinese medicine. This
channel interacts with the entire meridian system, while nourishing and
defending your body-mind. The meditation has two distinct flows. In
one, energy travels down the center line of the front of your body, under
and then up your back. In the second flow, a circle is created by energy
traveling up the internal central core of your body, the Hara-line, becom-
ing a fountain when it crests the top of your head, flowing down around
the boundary of your aura, and pooling under your Base Chakra. Here
it's gathered and recirculated up your core. The Circle of Life nourishes
and revitalizes all aspects of your physical, mental, and emotional being.
It helps prepare your nervous system to handle larger quantities of finer
frequency energy.

Benefits:
- Promotes balance between nourishment and defense.
- Supports your energetic constitution.
- Revitalizes, renews, and rejuvenates.
- Balances excess/deficient energy.
- Creates even distribution and smooth flow of energy.
- Clears your thinking and focuses your actions.
- Opens psychic perception.
- Prepares the body for finer spiritual frequencies.

Use to:
- Improve health and strengthen the immune system.

1.

2.

3.

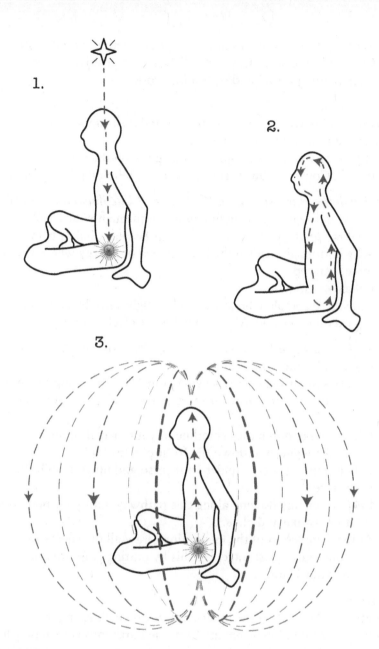

Circle of Life

- Regain physical strength after trauma, depletion, or exhaustion.
- Clear old, stagnant ideas and beliefs; create positive action.
- Prepare for spiritual and/or healing work.

Flow Pattern:
Sit comfortably with your back straight and well supported.
Center, ground, and let go of tension.
Relax your jaw and place your tongue lightly on the roof of your
    mouth. Contract your perineum as though holding your bladder.

Step 1: *Fill the Hara, see figure 1 in Circle of Life illustration.* Inhale
    and visualize energy as light coming in through your Crown
    Chakra, down your Hara-line to your Second Chakra below your
    belly button, also called the Hara or Sea of Energy where vital life-
    force is stored.
    Exhale tension.
    Take three complete breaths, inhaling light into the Hara and
        exhaling tension. Allow your body to feel vibrant and alive.

Step 2: *Establish the Flow, see figure 2 in Circle of Life illustration.*
    Inhale light into your Hara.
    Exhale, visualizing energy leaving your Hara, traveling down under
        your torso, up into your sacrum, up your spine, and over the
        top of your head.
    Inhale energy down the centerline of your face, through
        your tongue, and down the front of your body.
    Exhale, curling energy under your torso and up your spine as
        before.
    Keep the energy flowing along this pathway until your body-mind
        feels awake and alive.
    At the completion of the meditation, draw all the energy into
        your Hara for storage. Do this by putting your attention
        on your Hara.

Variations:
Variation for Activating the Inner Central Channel; see figure 3 in Circle
of Life illustration. Inhale energy from the Earth into your Base Chakra
at the bottom of your torso and draw the energy from your Base Chakra
up your Hara-line.

- Exhale and visualize the energy spilling out the top of your head
  like a fountain.
- Keep the circle flowing, allowing the energy to form a torus of
  energy that looks like a donut. (See illustration.)

It's easy to become overstimulated with this exercise. To avoid this, begin your practice with shorter sessions. If you do become overstimulated, send the excess energy out your hands and feet. With practice, you will be able to handle both larger quantities and higher frequencies of energy.

Chakra Clarity

Keyword: Growth

Description: This meditation activates all seven of the major chakras. Chakras are vortices, often called "wheels of light," that emerge from the Hara-line and project outward into the aura. Chakras are centers of finer frequency that accumulate and transmit vital life energy. Chakras are involved in all aspects of health, growth, and spiritual development. Each chakra governs a specific aspect of evolving consciousness and is associated with a specific color, sound, spiritual challenge, gift, and set of emotions. Working with the chakra system is an intricate, lifelong process. Although this is a basic meditation, it can take you into a very deep practice.

Benefits:
- Improves emotional balance and clarity.
- Enhances spiritual awareness and personal development.
- Promotes the specific benefits of each chakra. (See Chapter 7.)
- Helps clear self-limiting attitudes, beliefs, and behaviors.
- Helps to discover inner resources.

Use to:
- Expand your spiritual practice.
- Promote inner to outer balance.
- Understand and shift self-sabotaging behavior.
- Balance extremes of emotion during times of stress.
- Explore obstacles on your path.

Flow Pattern

Preparation: Visualize the seven physio-energetic vortices called chakras (if you want more info, see Chapter 7). Feel them as a vibration in the area of the body where they live.

Sit or lie down with your spine as straight as possible or, if you can't sit down, imagine sitting with a straight spine.

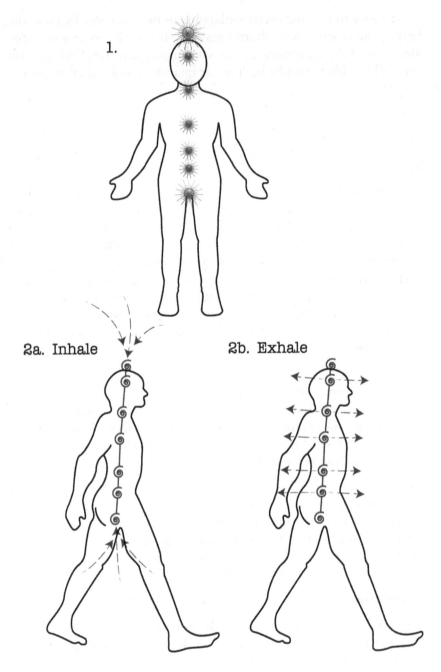

1.

2a. Inhale   2b. Exhale

Chakra Clarity

Relax. Calm the mind and open the Spiral Pillar of Light to hold space for your exploration.

Step 1: *Exploring the Chakras, see figure 1 of Chakra Clarity illustration.* Begin with the Base Chakra (lowest) and explore each chakra. Notice what each looks like, how it feels, and what the quality is. There's no need to change anything, just notice.

What color is it? What is the shade and quality of the color? Is it clear, cloudy, vibrant, dull?

What shape is it? Is it round, oblong, cylindrical? Is it symmetrical, lopsided, bulging, have pieces cut out?

Is the chakra full or empty, hot, cold, or neutral?

How far does the energy radiate?

Does the chakra leak?

Is the vortex tight, expansive, energized, depleted?

Is the chakra spinning? Fast, slow, counterclockwise, clockwise?

Does the chakra have an emotion?

Ask any questions that come to mind.

What do you feel/sense/experience and imagine as you connect?

Does one chakra draw your attention more than another?

Is it asking for something? Perhaps a color, more light, vibrancy, or space.

Inhale and imagine your breath providing the chakra whatever it needs. Notice what thoughts, emotions, feelings get in the way of receiving and also notice what assists you in being able to receive.

Does this area have a message for you? No need to change anything, just notice.

Take a wider view. Do any feel isolated? Do two chakras need balancing with each other?

Hold two chakras with uneven flow in your attention simultaneously.

Is there flow between them? Examine the relationship: Is one larger, clearer, more energized than the other? Does one overshadow the other? What is the flow like between them? Does one drain the other? What does each need from the other?

Offer an opportunity to balance.

Do this with as many chakras in as many combinations as desired.

Step 2: *Clear and harmonize the system, see figures 2a and b of Chakra Clarity illustration.* Inhale through your Base and Crown Chakras and down the Hara-line.

Exhale through the front and back of all the chakras.

Continue to inhale through Base and Crown and exhale through front and back.

With each inhalation, intend to charge the chakras.

With each exhalation, intend to release that which you no longer need.

Sit and enjoy the sensation of your chakras vibrating in harmony with each other.

Write down your experience.

Variation:

Tone the Chakras. Sound is a powerful healer. Use your voice to balance the chakras by humming or chanting a note that vibrates specific areas of the body and chakras. Start at the base and work your way up, or tone the chakra that is most in need.

Explorations in Light

Chakra Fibers (Light Filaments)

Keyword: Connection

Description: The Chakra Fibers meditation expands your ability to engage subtle energy while remaining grounded. A chakra can be experienced as a rotating vortex, as in Chakra Clarity, or as a nexus of energy filaments, or fibers, used to explore and connect with your environment. Where you place your attention is where your filaments explore. When your filaments anchor in one place, you become grounded in that reality and way of seeing the world. When they are unattached, you have free attention to explore new ways of being and perceiving. A balance between anchored and unattached fibers allows for stability and commitment while fostering flexibility of thought and openness to new ideas.

Benefits:
- Anchors your perceptions.
- Deepens your connection to other life forms.
- Explores your physical and energy environment.
- Maintains grounding and direction.
- Provides creative inspiration.
- Increases intuition.

Use to:
- Deepen connection in relationships, human and nonhuman.

Chakra Fibers

- Release outgrown attachments and old relationships.
- See different perspectives and approaches to life.
- Strengthen connection and ability to perceive subtle energy.
- Release our old "stories," providing freedom from limiting beliefs.

Flow Pattern:

Sit or lie with straight spine. Relax, center, ground, and establish your boundaries.

Take three chakra clearing breaths, inhaling through the top of your head and your Base Chakra and exhaling through the front and back of your chakras.

Focus your awareness on a chakra that draws your attention. If you're not drawn to one, use the Third Chakra.

Visualize the energy fibers flowing from this chakra into the space around you.

Notice their color, thickness, flexibility, length, amount of light, and
   so on. Do they move freely? Are they tangled? Are they lively and
   awake? Dull or asleep?
Based on what you feel, what percentage are fixed and what percentage
   are free to explore? Is it the right balance for you at this time?
Respectfully extend your fibers to explore your environment, touching
   and assessing objects, plants, animals, and beings around you.
When you're finished, breathe vitality into your fibers and imagine
   them full of life, freedom, and joy.
Focus your attention and call your fibers home. Visualize them coiling
   into a nest of light.
Ground, center, and relax.
In a journal consider the light filaments in the chakra you explored and
   write down your perceptions.

Weaving the Nadis

Keyword: Serenity

Description: This meditation impacts the quality rather than quantity
of your energy. The Nadis are pathways of energy. Three of the major
Nadis link the seven major chakras. These Nadis sustain a smooth flow
of energy. When they're too tight or loose, flow is uneven, creating wild
rapids and stagnating pools. Clear-flowing Nadis help prepare the ner-
vous system for managing finer frequency and amplitude of energy. They
also prepare for the rising of Kundalini, a spiritual energy residing in the
sacrum that rises naturally as awareness expands. This meditation is the
sweetest of all, providing a truly sublime serenity.

Benefits:
   • Regulates the flow of energy.
   • Promotes peace and harmony.
   • Enhances communication and integration among chakras.
   • Nourishes and cleanses chakra energy.
   • Prepares the Hara-line for receiving Kundalini.
   • Increases psychic perception.
   • Maintains balance between left and right; up and down.
   • Integrates insight derived from life experiences.
   • Improves the quality of energy used for daily living.

Use to:
   • Calm the mind and soothe the spirit.

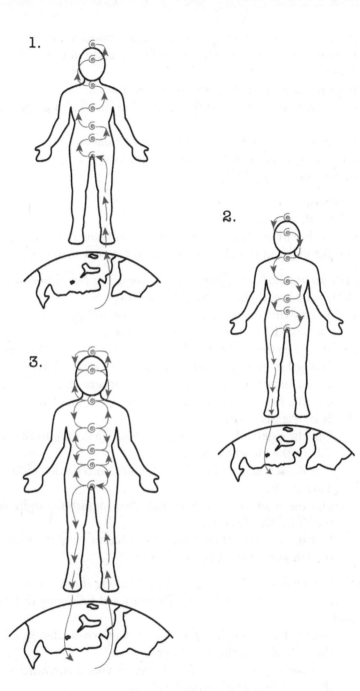

Weaving the Nadis

- Reduce fatigue by stimulating stagnating pools of energy.
- Improve focus by reducing the frenetic quality of undirected energy.
- Improve quality of sleep and reduce insomnia.
- Calm vibrations in legs and sacrum from Kundalini preparing to rise.
- Integrate emotional trauma and restore balance.
- Increase unconditional love and acceptance.
- Invite spiritual uplifting.

Flow Pattern:

Sit or lie with straight spine.

Using your breath and attention, invite the movement of energy into and through your chakras in a spiraling ascent then descent.

Step 1: *Upward Path, see figure 1 of Weaving the Nadis illustration.*
With your breath, fill each chakra with light:
Inhale, drawing energy into your left foot and up your left leg to enter the left side of your Base Chakra.
Exhale the energy out the right side of your Base Chakra and upward to enter the right side of your Sacral Chakra.
With your breath, continue inviting the progression of energy:
- Out the left side of the Sacral Chakra, into the left side of the Solar Plexus Chakra.
- Out the right side of the Solar Plexus Chakra, into the right side of the Heart Chakra.
- Out the left side of the Heart Chakra, into the left side of the Throat Chakra.
- Out the right side of the Throat Chakra, into the right side of the Third Eye Chakra.
- Out the left side of the Third Eye Chakra, over the head into the left side of the Crown Chakra.

Step 2: *Descending Path, see figure 2 of Weaving the Nadis illustration.*
With your breath, exhale energy downward following this progression:
- Energy flows out the right side of the Crown Chakra and enters the right side of the Third Eye.
- Out the left side of the Third Eye, curving downward and into the left side of the Throat Chakra.
- Out the right side of the Throat Chakra, curving downward into the right side of the Heart Chakra.

- Out the left side of the Heart Chakra and into the left side of the Solar Plexus Chakra.
- Out the right side of the Solar Plexus Chakra and into the right side of the Sacral Chakra.
- Out the left side of the Sacral Chakra and into the left side of the Base Chakra.
- Out the right side of the Base Chakra, down the right leg and out the right foot into the Earth.

Step 3: *Complete the Circuit, see figure 3 of Weaving the Nadis illustration.* Continue the circuit for three full rounds.

When you're comfortable with the flow, bring energy up through every chakra on one inhale and take it down through every chakra on one exhale.

Five-Hearts Open

Keyword: Sensitivity

Description: The Five-Hearts Open meditation is used to enhance your awareness of the subtle energy within matter. The five "hearts" of Chinese medicine consist of four small chakras, one in the palm of each hand and in the soles of the feet, plus the large Heart Chakra in the middle of the chest. The chakras in the palms of your hands feel the world around you; the chakras from the soles of your feet connect to the ley lines of the Earth. Five-Hearts Open is a moving meditation that opens awareness to the energy within physical form, increasing your energy sensitivity. It plugs you into the Earth's energy circuit and enhances the direct experience of how interconnected all life is.

Benefits:
- Increases energy sensitivity and awareness of energy connections.
- Increases contact with the people around you.
- Increases connection to nature and the natural environment.

Use to:
- Increase energy sensitivity.
- Better feel auras in people, animals, crystals, and so on.
- Feel the energy flows in Earth.
- Understand the energetic quality of a place or past event.
- Plug into Earth energy and charge your energy system.
- Explore and discover deeper connection and meaning in life.
- Increase inspiration and guidance.

Five Hearts Open

Flow Pattern:
Ideally, this meditation is done outdoors, although indoors works as well.

Sit quietly and do an opening meditation, creating sacred space.
Using awareness and breath, direct your attention to your Heart
   Chakra.

Step 1: *Charging the First Heart, see figure 1 of Five-Hearts Open.*
   With each inhalation, draw conscious, living light into your Crown
   Chakra and down your Hara-line to your Heart Chakra, expand-
   ing it with light and joy.
   Let light shine from your Heart Chakra into the space around you.
      Become an extension of light as your fibers explore. Bring your
      awareness and energy back to your Heart Chakra. Using your
      breath, recharge your Heart Chakra.

Step 2: *Charging all the Hearts, see figure 2 of Five-Hearts Open
illustration.*
   Focus on your hands and feet.
   Send streams of living light from your Heart Chakra, down your
      arms, and into your hands. You may notice your palms tingling
      and/or becoming hot.
   Open a pathway from Heart Chakra heart to the soles of your feet,
      allowing them to come alive with awareness.

Step 3: *Exploring, see figure 3 of Five-Hearts Open illustration.*
   When all five hearts are open, stand up and visualize the energy
      streaming from your feet descending deep into the Earth.
   Walk slowly and deliberately, engaging your entire foot as your
      weight shifts.
   When your foot lifts, keep your focus on the connection it still has
      to the Earth. No matter how far off the ground your foot rises,
      feel energy streaming out of the sole, plugging into the Earth's
      energy circuit.
   Breathe Earth energy up into your body through your feet,
      charging your system.
   Approach a tree or plant and ask permission to connect with its
      spiritual essence.
   Stream energy out of your Heart Chakra and hands to engage.
   Explore the space around the plant, feeling for the radiance ema-
      nating from its core. Pulse your hand toward and away from
      it, building energy. You may notice a magnetic repulsion/attrac-
      tion between your hand and the plant.

Notice changes inside yourself as you connect energetically with life.

Variation:
Do the same as above, only blindfolded. Be sure to have a friend present for safety.

Queen Nefertiti's Headdress

Keyword: Perception

Description: This meditation brings freedom from old, emotional patterns by recreating the ancient Egyptian headdress worn by queens and pharaohs. The headdress is a unique energy amplifier. Shaped like a cone and worn with the narrow end around the head and the wide end opened to Spirit, it channels spiritual energy downward into the Crown Chakra. The layered striations of the headdress align with the seven layers of the aura. Each striation connects to its associated layer. As finer frequencies are drawn into the headdress, the aura begins to vibrate. Each layer of the headdress, and thus each layer of the aura, vibrates at a different rate. Thought-forms, limiting beliefs, and old emotional patterns burst and disperse, allowing new inspirations to emerge. This meditation brings upliftment, expanded consciousness, and freedom from limitation. It allows you to perceive reality without your standard lens and bias.

Benefits:
- Cleanses and purifies the aura.
- Expands consciousness.
- Raises frequency for higher connections and guidance.
- Removes bias and outmoded perceptions.

Use to:
- Remove negative thought-forms and old emotional patterns.
- Remove energy attachments.
- Eliminate energy projections from other people or situations.
- See situations, people, and self clearly.

Flow Pattern:
Sit comfortably; do an opening meditation to create sacred space.

Step 1: *Establish the Headdress, see figure 1 of Queen Nefertiti's Headdress illustration.* In your imagination, put on the cone-shaped Egyptian headdress so that the narrow end rests on your head and the wider end opens to the heavens.

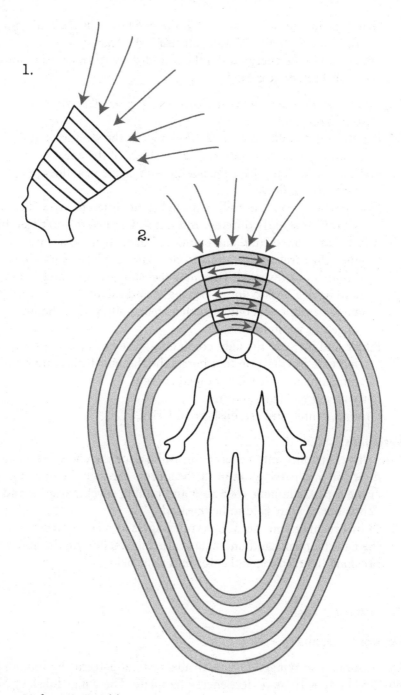

1.

2.

Queen Nefertiti's Headdress

Gently drop your chin and stretch the back of your neck, aligning the cone heavenward and activating the Hara-line.

Inhale and invite energy to fill the headdress with increasing intensities of finer vibration.

Step 2: *Distribute Frequency, see figure 2 of Queen Nefertiti's Headdress illustration.*

Exhale and visualize the energy flowing out the striations of the headdress into the corresponding layers of the aura.

You do not need to direct the energy into layers or influence the direction of flow.

Notice that as your aura fills with light, the different layers begin to vibrate at slightly different rates. It's okay if you don't feel this.

Allow and invite mental and emotional disturbances, negative thought-forms, projections from other people, and psychic hooks to be revealed. They may feel sluggish, blocked, dense, and have a dark color or be jagged and excitable. You may notice emotional content such as fear, guilt, greed, shame, anger, or victimization.

Inhale and increase the light coming into the headdress. Notice the increase in vibration that bursts the thought-forms and frees attachments, releasing trapped energy.

Let yourself feel light and free.

Ground, center, and establish boundaries.

Variations:

After dispersing unwanted energy forms, imagine the energy reversing direction and passing out of the headdress through the opening at the top, vacuuming your aura and pulling psychic residue and debris out of your field to be released.

Finish by brushing your aura. Use your fingers as a comb to separate the light filaments and untangle snarled areas, fluffing the aura by brushing light, space, and color into your field.

The Winged Disk

Keyword: Healing

Description: The Winged Disk activates healing patterns by linking the physical body with its perfect energy template. The winged disk symbol of ancient Egypt, like the Zuni Eye of God, recognizes the God force at

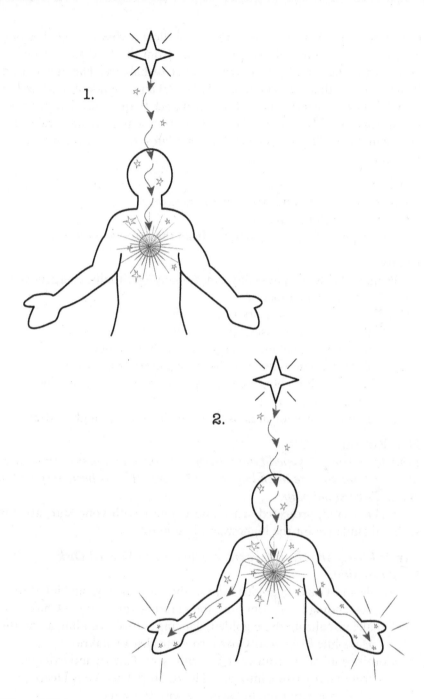

1.

2.

Winged Disk

the heart of all creation. The winged disk flew across the sky, keeping watch over creation and bringing energy from the God side of reality onto Earth when the Earth plane was out of balance. This meditation focuses on health as an outcome of balanced and abundant life-force. It channels healing energy in the form of higher frequencies that promote transformation. The Winged Disk meditation acts as a star-bridge for people in the healing arts, channeling templates for physical reality from the Source.

Benefits:
- Increases vitality and free flow of energy.
- Brings in spiritual energy.
- Opens powerful flows of energy from the creative life-force.

Use to:
- Promote healing—physically, emotionally, spiritually, energetically.
- Enhance immune function.
- Assist during healing work of all kinds:
  - To energetically assess life-force, flow, and obstruction.
  - To align and balance energy flow within the body.
  - To transmute frequencies holding patterns of disease.
  - To transmit higher frequencies of unconditional love, the source of all healing.
  - To manifest your dreams that are aligned with higher ideal.

Flow Pattern:
Prior to starting this meditation, be sure to have permission from any-one to whom you are intending to send energy. This is basic respect for another's personal path.

Open sacred, protected space and connect with your Star; ask for spiritual guidance for the highest and best good.

Step 1: *Charge the Heart Chakra, see figure 1 of Winged Disk illustration.*
Inhale and visualize golden light in the form of tiny, dancing stars descending from your Star and entering your Crown Chakra.
Exhale, visualizing these golden, dancing stars descending along the Hara-line from your Crown to your Heart Chakra.
Continue inhaling from your Star into your Crown and exhaling from your Crown into your Heart. Stop when your Heart Chakra is vibrating in harmony with the stars.

Step 2: *Send Energy through the Hands, see figure 2 of Winged Disk illustration.*

Inhale into your Heart Chakra and exhale, inviting the dancing stars to flow down your arms into your hands.

Using your breath as a pump, inhale energy in through the Crown Chakra, down to your heart, and into your hands.

Exhale energy out your hands to an imbalance in any person, location, situation, goal, event, or place on your body that needs support. Hold an image in your mind's eye of where you want the energy to flow.

If you want, place your hands on the imbalanced area or a picture of the person or place you're offering support to.

Acknowledge that every person is their own healer and only they know what they need. They have the right to accept or reject your support.

Imagine molecules vibrating into alignment with ideal reality, reflecting the perfect template that already exists in the energy matrix.

Release all judgment of what the ideal is "supposed" to look like and allow it to be whatever it is.

Allow your hands to intuitively move until you feel the flow decrease, indicating the conclusion of the session.

Continue to hold sacred space, allowing thoughts, impressions, and feelings to emerge.

Close the channels to your hands and continue to let your heart fill with light.

End the meditation with your own heart full of light, energizing all the pathways in your body.

Celtic Cross

Keyword: Protection

Description: This pattern provides a protective shield when in physical, psychological, or psychic danger. The Celtic Cross consists of four energy balls that are satellites around you. When the satellites are connected in the Celtic Cross pattern, an impenetrable field of safety is created. Any ill-intentioned energy sent toward a person or place protected by the Celtic Cross is blessed and reflected back to the sender. This formation magnifies your energy field, expands your personal space, and creates strength. It activates your survival instincts while calling on higher

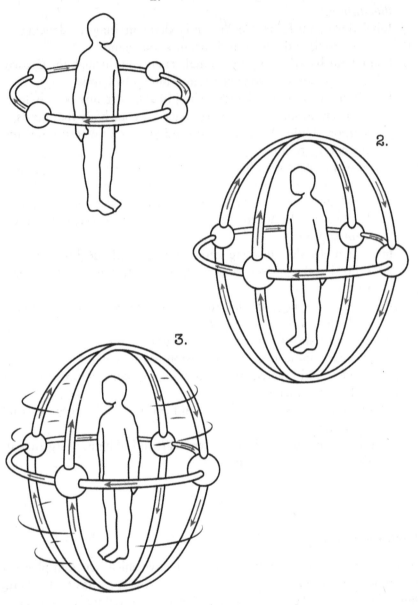

Celtic Cross

powers to assist your safety. Although not an aggressive pattern, it's fully protective. It can also act as a filter, allowing higher energy to come in while shielding you from thought-forms, projections, and hooks. (See Chapter 12.)

Benefits:
- Creates an energetic shield around yourself, people, objects, and places.
- Helps to focus and solidify your attention.
- Gathers all your resources necessary for strength and action.
- Facilitates the highest and best outcome for all involved.
- Allows you to rest when under extended external pressure.
- Filters harmful energy from the matrix of energy you receive.

Use to:
- Protect from psychic attack or extreme situations.
- Maintain boundaries and facilitate peaceful resolution during conflict.
- Assist a safe outcome when in physical danger.
- Help protect and shield loved ones.
- Protect property.
- Activate filtered protection when in group situations, and during telepathic or psychic explorations.
- Act as vehicle for out-of-body exploration.

Flow Pattern:
Activate the Spiral Pillar of Light.
Align the outer edge of the pillar with the outer edge of your aura.

Step 1: *Construct the Ring, see figure 1 of Celtic Cross illustration.*
Imagine four spheres/balls of light circling just beyond your aura: one in front of you, one behind, and one to either side of you. They are connected through a tube of light circling your torso.

Step 2: *Construct gyroscope, see figure 2 of Celtic Cross illustration.*
Visualize a tube of energy flowing from the front sphere, over your head and through the ball behind you, then flowing under your feet and returning to the ball in front. Maintain energy flowing along this circular tube.

Step 3: *Active Protection, see figure 3 of Celtic Cross illustration.*
Imagine a tube of energy flowing from the sphere on your right, over the top of your head through the ball on your left, under your feet, and back to the ball on the right. Keep energy flowing along this route.

Maintain a continuous energy flow in all three circuits.
Spin the entire construct, creating a gyroscopic field that repels
and/or filters approaching energy.

Variations:
Use color to magnify the effect; metallic silver is one of the strongest.
Construct this pattern around your house, family, individuals, animals,
personal property, or objects that need extra protection.

Master Activations

Mystic Triangle

Keyword: Intention

Description: The Mystic Triangle is a master communication tool. It
aligns with and opens the Third Eye Chakra, promoting high level communication. It magnifies the ability to both see greater truth and manifest it in the physical world. It can open a portal between dimensions,
different levels of reality, or different places in time and space. This is a
Master Activation and requires a developed nervous system to sustain.
It invokes the archetype of the Earth Mother, the Spiritual Mother who
gives birth to higher truth and nurtures it in this reality. This is a protective and sustaining activation.

Benefits:
- Establishes mental, emotional, and spiritual clarity.
- Creates a portal to higher planes.
- Connects with guides, guardians, the angelic realm, and Nature
  Spirits.
- Manifests spiritual principles and aligns to higher path and purpose.
- Provides connection between people in different locations or times.
- Enhances telepathic ability.
- Activates the pineal gland and the Third Eye Chakra.

Use to:
- Provide inspiration for creative projects (art, writing,
  problem-solving).
- Communicate telepathically with others.
- Remote view distant events or places and explore psychic realms.
- Enhance therapy sessions, healing work, prayer, meditation, manifestation.
- Channel or develop intuition and extrasensory perception.

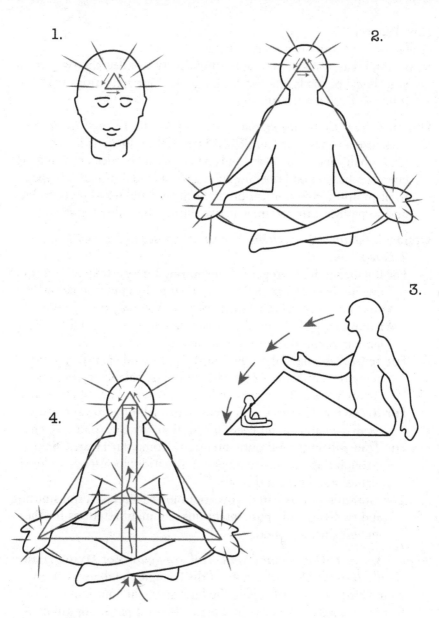

1.

2.

3.

4.

Mystic Triangle

Flow Pattern:

Center, ground, and open sacred space.

Sit or stand with arms at your side, about forty-five degrees away from your body, palms facing forward. Use the four activations that follow for different purposes.

Option 1: *Increase Intuition, see figure 2 of Mystic Triangle illustration.* Visualize a triangle at your Third Eye Chakra. Imagine it as electric, cobalt blue with energy pulsing along the borders, creating an energetic beacon and opening to receive spiritual insight. Be open to inspiration, communication, upliftment, heightened perception, and so on. Keep this triangle active during the following steps.

Option 2: *Balancing, Receiving, Transmitting, see figure 3 of Mystic Triangle illustration.*

For Balancing, Receiving, or Transmitting Energy: Imagine energy flowing from the triangle in your Third Eye into the palms of your hands creating a larger triangle. You may notice your palms getting hot and the entire triangle vibrating. Hold this large pyramid open during the next three steps.

For Self-balancing: Allow the Third Eye to send energy in a flow along the perimeter of the large triangle, balancing your entire energy system. The flow can be clockwise or counterclockwise.

For Receiving: Connect with your higher self or guide and ask to receive whatever you need: inspiration, insight, solutions, etc.

For Transmitting: Send pure intentions from your Heart Chakra through this triangle to a person, situation, location, etc. for the highest and best good of all.

The vibration of this pattern overrides lower impulses, transmitting and receiving only pure intentions and manifestations for the highest spiritual good.

Option 3: *Create Communication Portal, see figure 3 of Mystic Triangle illustration.* Allow the apex of the triangle to fall away from your Third Eye while keeping the base stable in your hands. This forms a triangle in a horizontal plane. Invite a person or guide to sit in the apex for the purpose of communication. This activation protects you from lower-level influences or attachments.

Option 4: *Charging Your System, see figure 4 of Mystic Triangle illustration.* Visualize a triangle with its apex in your Third Eye and its base in the palms of your hands. Create a smaller triangle within the larger triangle, sharing the same base between the palms of

Subtle Energy Work

your hands, with the apex at your Second Chakra. Draw Earth energy up from your Base Chakra into the smaller triangle.

When the energy feels full, invite it to flow up from the apex using the Hara-line to the apex of the larger triangle in your Third Eye, activating the Solar Plexus and Heart Chakras as it passes. Attune to the finer vibration and charge your system.

Pyramid Purification

Keyword: Cleansing

Description: This is an advanced cleansing activation. Spiritual growth requires that we own both our light and the shadow it casts. Our thoughts and emotions generate energy forms that fill the aura and atmosphere of Earth and travel beneath the surface of the planet on ley lines. Heart-centered thoughts and emotions create connection and advancement. They stabilize the planet and promote the harmonics of spiritual growth. Destructive thoughts and emotions create energetic pollution, poisoning the planet energetically just as industrial pollution poisons the air, water, and soil. This activation cleanses and purifies destructive emotional manifestations, which are then transformed and broadcast as unconditional love. This construct provides the opportunity to call home our shadow and embrace it, merging the shadow with light, accepting wholeness.

Benefits:
- Encourages inner congruence.
- Promotes self-acceptance, self-love, inner peace, and forgiveness.
- Removes obstacles to healing.
- Transmutes karma.
- Cleanses old pain, trauma, anger, and destructive patterns.
- Creates spiritual upliftment and freedom.
- Cleanses and clears Earth.
- Harmonizes Earth's aura and stabilizes Earth energy.

Use to:
- Generate love, peace, light, forgiveness, and grace.
- Cleanse personal space, houses, offices, etc., especially after conflict.
- Clear the land of trauma, such as the sites of battles, massacres, prisons, and murder.
- Take responsibility for your choices and actions.
- Make an intention of peace on the planet.
- Clear energetic pollution.

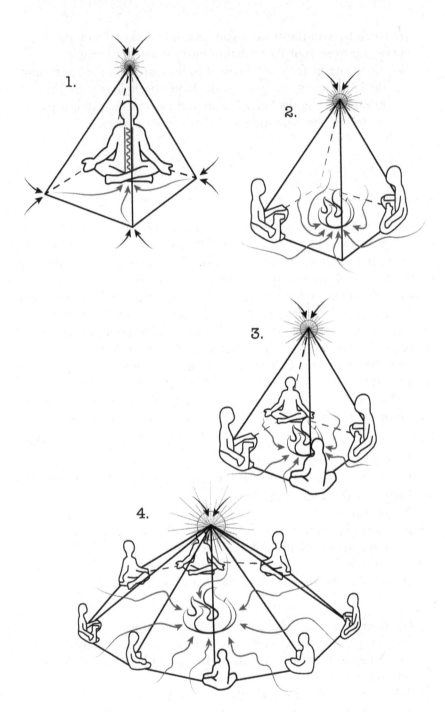

Pyramid Purification

Subtle Energy Work

Flow Pattern:

Sit with straight back in cross-legged position or on chair, feet flat on
the ground. Activate the Spiral Pillar of Light.

Notice that you have high-level energy centers in your aura that align
with your dimensional self and link to multidimensional planes.
Their function is to tune into spiritual reality.

The base of the pyramid is connected to lines of energy within the
matrix of the planet.

As the pyramid activates, past, destructive energies are drawn into the
base for the clearing.

Option 1: *Individual Cleansing, see figure 1 of Pyramid Purification
illustration.*

Imagine yourself sitting in a four-sided pyramid with the apex
above your head at the level of one of the higher energy
centers.

Activate the pyramid by focusing on the apex while holding
the intention to take responsibility for all of your emotions,
thoughts, and actions.

Draw energy in through the apex and visualize it filling the pyra-
mid with pure white light or any color you would like.

Imagine a vortex of spiraling energy forming along your Hara-line,
drawing energy up through your chakras and out the top of the
pyramid. The spiral may appear as a violet flame.

Call home all your harmful projections, all the disowned parts of
self. You may see dark vapors pulled into the base of the pyra-
mid and fed into the violet flame vortex.

Witness all returning energies being transformed into pure white
light.

Embrace your shadow, the small, hurt part of self, and welcome
yourself Home. Allow all the cells of your body to be bathed in
love and acceptance. Feel the rips and tears in your light-body
mend as you expand.

Option 2: *Two-Person Cleansing, see figure 2 of Pyramid Purification
illustration.*

Use to repair fractured relationships or join with another to clear
harmful impacts from Earth.

Sit facing each other in cross-legged positions. Create a pyramid
with each of you in opposite corners and the apex about two
feet over your heads.

Open the Spiral Pillar of Light around the pyramid you've con-
structed and connect with each other in love and acceptance.

Hold the intention of purifying a specific issue, situation, place, etc.

Draw energy in through the apex of the pyramid to stream into the
pyramid, filling it with light.

Imagine a spiraling violet flame burning between you in the center
of the pyramid.

Call in the energy being purified; see it coming into the base of the
pyramid and into the violet flame.

Energy is released from its negative pattern and transformed into
the white light of unconditional love. Allow it to flow out the
apex of the pyramid.

Option 3: *Four-Person Cleansing, see figure 3 of Pyramid Purification illustration.*

Create a square with the placement of four people, each in a corner
of the pyramid. The apex is about four feet above your heads.
Use as in the Two-Person Cleansing to cleanse Earth of destruc-
tive, human-based activity.

Option 4: *Larger-Group Cleansing, see figure 4 of Pyramid Purification illustration.*

Add as many people and sides to the pyramid as you have in your
group and proceed as in the Four-Person Cleansing.

The Living Matrix

Keyword: Transcendence

Description: The Living Matrix is the Master Activation for expanded consciousness. According to the ancient Maya, three-dimensional consciousness is woven on a loom of twenty vertical warp lines and thirteen horizontal weft lines, creating the matrix of life. Everything we see and experience resonates to the ratio of 13:20. This is the golden ratio of nature; it governs the cycles of time and harmonizes the music of the celestial spheres. The human body is woven into the matrix through the twenty fingers and toes. Thirteen major joints (ankles, knees, hips, wrists, elbows, shoulders, and neck) create connecting points to the galaxy. When your toes anchor your meridians into the ley lines of the Earth and your fingers weave your meridians into the energy pathways of the heavens, the thirteen joints become portals to dimensional reality.

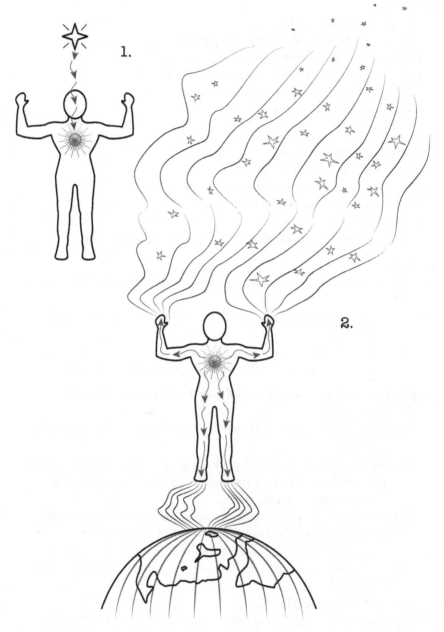

The Living Matrix

Benefits:
- Expands consciousness.
- Harmonizes and uplifts your frequency.
- Opens dimensional perception.
- Activates the light filaments in your DNA.
- Brings singularity consciousness into expression.
- Increases planetary love.

Use to:
- Activate your intuition.
- Merge with your higher self.
- Manifest your dreams and goals.
- Envision, create, and anchor an expansion of reality.
- Align with new frequency.
- Bring humanitarian ideals for all life into consciousness.

Flow Pattern:

Step 1: *Open the Heart Chakra, see figure 1 of Pyramid Purification illustration.*

Stand with your arms up, fingers toward the sky, and legs hip width apart.

Breathe in through your Crown Chakra and invite energy from your source into your Heart Chakra, filling it with light.

Step 2: *Link to Earth and sky, see figure 2 of Pyramid Purification illustration.*

Imagine the light in your Heart Chakra streaming into your arms and legs.

Imagine the energy in your legs flowing out your toes into the ley lines of the Earth. Feel yourself as an anchor for higher frequency into the Earth plane.

Imagine energy in your fingers flowing out into the energy pathways of the sky. Feel yourself as part of the Universe.

Maintain awareness of flow from your Star, into your Crown, down to your Heart Chakra, out your fingers and toes, into Earth and sky.

Join in The Living Matrix.

Experience yourself as one link in a network grid of light. All of your mentors are before you, you are a mentor to those behind, and all are part of one whole.

Know that we are all part of the shift underway: none of us makes it unless all of us do.

Send energy and light to humanity. Consider the Mayan phrase, In lak'ech—I am another yourself.

Let go of judgment and condemnation. Become pure light, pure love.

Align with pure light, pure love.

Variation:

Send this energy to the highest and best vision you have for the world we are creating.

Integration Exercise

Dancing with the Elements

(A gift from Louisa Poole)

Keyword: Exploration

Description: All life is interconnected and interdependent. Energy flows into, through, and around matter, forming and un-forming, in a perpetual exchange between energy and matter. Quantum physics is based on the realization that light can be either a particle or a wave. It can be either the matrix or the form within the matrix. Each particle is a specific window into reality, a perspective, a unique and small experience of the whole. We choose whether we are the whole or the part, but either way, each contains all. Dancing with the Elements is not an activation; it's the celebration of all that is awake within us.

Benefits:
- Awakens energy awareness.
- Deepens or awakens connection to nature, self, and the universe.
- Increases gratitude and appreciation.

Use to:
- Celebrate being alive.
- Overcome depression.
- Wake up the senses.
- Play and have fun.
- Experience and express joy.
- Honor and experience the sacred in nature.
- Get over one's self importance.

Flow Pattern:

Wear loose, comfortable clothing; barefoot is best if your feet can do it.

Stand outside at dusk, dawn, or early night. (Well, okay—any time is fine!)

Open the Spiral Pillar of Light and create sacred space.

Open the Hara-line and feel yourself suspended between Earth and sky.

Become a puppet whose strings are controlled by the elements. Focus on your senses and let yourself be moved by what you feel, see, and hear.

Follow the wind. Let it push you, pull you, send you down the road, across the beach, into the field.

Conduct the orchestra of the birds, the cars, the waves.

Follow smells, low down, up high, swirling into and out of. How does wind smell? How does it move? Where does it go? Does it have shape? Can you dance to it?

Move with the insects, move with the flowers, move with the clouds, move with the sunlight, moonbeams, starlight.

Send your energy out of your arms, out of your legs, out of all parts of your body. Send your energy into the wind, into the Earth, into the sky. Can you say if the wind moves you or you move the wind? Can you say if the birds call you or if you call the birds? Who is the leader? Who is the follower? Is there a difference?

Variation:

Dance with the elements blindfolded. Be sure to have a guide who keeps you safe and stays out of the way.

Chapter 4

Troubleshooting

Trouble engaging with these meditations or any in this book may have simple causes. Consider that you may:

- Need a better foundation in the practice of meditation. If you've never meditated before, start a standard meditation practice or join a meditation class. Return to these activations after you've developed basic focusing skills.
- Be having difficulty with the more advanced activations because you don't have enough energy in your aura to maintain the complexity of the patterns. Stay with the foundational patterns until you're able to establish and maintain the flows comfortably and have built energy in your field before moving to the more complex patterns.
- Have too much investment in the outcome. These are processes and the object is to experience them; outcome orientation limits possibility and creates self-doubt. Release any expectations and do the meditations for fun. Whatever happens, happens. If nothing happens, that's something, too. Accept the experience and continue to practice just for the sake of it.
- The directions are described in very visual terms. You may not be a visually oriented person. Try translating the instructions into terms you can relate to, such as auditory or kinesthetic.
- Engage your auditory sense. Instead of using light as a metaphor, use sound or tones. Instead of creating visual structures, create sound architecture.
- Engage your kinesthetic senses:
- Try drawing the patterns, letting yourself feel them in your body.
- Draw the patterns very large in your backyard or driveway. Walk them until you feel them in your body.

- You may have difficulty with the subtleness of the energy experience, needing more practice and time. Look for less, rather than more. Maybe you're separated from the feelings and sensations in your body, or maybe this is so different that you're unsure of what you're experiencing. Working with an experienced, trained energy practitioner can boost your confidence and awareness. A few good energy sessions should help you in discerning your inner energy flows.
- If you find yourself falling asleep during your practice, don't discount your experience. You may be accessing other realms in your sleep state. Ultimately, you want to be able to access deeper brain wave states while maintaining conscious awareness. You might want to practice your meditations while sitting up, or start with the moving meditations until you can maintain wakefulness while in a deep meditative state.
- If you have trouble staying focused or taking the work seriously, practicing alone may not provide enough initial support. Practicing with other people can magnify energy and also provide validation for your experience.
- Some people need an intellectual construct to align to. If your mind needs further engagement, read Part II of this book before continuing with the meditations.
- Be sure your ego isn't sabotaging you with feelings of self-doubt.

Part II

The Sea of Life-Force

Part II provides constructs of subtle energy. Constructs are models for organizing information. They're not written in stone. They evolve with new information, as we see every day in the development of science. The structures that organize energy in the body, the aura, chakras, and meridians, are themselves simply constructs. As humans evolve and as the planet's energy changes frequency, our energy structures are changing as well.

The information in Part II is a guide for how things might be, not a directive for how they have to be. Your body will confirm what's true for you and what isn't. Don't let intellectualizing get in the way of understanding. Your experience is what's important.

Chapter 5

Holographic Consciousness

The discovery of holograms changed the scientific view of the universe and consciousness to one of an all-pervasive and indivisible whole. But what exactly does a hologram have to teach about subtle energy?

The flow of our internal energy—its amplitude, clarity, vibration, and the connection between one structure in our energy anatomy and another—is a reflection of our consciousness and how we perceive reality. Interacting with the movement of our energy flow opens our mind to new levels of awareness, promoting expansion. Understanding the connection between subtle energy and consciousness helps clarify how the meditation practices in this book can expand our lives.

Holograms are quite common in our everyday world. There are holographic ID cards, advertisements, and knickknacks in every store. They've become so commonplace we rarely consider them beyond a three-dimensional photograph. However, that's the smallest part of what holograms offer our understanding.

The Making of a Hologram

To make a holographic photograph, an object is illuminated with a laser beam of highly coherent light. Coherence is the reason for a laser's brilliance. A second laser beam is bounced off the reflected light of the first laser beam, creating an interference pattern. The interference pattern is captured on film, looking like a meaningless swirl of lines, but when they're illuminated by a third laser beam, these meaningless swirls give rise to a three-dimensional image of the original object.

Have you ever looked at a Magic Eye picture? This is utilizing the principles of holography, with your brain creating the coherence that allows the emergence of a three-dimensional picture.

One of the remarkable things about a hologram is how information is contained in the picture. If a holographic picture is cut in half, we don't have two halves of the picture as with an ordinary photograph cut in half. Instead, each half contains the entire image. If the halves are divided again, each piece still contains a smaller, but intact version of the original image.

In fact, every part of a hologram contains all the information possessed by the whole, but with a distinct difference. Each part contains all the information for the whole from the perspective of where it was in the picture! That's why the eyes in a holographic photograph of a person seem to follow us as we move. This concept has changed scientists' view of nature, consciousness, the universe, and the functioning of our brains.

In holographic consciousness, the universe is not made up of separate, unrelated, individual "I's." Rather, each individual is part of the whole, contributing their unique perspective to the awareness of the whole. Every part of this awareness is important. Every type of experience, from every perspective within the hologram, is integral.

What this means is that wherever we are within the whole, becoming fully awake, aware, and alive is what matters. Each perspective is unique and our perception is our contribution to the whole of consciousness. Every so-called mistake, every challenge overcome, everything we learn provides growth for everyone.

Dimensions within the Hologram

The term *dimension* has different meanings in different contexts. What we call three-dimensional reality, Einstein expanded to four: the three dimensions of space (height, depth, and width) and the fourth dimension of time. The string theory of physics predicts that physical space has ten to eleven dimensions (some say twenty-six) that can't be seen or measured due to the folding of space.

In the many-worlds theory of quantum physics, every possible choice creates a split in the universe. In other words, "the universe makes copies of itself to account for all possibilities and these duplicates proceed independently. Each of these universes offers a unique and independent reality that coexists with other parallel universes."[1] This implies that the universe we inhabit is created by the choices we make, joining physics with metaphysics. In both, a dimension is a state of consciousness, a reflection of our unique perspective.

According to the Hindu Vedas, humans are connected to multiple dimensions through the energy structures in our body. Each chakra is linked to a specific dimension. As we expand our awareness, we are able to inhabit all levels of consciousness, becoming multidimensional. This doesn't mean moving awareness from one dimension within the hologram to another, or one chakra to another. Multidimensional consciousness means becoming aware of ourselves through all chakras simultaneously within the entirety of the hologram, able to experience and perceive among different dimensions at will.

Singularity Consciousness

Awareness of the whole is sometimes called singularity, or unity, consciousness and is often translated to mean "we are all one." More directly, however, singularity consciousness challenges the concept of duality. Western culture deifies two forces, one good and one evil. In singularity consciousness there is one force. If we call that one force light, then darkness is not a separate force; it is the lack of light.

Perhaps because we consider spiritual good and material bad, we look to the heavens as being more spiritual than Earth. Yet, of course, Earth is also a celestial body traveling through the heavens. We look at higher frequency as more spiritual than lower frequencies. Yet low-frequency brain waves take us deep into trance states where we can travel through dimensions. As seen in cymatics (see Chapter 6), lower-frequency sound waves produce less complex forms, while higher frequencies produce more complex forms, but is one more elevated than the other? Is a sphere less valuable than a snowflake? Higher frequency creates more complexity than lower frequency, yet both are essential and both have function. Problems arise when we become stuck in only one frequency, using it for all situations. Most important are the clarity, purity, and intensity of a frequency and how well it resonates with a particular need.

Singularity consciousness asks that we accept that matter and energy are the same stuff, vibrating at different frequencies, and each frequency has a unique, important contribution to the whole. This is probably the most important concept in energy awareness. As soon as we create a separate, negative force, we invest it with energy and bring it to life. Then we can offload everything we don't like about self onto this force and avoid dealing with it. To become conscious, however, we must integrate our shadow, the part of our self we judge and cast out.

How the Meditations Work

Attitudes, emotions, and beliefs create thought-forms with geometric structures in different layers of the aura. They link together in patterns of energy that interact with other parts of our energy structure. At the same time, these flows of energy network with the world around us, anchoring us into the larger picture. (See Activating Energy in Chapter 2.) In this manner, we're interconnected with specific people, places, and so forth.

Energy pathways in the body are similar to neural networks in the brain. Stanford neurophysiologist Karl Pribram illuminated the study of the brain with holographic models as explained by Michael Talbot in his book *The Holographic Universe*. An article posted on *spaceandmotion.com* reports:

> Pribram believes memories are encoded not in neurons, or small groupings of neurons, but in patterns of nerve impulses that crisscross the entire brain in the same way that patterns of laser light interference crisscross the entire area of a piece of film containing a holographic image. In other words, Pribram believes the brain is itself a hologram.[2]

Energy perception is stored in patterns of light in the same manner that information in the brain is stored as patterns of neural activity. The geometric thought-forms create magnetic charge in our biofield that influence the direction and configuration of energy flow. When we act in habitual ways, our energy flows in predetermined patterns. The meditations in this book activate new configurations, new pathways of energy, creating new relationships and awareness. They are portals into different aspects of the hologram.

Chapter 6

Understanding Subtle Energy

The sea of energy coursing into, through, and around us organizes matter into form. This doesn't happen randomly. Humans have energy structures in and around the body that filter incoming energy and radiate outgoing energy in an organized manner. They consist of the aura, a field of energy that surrounds the body in seven distinct layers; the chakras, seven energy centers originating in the layers of the aura and permeating the physical body; and the meridians, channels within the body that feed each cell with vital life-force (see Chapter 7, Human Energy Systems).

The Frequency of Life

Subtle energy, chi, or life-force is not a supernatural concept. According to Einstein's famous equation, the speed of light is the reference point for the exchange of matter and energy. $E=mc^2$ (energy equals matter moving at the speed of light squared), means that matter and energy are the same substance, just moving at different speeds. Matter doesn't necessarily move faster and faster in a straight line until it reaches the speed of light squared and transforms into energy. Movement is also vibration. Matter vibrating at a high enough frequency becomes energy.[1]

The physical world—everything we see, feel, hear, and experience—is an expression of vibration. Quantum physicists describe light as the building block of matter. The basic unit of light is a photon, and all photons travel at the speed of light. Photons are considered to be subatomic particles and carriers of the electromagnetic field.[2] The grandfather of quantum physics, David Bohm, went so far as to describe matter as frozen light. While light is commonly thought of as energy, as the interface between matter and energy, it's both a particle and a wave.

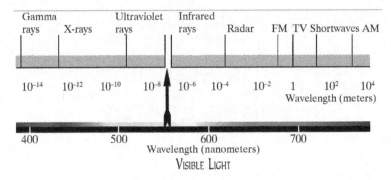

Electromagnetic Spectrum. The physical world is comprised of vibration expressed along an electromagnetic spectrum from low frequency to high.

Subtle energy exists outside of the current measurable electromagnetic range. That doesn't mean it's supernatural. It means science hasn't discovered the technology to measure its frequency. As with radio waves and microwaves, it's only a matter of time before subtle energy is scientifically verifiable.

Metaphysically, subtle energy provides the matrix from which matter is formed. Vibration within this matrix organizes form. Light carries information from the vibration of energy into that of matter. The fact that all spiritual traditions associate inspiration, healing, and spiritual connection with light is testament to the awareness that light is an organizing principle of matter and matter is infused with light.

The idea that higher frequency is better than lower frequency is prevalent in our thinking. Consider, however, that the resonant frequency of Earth is 7.8 Hz, while light is measured in trillion Hz or THz, which is Hz times 10^{12}. Duality thinking causes us to separate matter and light, Earth and Heaven, into good and bad when, in fact, all matter is infused with light. Truthfully, spirit exists throughout, and within, all levels of reality. Only judgment creates separation.

Organizing Principle

The field is the sole governing agency of the particle.

—Albert Einstein

Energy is an organizing principle. Gravity organizes the orientation of life; trees, people, and animals grow vertically, oriented to the field of gravity. The forces within chemical bonds create the geometries inherent in nature. Ice crystals look the way they do based on the amount of energy in the bonds between water molecules. And as we remember from grade school, electromagnetic fields organize magnetized particles.

Dr. Hans Jenny, a Swiss medical doctor and naturalist, investigated vibration as an organizing principle in a science he named "cymatics." Using audible sound frequency, he demonstrated that sound frequencies vibrate material substances into geometric patterns. Different frequencies, he found, vibrate particles of sand suspended in oil into unique, complicated, and sustained designs. Alternating frequencies creates undulating, or moving, patterns.[3]

Although Jenny used audible sound frequency, the action of higher, inaudible frequency has the same impact. His experiments show the higher the frequency, the more complex the pattern. Jenny's work provides a visual for how frequency creates energy templates for matter. Changing the frequency of the vibration changes the pattern of the template and therefore the physical structure.

A demonstration of how this principle works with the frequency of thought and emotion comes from author Masaru Emoto. His work reveals that the crystalline structure of frozen water is impacted when exposed to different thoughts. Water that was focused on by people holding thoughts of love when frozen developed more elaborate and symmetrical crystalline structures than those that formed when focused on by people holding negative thoughts.[4]

The idea that thoughts have a specific frequency, or vibration, and are active rather than passive is not new. Many believe the change in the crystalline structure of Emoto's water indicates that the energy of thought, the force measured in an EEG, is absorbed by the water molecules, changing their bond angles. Regardless of the mechanism, the experiment demonstrates that physical structure can be changed through conscious intent. To that end the tools in this book are powerful agents of change.

Biological Information Codes

Subtle energy provides information transmitted as frequency coded on energy carrier waves. Human bodies receive this information and decode it. Sound waves are coded with information received by your ear; light is coded with information received by the eyes; both are decoded by the brain. Vibrations in the body transmit information in cell-to-cell communication and along neurocircuitry. As described in Chapter 7, vibration transmits information through the body's energy structures as well.

Communications technology is based on natural laws and works the same way. Consider radios and cell phones. Radios receive and decode frequency coded on radio waves, transmitted from the station. Cell phone transmissions are coded as frequency on microwaves. Encoding information on energy carrier waves, as with all of our technology, is based on mechanisms discovered in nature.

In short, subtle energy is the carrier of information coming to us through the ambiance. It's responsible for the "vibe" of a room, intuitive insight, telepathy, contacting the unseen realms, and more.

Interacting with Subtle Energy

Subtle energy, being both particle and wave, can be experienced in several distinct modes. Direct contact, feeling the radiation of it in our hands and body, is associated with its substance. We think of electromagnetic particles radiating through space, or a wave propagating from one place to another. However, subtle energy is also experienced through resonance and quantum entanglement.

Subtle energy can be felt as vibration and flow. This is the mode most hands-on energy-balancing techniques use, as well as acupuncture in the body and standing stones in the landscape. This mode of interaction is dependent on direct contact with the energy being felt and/or influenced.

We can also interact with energy through sympathetic resonance. This occurs when any item—an object, string from a musical instrument, human body—is influenced by another item it has sympathy or correspondence with. Sympathetic resonance is happening when a C string on a harp is plucked and all the C strings of different octaves vibrate and produce sound as well. Important to note is that notes other than C don't vibrate as they don't share correspondence.

Two other examples of sympathetic resonance exist with grandfather clocks and fluorescent light bulbs. In a room filled with grandfather clocks, the pendulums may start out in different phases of their swing, yet within a short time they all synchronize, swinging together in the same phase. With fluorescent light bulbs, a fluorescent light that is turned on can stimulate a nearby fluorescent bulb that is not plugged in to illuminate. Fluorescent particles from one don't flow into the other; the vibration of atoms in the lighted bulb excites the atoms in the unlit bulb.

Subtle energy interaction using direct contact or sympathetic resonance requires proximity to work. Interacting with energy from a distance relies on quantum entanglement. In what Einstein labeled "spooky action from a distance," entanglement happens when one subatomic particle changes simultaneously in relation to another subatomic particle, no matter where the other particle is. The condition is that they have to know each other. Particles that don't have a relationship don't affect each other.

The reality is that we engage and influence subtle energy in everything we do. Our thoughts and emotions have frequency and electromagnetic radiation that is measurable. They interact with other subtle energy systems we have a correspondence, or relationship, with. Energy awareness is the journey of becoming conscious of how we engage and interact with subtle energy, taking responsibility for how we impact the world through what we think, feel, say, and do.

Chapter 7

Human Energy Systems

For thousands of years, cultures across multiple continents developed ideas of what human energy anatomy looks like and how energy "organs" function. Tibetan monks, Native Americans, Hindus, mystics, and present-day metaphysicians developed systems of healing, meditation, and self-realization based on these structures. What they describe and the techniques they developed are surprisingly similar.

The names and descriptions of the energy anatomy in this book blend the Hindu Vedic system, Asian medical systems, and metaphysicians of the early 1900s with my own awareness. You may already know all you need to on the subject of energy anatomy, but if this is new territory for you, the information here is a foundation. If you're curious to learn more, there are recommended books in Appendix B.

The Interacting Energy System

The energy structures of the aura, chakras, and meridians interpenetrate each other and are interactive. They occupy the same space, distinguishing their separateness by vibrating at different frequencies. Each structure interacts with all other energy structures in holographic synergy. As growth occurs in one structure, all undergo corresponding change.

The aura engages frequency in the environment that is stepped down by the chakras into frequencies the body can sustain without overwhelming our circuits. Consider plugging an American hair dryer meant for 110 volts at 60 hertz into a British system that transmits 240 volts at 50 hertz. The circuits of the hair dryer get blown. Chakras are the transformers that ensure the circuits of our nervous system don't get blown.

Chakras digest energy information and distribute it to the meridians, nervous system, and endocrine glands where it's converted into metabolic activity and awareness. The transmission is two-way. At the same time that information is being received, our thoughts, attitudes, and beliefs are being transmitted outward to become our presence that attracts people, opportunities, and challenges into our circumstances.

Every day, we're in the midst of a continual stream of energy. Frequencies we resonate with activate different energy structures that interact with each other, forming unique patterns. These patterns stimulate emotions and thoughts and direct our actions and reactions.

High frequencies are expansive and stimulate our capacity to love, create, and serve. Lower frequencies focus awareness on detecting danger, finding shelter and food, and developing survival strategies. All frequencies are essential. All centers need to be able to function to their highest potential.

What makes a frequency, emotion, or thought-form destructive or dysfunctional isn't necessarily its frequency; it's our consciousness around it. If we're stuck in survival mode, we interpret everything as a survival issue. Even high frequencies, however, can be dysfunctional. Consider being so addicted to spiritual bliss that the need for physical survival is ignored, causing a person to lose the opportunity of physical reality.

Trauma, conditioning, and limiting patterns shape the interaction and transmission of energy. The thirteen energy meditations help clear and fine-tune our energy system to activate deeper levels of awareness.

The Aura

The aura is a field of luminosity, the radiation of life-force that surrounds people, animals, plants, and objects. The human aura is described as a "luminous egg," because emanations at the base are wider than at the top. The average human aura extends three feet from the body, although it can be much larger or smaller.

The aura is more constricted when we're processing and integrating information, doing our inner work, or need protection. It extends further outward when we're expressing, exploring, seeking, when we feel safe and content, or are undergoing spiritually expansive experiences.

The aura is bounded by a geometric Energy Template that's linked to the collective consciousness. This template establishes our energetic constitution, physically, emotionally, mentally, and spiritually. It connects to deeper spiritual realms and holds our path, purpose, and the blueprint for our major life experiences.

Our energy constitution aligns with the experiences of past incarnations and changes as we evolve. The consequences of our choices are reflected through the denseness, clarity, and patterning of energy and flow within our aura. They are also reflected in geometric thought-forms made from intentions, beliefs, and attitudes that are invested with emotion. Thought-forms are often seen as geometric patterns of energy in different auric layers. They link with other resonant thought-forms in separate layers of the aura and influence our perceptions. They're part of our presence, the magnetic force that attracts people, situations, events, and conditions into our life.

Thought-forms can develop a life of their own and feel like entity attachments. The more emotion they're given, the more magnetized they become, regardless of whether the thought-form carries high or low frequency. Highly magnetized thought-forms can attract entities, making it important to maintain a practice of clearing the aura. Queen Nefertiti's Headdress on page 36 is excellent for this.

The aura is not just a field of energy. It's comprised of filaments of light that emanate from our inner core. The light changes in frequency

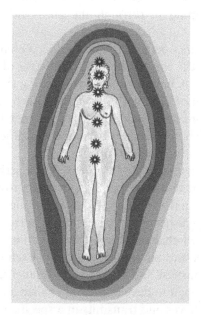

Seven layers of the aura and the corresponding chakras

and therefore density and color as the filaments radiate outward, giving the appearance of layers of energy. There are seven changes in color, or layers, in the aura. The slowest in frequency is closest to the body and the fastest is furthest away. Each layer directs specific functions through a corresponding chakra.

The aura is the organizing field of the physical body. It's not a new idea that an energy field might organize the body. It was hypothesized in the 1950s by Dr. Harold Saxton Burr, a Yale University professor of anatomy. Burr was studying cell differentiation in the developing embryo and looking at the long-standing question: If all cells have the same DNA blueprint, what activates the DNA in one cell to become a toe and another to become an eye? Through his research with salamander embryos, Burr determined that cellular development was activated and organized in accordance with a biological electromagnetic field, which he called the L-field, or life-field.[1]

Chakras

The chakras are seen within the luminous field of the aura as vortices of swirling rays of light. Although there are hundreds of chakras in the body, there are seven main physio-energetic centers. These link the energy coming in through the aura with the physiology of the body.

Each chakra is anchored in the Hara-line, a channel of energy that enters and exits at the top of the head and base of the spine through the Crown and Root Chakras. Energy runs along the Hara-line in both directions: a column of light with two tracks. Each chakra projects into the aura with a front and back emanation, except for the Crown and Root Chakras, which are actually two aspects of the same chakra with an upward and downward emanation.

Chakras are organs of development. They assimilate experiences and provide context, meaning, and avenues for growth. In this regard, they guide our spiritual evolution. Author and metaphysician Carolyn Myss explains the chakras as a progression of personal identification.[2]

Each of the seven chakras is associated with a major nerve plexus, an endocrine organ, and an area of the body. Each correlates to a specific level of consciousness and stage of development, and expresses as a color, sound, emotion, and developmental challenge.

Each chakra receives and transmits in a specific range of frequencies reflected as undulating rays. In paintings, the rays are often depicted as flower petals or flames. Frequency increases from lower to higher chakras, represented in pictures as an increase in the number of petals. Remember that all frequencies are essential and meant to work together to create our vehicle of consciousness on this plane of existence.

Anthropologist Carlos Castaneda, author of *The Teachings of Don Juan: A Yaqui Way of Knowledge,* describes rays of light in the aura as "fibers" of light.[3] These chakra fibers are thicker and denser than the filaments of light in the aura.

Castaneda's fibers have two functions. Some of them anchor us in the world, providing a frame of reference and continuity of experience. Others are unattached and extend outward, feeling and sensing the environment. The more fibers that are attached, the more secure we feel; the more fibers that are free, the more attention is available to explore new ideas, creativity, and experiences. Life is a constant interchange between security and freedom.

The Power of Seven: Layers of the Aura and Corresponding Chakras

The aura and chakras are constantly changing in size, shape, color, clarity, and density depending on our actions and reactions. The flow of subtle energy—its amplitude, clarity, and the connection between one energy structure and another—is a reflection of our consciousness. When we consciously interact with our energy patterns, we open our awareness and expand.

Traditional systems describe the aura as having seven layers with seven corresponding chakras. This seven-tiered system directly interfaces with our physical bodies. Additional auric layers and chakras exist in both higher and lower frequencies and are guiding our spiritual evolution. Rudolf Steiner, a 20th-century metaphysician, explains that as evolutionary forces drive us to change, the change happens first in our energy structures. The energy structures of today are not exactly the same as they were two thousand years ago.

The Table of Chakras: Quick Reference on page 80 provides a list of the physio-energetic chakras and auric layers along with their qualities and functions. Information in the charts will not be repeated in the following short descriptions, including sound, color, and emotion. The world is in flux and so are we. If the information about the chakras doesn't match your inner knowing, always trust yourself.

1: The Etheric-Physical Layer of the Aura and the Root Chakra

The Etheric-Physical Layer of the aura extends about two inches beyond the physical body. The inner part of it contours and permeates the body to envelop every tissue, organ, and cell. It's seen as a bluish-white webbing of light. Energy pulses along different paths within this webbing for various functions, creating mutable geometric patterns. The patterns are in constant flux, reflecting our energetic response to our internal and external environment. This layer looks and behaves remarkably like the neural pathways in the brain, changing with every thought, memory, and feeling.

Not surprisingly, the Physical Layer is associated with physicality, especially touch and physical sensation. It governs developmental stages from birth to death. Because it supplies vital life-force, imbalances can reflect illness, pain, or dysfunction.

Energy patterns in this layer hold the cellular memory of past physical pain and trauma as well as pleasure and health. While trauma can be reactivated under stress, memories of past health and upliftment can also be reactivated as a healing resource. Restoring full flow through the weblike pathways supports physical well-being.

The Physical Layer of the aura corresponds with the Root Chakra that's located near the base of the spine in the sacrum. It's also called the Base or First Chakra. The Root Chakra connects the Hara-line to the spiritual wisdom of Earth and provides grounding and support. It's the storage site of dormant, spiritual energy called Kundalini that rises up the spine during spiritual awakening. The Root Chakra draws the energy of the Crown Chakra down into the body and together the two coordinate our spiritual path.

The Root Chakra maintains physical vitality and determines the quantity of our physical energy. It's the part of our identity that understands we are part of Nature, born of Mother Earth. We tend to resonate in the Root Chakra with specific places on the planet that feel like home.

Developmentally, this chakra deals with shelter, security, nourishment, finances, medical needs, and our standing in the community. The primary motivation is survival and, emotionally, it deals with the apparent opposition between fear and faith: fear of mortality, our ability to survive financially, to belong; and faith to face problems with confidence, to believe in ourselves, and to know our place in the universe.

In the Root Chakra we learn about self in relation to the natural world and physical reality. The developmental lesson is to know that however things look, resources are available, and God is Nature.

2: The Emotional Layer of the Aura and Sacral Chakra

The Emotional Layer extends about three inches from the body and holds the template of our emotional constitution. To be clear, emotions are received and transmitted through every layer of the aura and managed in every chakra. The frequency of a given emotion determines what layer of the aura receives it and what chakra manages it.

The Emotional Layer of the aura reflects our emotional wiring, the specific constitution that determines our initial response to life. Our emotional constitution is established through genetics, spiritual lineage, past or parallel lives, and our design in this life. This layer is not as fixed as the Etheric Physical Layer and responds more fluidly to emotional growth so that our constitution changes with self-development. While the Physical Layer dealt with muscles and strength, this layer regulates the autonomic nervous system, overseeing metabolism, circulation, hormones, and respiration.

The Emotional Layer doesn't have a set color. It fluctuates with changing emotional states. Throughout the aura, emotional trauma shows as dark, thick clouds of dense energy that move slowly, if at all. Elevated emotions are clear, vivid, and full of movement. Both are found in all layers and colors. Emotional clarity expresses as intense brilliance.

The Emotional Layer of the aura channels energy into and receives energy from the Second or Sacral Chakra. This chakra is located above the pubic bone and beneath the naval in an area called the Hara or Tan Dien. It's also called the Sea of Energy or Sea of Nourishment, reflecting the role of this chakra in generating our vitality. The Sacral Chakra governs how we process and express emotions. It reflects our level of emotional maturity and intelligence and ability to maintain emotional boundaries.

The Second Chakra deals with creative impulse, emotional intelligence, reproduction, sexuality, partnerships, and commitment to family and community. We learn how to express emotions without projecting, and how to respect another person's emotions without abandoning our own.

In this chakra we learn about self in relation to others. It deals with opposition of shame and creative fulfillment. Its developmental lesson is identifying self versus not self.

3: The Mental Layer and Solar Plexus Chakra

The Mental Layer extends approximately eight inches out from the body. The quality of color reflects our mental clarity as this layer contains the template for our mental constitution, our intellectual approach to life. Thought-forms are generated here and projected into the layers of the aura that they resonate with.

The Mental Layer channels into the Third Chakra, called the Solar Plexus Chakra. This chakra is located in the space beneath the chest bone between the left and right halves of the lower rib cage. It's the center of personal identity and ego and deals with personal power, ambition, willpower, and the ability to manifest our goals. The Solar Plexus Chakra relates to our unique place in the universe, our impact in the world, and our distinctive gifts. It works with motivation, the ability to turn plans into reality, decision making, accessing inner and outer resources, and ambition.

In this chakra, we learn empowerment. We learn to let go of the self-denigrating, control-oriented voice of our disempowered ego-mind. The Solar Plexus Chakra is a major psychic center, converting the awareness of our energy senses into gut feelings.

In this chakra, we learn about self in relation to self. It deals with the emotional polarity of anger and joy. The developmental lesson is how to be personally empowered without damaging others, including people, plants, animals, and Earth.

4: The Astral Layer and Heart Chakra

The Astral Layer extends approximately twelve inches away from the physical body. It's the transitional layer of the aura. The inner three layers are oriented toward the physical world, the outer three layers toward the spiritual ideals that enliven the physical.

The Astral Layer generates the frequency of unconditional love. Its primary purpose is delivering pure frequencies of love from higher spiritual planes into its corresponding chakra, the Heart Chakra. Without love, spiritual frequencies can't ground in our energy network.

The Heart Chakra is the seat of our spirit, the place where our deepest truth resides. It's our center where we understand our path and purpose. The Heart Chakra deals with issues of forgiveness, compassion, harmony, acceptance, and empowered relationships. It allows us to remain neutral, seeing all experiences in terms of learning. Here there are no mistakes, only growth.

A fully functioning Heart Chakra allows us to learn from the story of our life without being attached to it. Once we're no longer attached to the story, forgiveness of self and others is possible. Without forgiveness, we become critical, rigid, and hard to please. Self-acceptance allows us to also accept others without the need to change or "fix" them. People find it easy to be with us because we're easy in our own company. Acceptance is the basis of peace.

In the Heart Chakra we learn about self in relation to unconditional love, respect, and acknowledgment. The emotional polarity is unity versus envy. The developmental challenge is shifting out of relationships based on power to ones based on connection.

5: The Etheric Template Layer and the Throat Chakra

The fifth layer of the aura extends as far as two feet from the body. Like the Etheric-Physical Layer, it's visualized as a grid-like web. It surrounds the inner layers, links to them, and binds them together, creating what's called an auric body, or group of related layers.

The Etheric Template Layer holds the blueprint of the human ideal. The first layer, the Etheric-Physical Layer, holds the blueprint of the physical body as expressed in this life—a reflection of the learning goals and contracts held in our DNA. The Etheric Template Layer holds the ideal of our potential. Drawing energy from this level into the first layer helps activate patterns for healing and growth.

The Etheric Layer connects us to the scaffolding of everything that exists in the material world. When connecting with this layer, we shake hands with the creator. This layer corresponds to the Throat Chakra, located in the center of the throat, and works with the manifestation of reality through vibration. Here we learn that what we speak and say matters. Our voice sends vibration into the ethers and creates form. We learn the importance of speaking our truth and aligning with higher will.

The Throat Chakra deals with information, communication, and speaking from our authentic self. It relates to psychic levels of communication and governs clairaudience and channeling. In this chakra we learn how to listen to our inner guidance and speak our truth. People enjoy being around us because we honor our path and theirs.

In the Throat Chakra, we learn about self in relation to higher will. The emotional polarity is wonder versus illusion. We question what is real and what is imagined and how we can tell the difference. The developmental challenge is discernment, knowing how to identify what's real and what's a projection of our own fears, hopes, and dreams.

6: The Celestial Layer and Third Eye Chakra

The Celestial Layer of the aura extends about two and a half feet from the body and has a shimmering quality with opalescent color. It connects us to spiritual knowledge and divine wisdom. It's the origin of spiritual experiences, the place where we find connection to the holographic whole. In this layer we find connection with the Other Side and communication with the world of spirit.

The Celestial Layer connects with the Third Eye Chakra, located in the center of the forehead, slightly above and between the eyebrows. The Third Eye Chakra is the center for clairvoyance. It communicates our life path and links us to our spiritual community. It's the seat of intuition and imagination. The spiritual vision received in this center directs the rest of the chakras.

The Third Eye Chakra brings us face-to-face with the great mystery. The more we learn, the less we know, and the more we understand we are governed by a larger force or truth. Rather than seeking control, this chakra seeks to maintain our frequency and surrender to the larger design of the Universe.

Third Eye vision sees the whole picture without judgment. It gives a God's-eye perspective, releasing us from the need to be right. In this chakra we can let go of duality, right and wrong, and see into the heart of matters. Guided by intuition, we find win-win solutions. Our intellect is sharp yet we don't rely on intellectualizing to understand what is real.

In this chakra, we learn about self in relation to nonphysical reality and understand that there's truly no separation between spirit and matter. The emotional polarity here is mystery versus rationality. The developmental challenge is surrender.

Level 7: The Ketheric or Causal Layer and the Crown Chakra

The Ketheric Layer of the aura extends about three feet from the body and is gold-silver in color. It's a weblike outer casing that resonates with spiritual reality. The outermost edge of this layer is where the geometry of the Energy Template exists. The Energy Template maintains the vibrational matrix that holds us in form.

The Ketheric Layer teaches that spiritual reality is not something that exists out there or up above. It's here, inside of self, in Nature, in Earth, in matter. This layer of the aura receives frequency from the deepest spiritual plane and links us to the higher consciousness and Source energy that lies within.

The Ketheric Layer feeds the Crown Chakra, located at the top of the head. This chakra is our center of higher consciousness, higher mind, and inner knowing. It's the seat of our spiritual identity and resonates with bliss.

Through the Crown Chakra, we experience direct connection to our spiritual identity. We feel the presence of the masters that guide us and the ancestors and spirits that accompany us on our path. When connected with this center, there's no longer any need to look for outside answers. We lose our dependency on gurus without losing respect for other people's paths.

The Crown Chakra draws Earth energy up through the body, connecting the spiritual wisdom of Earth, physical-side of Source, with the spiritual wisdom of the energy-side of Source. These chakras are the yin-yang of the whole and together guide our path to awakening.

In the Crown Chakra we discover self through the reflection of the greater mystery. The developmental challenge is to realize we are never alone, never apart from all of creation, all that is. There is no emotional polarity here, only awakening.

Meditations for Clearing the Aura and Chakras

Shifting the patterns of energy within our energy field alters our perception and expands our awareness. Meditations that strengthen and clear the aura are the Spiral Pillar of Light on page 17 and Queen Nefertiti's Headdress on page 36. Meditations that work directly with clearing and exploring the chakras are Circle of Life on page 22, Chakra Clarity on page 24, and Chakra Fibers on page 28.

Table of Chakras: Quick Reference

Chakra** Aura Layer	Keyword	Color	Music Note	Organ Nerves	Motivation	Themes
1st Root Chakra ** Etheric-Physical Layer	Abun-dance	Red ** White-blue web	Low "C"	Adrenal glands	Security	Survival Mortality Finance Security Nature Earth Service
2nd Sacral Chakra ** Emotional Layer	Creativity	Orange ** Red opal	"D"	Repro-ductive organs	Intimacy	Sexuality Creativity ** Family Change Partnering
3rd Solar Plexus Chakra ** Mental Layer	Power	Yellow ** Yellow	"E"	Pancreas and adrenal glands	Ambition	Manifesting Career ** Empowerment Cooperation Self-expression
4th Heart Chakra ** Astral Layer	Love	Pink/green ** Pink opal	"F"	Thymus	Unity	Forgiveness Self-worth Self-love Acceptance Compassion Love
5th Throat Chakra ** Etheric Template Layer	Commu-nication	Cobalt blue ** Blue and silver	"G"	Thyroid	Truth	Self-expression Truth Divine will
6th Third Eye Chakra *** Celestial Layer	Vision	Indigo or violet ** Violet	"A"	Pituitary	Purpose	Psychic perception Inner truth Divine inspira-tion Oneness
7th Crown Chakra ** Causal Layer	Divine Wisdom	Purple or white ** Gold and silver	"B"	Pineal	Awakening	Higher con-sciousness Service Spiritual con-nection

Meridians

Meridians are channels of subtle energy flowing through the body as vital life-force. Most of the major meridians are vertical pathways, supplying life-force to ever smaller channels to supply all parts of the body-mind. Acupoints are locations on the meridians that are close to the skin's surface, have low resistance, and are able to be stimulated in acupuncture and acupressure treatments. In Traditional Chinese Medicine (TCM), there are six pairs of organ meridians, and four pairs of extraordinary meridians that are often called Strange Flows.

All meridians are grouped in pairs of yin and yang partners. Yin and yang refer to complementary polarities of one whole necessary for physical creation. In TCM, all matter manifests through the energy created by the tension between the forces of yin and yang. The five elements of metal, water, wood, fire, and earth are the first divisions of yin and yang and govern the twelve organ meridians.

Yin meridians are integrative, nourishing, moistening, and substantial. The yin meridians generate emotions and emotional information. Yang meridians are active, externally oriented, and deal with manifestation. They transmit the emotion and information generated by their partner. The six paired yin and yang meridians are each associated with a specific element. Here is a quick reference to the meridian associations.

Quick Reference to the Meridians

Element	Meridian	Association
Earth	Yin—Spleen Yang—Stomach	Self-care, nourishment, mental energy, thinking, worry, satisfaction, reminiscence, and nostalgia
Metal	Yin—Lung Yang—Large Intestine	Boundaries, letting go and taking in, grief, happiness, old patterns
Water	Yin—Kidney Yang—Bladder	Ancestral energy, vitality, survival, fear, faith
Wood	Yin—Liver Yang—Gallbladder	Planning, supervising, decision-making, anger, depression
Fire	Yin—Heart Yang—Small Intestine	Joy, optimism, over-joy, shock, love, sadness, seat of the spirit, directions from the divine essence
Supplemental Fire	Yin—Pericardium Yang—Triple Heater	Protecting the heart and maintaining the flow of heart energy through the body-mind

Meditations for the Meridians

Balancing the energy flow within meridians creates balance in the body and mind, improving health, well-being, and creative engagement in life. The Circle of Life on page 22 directly activates and balances the meridians through the Central Channel Strange Flow. Weaving the Nadis on page 30 and The Living Matrix on page 50 also activate meridian pathways.

Evolutionary Energy Structures

Energy structures have two main functions: to maintain our physical bodies and to guide our spiritual evolution. Evolutionary energy structures are less involved with physical health than our physio-energetic chakras and meridians. They awaken our spiritual impulse through finer and clearer frequency energy. We are wired for the evolution of the soul and these evolutionary structures compel us to grow.

The Nadis

According to the Hindu Vedas, there are more than seventy thousand subtle-energy channels in the body called Nadis. Like meridians, their function is to transport vital life-force to every cell, as well as to connect various parts of our energy anatomy.

Three main Nadis, the Ida, Pingala, and Sushumna, flow along the spinal column and maintain the smooth flow of energy between the chakras. They connect the Base Chakra to the Crown, facilitating communication among the chakras and assisting the rising of Kundalini. The path of the three Nadis is depicted in the symbol of the caduceus used to signify medicine.

The Ida and Pingala run in spirals along the spine, weaving in and out of the chakras. The Ida is yin and represents the right hemisphere of the brain. The Pingala is yang and represents the left hemisphere of the brain. The third primary Nadi is the Sushumna and is part of the Haraline, directly connecting all the chakras through the Base and Crown.

When Ida and Pingala are clear and free-flowing, they rise to the Crown, gathering energy, then descend back to the Base Chakra to activate the spiritual force of Kundalini. Once activated, Kundalini rises from its home in the sacrum, up the Sushumna pathway to the Crown, completing the elevation of consciousness.

Kundalini

Kundalini is a finer vibration energy than the palpable subtle energy that makes up our physio-energetic anatomy. Many people see human energy fields and most people feel them. The Kundalini embedded in the Root Chakra is more difficult to detect. It carries the vibration of our spiritual identity. This frequency is the seed of awakening that exists in the most material aspect of our chakra system.

Awakening Kundalini is part of our spiritual path; however, it can be a double-edged sword. Ultimately it brings enlightenment, opening the doors to spiritual understanding, psychic ability, and higher states of consciousness. If it rises prematurely, however, it can wreak havoc.

Kundalini is highly charged and challenges the circuits of our nervous system when it rises, often producing uncomfortable sensations. As Kundalini prepares to rise, there can be a feeling of electric pulsations in the sacrum and vibrations shooting into the legs, often confused with Restless Legs Syndrome (RLS). Rising Kundalini can cause insomnia, mood swings, and anxiety, as well as sensations of alternating hot and cold.

As Kundalini rises, it passes through the chakras, magnifying unprocessed trauma and providing the opportunity to clearly see and resolve our mental and emotional issues. If we don't integrate the issues, they manifest externally as challenges that, if dealt with, create healing. Kundalini that gets blocked on its upward rise either descends back to the sacrum or remains in the area of blockage, sometimes creating physical pain as well as psychological imbalances.

Advancement to the Crown Chakra doesn't usually happen all at once. The progression often takes months or even years to complete. Activation can happen organically as part of our spiritual development, through spiritual practices, or be prematurely triggered by trauma that jars our awareness out of our physical body. This can include drug use and can lead to a psychotic break as well as damage to our energy structures.

While the side effects might seem daunting, nonetheless, humans are wired to seek enlightenment. Our spiritual identity demands it. Neuroscientist Candace Pert, who discovered the endorphin receptor in the brain, claims the brain is designed for the experience of spiritual bliss and the desire to attain it.[4]

The power of Kundalini is enormous. When activated, our vibratory capacity is increased. Kundalini integrates, harmonizes, and uplifts the chakras. Awareness is elevated and consciousness expands. As difficult as it can be, raising Kundalini and awakening our spiritual identity are the reason we're incarnate.

Weaving the Nadis on page 30 is a gentle practice to clear the Nadis and prepare the nervous system for the rising of Kundalini. If blockages occur, the Circle of Life on page 22 can help reduce discomfort. Meditation and Kundalini yoga are two good avenues of additional support.

Hara-line

The vertical line of energy that runs from the Earth through our chakras to the Crown creates a column of light in our central core. In her book *Light Emerging*, Barbara Brennan names this column of light the Hara-line.[5] The Hara-line connects us upwardly to our spiritual source and downwardly to the spiritual center of Earth. It's both grounding and uplifting, keeping us balanced, focused, and anchored in this life while embodying our spiritual identity. According to Brennan, the Hara-line activates intention and connects each person to the tasks and goals of this incarnation.

Difficulties encountered in spiritual work can be avoided if the Hara-line is actively engaged. Some of the pitfalls of spiritual work include getting caught in ego traps being invested in outcomes, becoming ungrounded, and damaging our energy structures. We might also engage in spiritual bypass, trying to engage spirituality without integrating our shadow.

The energy in the Hara-line is formed of light filaments structured in geometric patterns that emit high-frequency musical tones. Many people report hearing music, while others hear high-frequency pitches or internal tapping. Those whose intuition is not geared to auditory information often don't hear anything. These sound patterns are coded information that provides direction from within. Information in the Hara-line is reflected into the chakras.

The Earth and Sky meditation on page 19 directly activates and energizes the Hara-line, and the Circle of Life variation on page 22 energizes it.

Higher-Dimensional Chakras and Aura Layers

In addition to the seven physio-energetic chakras, two to three more chakras are emerging below the base chakra, one at the level of the knees, one at the level of the feet, and one embedded in Earth. More are also emerging above the head. These developing chakras are associated with additional auric layers, or subdivisions of the current layers. These structures represent evolutionary advances. The emergence of additional structures indicates that we're being anchored into additional dimensions of the universe.

In her book *Earth: Pleiadian Keys to the Living Library*, Barbara Marciniak channels from the Pleiadians that humans have twelve chakras in their energy system and, originally, human DNA was comprised of twelve strands as opposed to the current two. In her book, Marciniak writes that each of the twelve strands is connected to one of the twelve chakras.[6] The ten DNA strands beyond our two physical strands she claims, are light-encoded filaments.

The Spiral Pillar of Light on page 17 , Earth and Sky on page 19, and The Living Matrix on page 50 help us align with the higher-dimensional chakras.

Chapter 8

Earth's Energy Systems

Everything we eat, drink, breathe, and everything that goes into making our body, every resource we use to create our technology, comes from Earth. So it's not surprising that our energy structures are entwined with Earth's energy structures, and our frequency is entrained to hers as well. We act as though Earth belongs to us, but in reality, we belong to Earth. What quantum physics now posits is that the Universe, and everything within, is conscious,[1] has a subtle energy aspect (dark energy and dark matter)[2], and is part of the holographic totality.[3]

In Chapter 6, cymatics demonstrated that frequency creates the geometric forms of the physical world. The Schumann Resonance (SR), commonly called the Frequency of Earth, refers to the low-frequency electromagnetic waves that flow between the surface of the Earth and the ionosphere. Although the SR is stated as 7.8 Hz, or cycles per second, it's actually not a single frequency, but a set of harmonics. As when striking a C string on a harp and having all the C strings vibrate, the SR includes all the progressively weaker harmonics of 7.8 Hz, such as 14.3, 20.8, 27.3, and 33.8 Hz. As with the making of a hologram, the interference waves made by these harmonics may be part of what creates the sacred geometries within nature.

The Schumann Resonance has been described as the heartbeat of the Earth, the tuning fork that all life on the planet is entrained to. In humans, exposure to high amplitudes of the Schumann Resonance is shown to induce alpha brain-wave rhythms and stimulate altered states of consciousness.[4] Marie Jones and Larry Flaxman, in their book *The Resonance Key*, suggest that sacred geometry and structures of ancient megalithic sites are tuned to the SR and magnify its effect.[5] Can we assume that magnifying the SR effect was the intent of ancient sites, energizing ceremony and inviting celestial energy?

What we know is that when we harmonize with the Schumann Resonance, we feel uplifted, calm, and part of something larger than ourselves. The SR is stronger in Nature than modern, man-made environments because man-made, electromagnetic frequencies of all types—radio, hair dryer, TV, WiFi—are polarized and cause "disruption of the cell's electrochemical balance," which negatively impacts biological health.[6]

Earth Consciousness

Indigenous cultures respect Earth as a living being. They understand that human life is an interdependent cog within a larger planetary system. Although our scientific definition of life doesn't include planetary bodies, in the 1960s Dr. James Lovelock, PhD, proposed the first scientific theory for Earth as a living system. His theory, called the Gaia hypothesis, proposes that Earth is composed of complex, self-regulating, interactive systems that act in concert as a single organism to optimize conditions for life.[7]

The single-organism theory suggests that each person's individual transmission is reflected in the planetary whole. Every thought, behavior, and action of ours is part of the fabric of Earth consciousness that forms the vibration of our collective frequency.

Earth's Living Energy Systems

Earth seems to exhibit the same energy structures as humans with an aura, chakras (called vortices, sacred sites, or power spots), and meridians, referred to as ley lines or dragon lines. These structures receive and transmit information from the larger universe to the various life-forms of Earth.

According to the ancient Maya, Earth receives energy transmissions from spiritual dimensions through astronomical features, most notably the center of the galaxy. As part of a celestial matrix, the Earth's aura transmits outward our collective frequency. Earth, and life on Earth, is part of a feedback loop into the Universe, helping direct the evolution of the whole.

Awareness of Earth's energy anatomy was once widespread and common. Sites such as Stonehenge, the Giza Pyramids, and Mayan temples were built on Earth vortices to draw the inherent power into the function of the site. Ancient structures in all indigenous cultures were designed to interact with cosmic energy by aligning to the Sun during the equinox and solstices, to the movement of planets and constellations, and to other astronomical events. This awareness created societies that were in harmony with the flow of energy on the planet and the larger universe, something we might have need of today.

The Aura of Earth

Earth's aura is an energy field that streams energy to and from other celestial bodies. Clairvoyants describe the field as having multiple layers that, as with the human aura, receive and translate frequencies into the Earth's chakras, which are then transmitted across the planet through the ley lines. Collective emotion and thought-forms in Earth's aura look like clouds or vapors of energy with various colors, shapes, and densities.

Bruce Cathie, a retired airline pilot from New Zealand, mathematically determined the existence of an energy grid that surrounds the planet.[8] Cathie's calculations suggest that the geometric patterns of this grid maintain the harmonic frequency of Earth, which he believed provides the matrix for physical form. He claimed "that the whole of physical reality was in fact manifested by a complex pattern of interlocking wave-forms."[9] Like the first layer of the human aura, the Etheric-Physical Layer, the matrix Cathie mapped is the template that maintains physical health and seems to link to the template for every species on the planet.

Cathie's grid is not the only one that's been discovered. The Currie grid is a regular pattern of crisscrossing lines that is said to induce positive health effects. The Hartmann grid alternates positive and negative currents, and where the currents cross, generates harmful health effects. None of these grids seem to relate to each other and perhaps they represent different templates within different layers of Earth's aura.

Earth's aura stores the frequency of all emotions, thoughts, ideas, beliefs, actions, and behaviors of every species and individual within the species. Through Earth's aura the awareness of individuals within each species is linked together. Biologist Rupert Sheldrake theorizes that every species has its own Morphic Field that transmits information between members of a species, giving rise to the Hundredth Monkey Effect.[10] This concept suggests that when a certain number of individuals within a species learn a skill, that skill becomes available to all members of the species, regardless of physical proximity.

Human beliefs increase in amplitude within Earth's aura when they're fed by large numbers of people and invested with emotional intensity, whether the belief is beneficial or harmful. The higher the amplitude, the more people will be influenced. In its most destructive form, this is mob mentality where people engage in acts of cruelty they would never inflict on their own.

Spiritual practices take advantage of the amplification of thought frequency in Earth's aura with group meditation/prayer/intention-setting. In Lynne McTaggart's *The Intention Experiment,* she scientifically demonstrates that groups of people focused on a single outcome can generate significant change.[11]

Earth Chakras

Energy streaming into Earth through Earth's aura is grounded into Earth's chakra system. Like humans, Earth is thought to have thousands of minor chakras, or power spots, with seven primary chakras.[12] More probably, there are many more primary chakras spanning the continents and oceans, all synchronized with the frequencies of the planet and harmonizing Earth with the cosmos.

Imagine, as Earth spins on its axis, moves around the sun, and travels through the galaxy, the different sacred sites come into and out of alignment with other celestial bodies. They gather energy transferred in the alignment and convey it from site to site through connecting ley lines, maintaining the vitality of Earth. This immense power, amplified in sacred sites, has been used for centuries to boost ceremony and energy practices. The sacred sites keep us entrained with the cosmos we are part of.

Codices of the Maya suggest that as our solar system moves into different areas of the galaxy, finer frequencies are being encountered. Further, sacred sites are helping us awaken and remember our spiritual identity.[13] Fortunately, for those unable to travel, time and space don't limit the ability to receive these new frequencies or to connect with sacred sites. We can connect by focusing on the image of a particular site while meditating and sending energy from our Root Chakra into Earth. Exercises to help align with Earth energy and find your personal power spot are in Chapter 14.

In the craziness of modern times, we may have lost connection with Earth, but in the documentary *Planetary*, First Nation people remind us, Earth never lost connection with us.[14] We can all tap in to home.

Earth Meridians

Energy and information stream through Earth's subtle body in pathways called ley lines that are comparable to human meridians. Intersecting ley lines create vortices of energy that are easier to interact with. Similar to meridians, ley lines have either yin or yang qualities. They function as information highways and translate the frequencies from the chakras and aura into useable biological energy. As with meridians, these pathways can become blocked or damaged by human activity.

The ley lines that occur beneath Earth's surface are not the same as the grids around the planet, just as the meridians in our body are not the same as the grids in the layers of our aura. The original term *ley line* was coined by Alfred Watkins in his book *The Old Straight Track*. He identified a network of straight lines that connected sacred megalithic sites in geometric patterns across the landscape of England.[15] These straight paths were most likely made through human intention to connect power spots and channel Earth energy.

The original description of man-made ley lines is distinct from the undulating, living pathways of Earth energy described in Chinese and Indigenous teaching. Over time, however, the term *ley lines* has become synonymous with pathways of Earth energy and is used to denote both man-made straight lines and the naturally flowing energy lines of Earth.

In China, subtle energy pathways in the landscape are called dragon currents or dragon paths. Interpreting their influence forms the basis of feng shui. Buildings and communities, layouts of houses, and the timing of events employ feng shui to maintain harmony with the dragon currents. In the same way, ancient Maya built temples and pyramids to align with celestial energy to harmonize their human activity with the larger Universe. In today's culture, we've forgotten the need to harmonize with the natural world as technology has become the center of our personal universe.

We may struggle to stay harmonized with Earth and the Universe; however, we are part of the larger whole. In Chinese medicine, acupoints in the fingers and toes fix our bodies onto the loom of life and weave us into the Universe. The toe points link into the meridians of Earth and the fingers into celestial lines of force, suspending us between Earth and sky. The ancient Maya also believed the fingers and toes weave us into the Earth and sky. In addition, the Maya believed the body is connected through thirteen major joints to portals into specific harmonics in the galaxy. The joints are the ankles, knees, hips, shoulder, elbows, wrists, and the neck.

Meditations to Connect with Earth Energy

Our connection to Earth energy is innate and natural; we're alive and therefore connected. However, when we're inundated with modern technology, the Earth and Sky meditation on page 19 strengthens the links in the body with Earth and celestial energy. Circle of Life on page 22 creates a smooth flow of energy along the meridians, and The Living Matrix on page 50 directly weaves us into the matrix of the Universe. Using the activations not only helps harmonize and elevate our energy, it also projects our positive intentions into Earth's aura. Every person's contribution makes a clearer vibration for everyone.

Sacred Geometry

The forces behind and within the forms of nature are frequencies. Frequencies form foundational geometric shapes arranged in specific ratios as templates that create form. These foundational codes are repeated throughout nature as a blueprint for the visible and invisible universe.[16] The geometric patterns, called Sacred Geometry, represent a mathematical language that organizes and unifies creation.

Every natural pattern is built with a combination of one or more of the same basic geometric shapes: the sphere, square, triangle, pyramid, spiral, and the five platonic solids (tetrahedron, hexahedron, octahedron, dodecahedron, and icosahedron). These basic geometries are combined according to particular ratios that shape all the various forms of matter.

The most well-known code is the Golden Mean Ratio derived from the Fibonacci sequence. The Golden Mean is generated by adding the previous two numbers in the progression together to form the next. It begins as (1,1,2,3,5,8,13,21,34,55), so 1+1 is 2, 1+2 is 3, 2 + 3 is 5, 3 + 5 is 8, and so on. When a number in the sequence is divided by the number before it, the result tends towards 1.61803 the further you go into the progression. This is called the Golden Mean.

The Golden Mean Ratio produces the Golden Mean Spiral seen in pine cones, nautilus shells, sunflowers, fern leaves, beehives, the cornea of the eye, the helix of DNA, the spin of galaxies, and so forth throughout nature. Since these geometric patterns are the foundational codes throughout the Universe, at the basic level of our physical form, we have resonance with all other aspects of the Universe. We are expressions of the same base frequency.

The spiritual energy that powers life is amplified when we incorporate the principles and proportions of sacred geometry in buildings, art, symbols, and sacred sites. Aligning with the frequencies in this way brings us into balance with the Universe. It's notable that sacred geometry is apparent in the design of churches, synagogues, mosques, temples, and ancient stone circles. The ratio between the height of the Great Pyramid at Giza with the width of its base is the Golden Mean.

Incorporating sacred geometry into the spiritual work we do increases its effectiveness. More importantly, when we design using the principles of sacred geometry, we magnify natural energy and strengthen Earth. We amplify the Schumann Resonance rather than disrupting it. Consider highways, high-rise buildings, city plans, and other manifestations of today's world. Imagine how different they might look and feel if designed in proportion with fundamental geometric patterns. Consider how that might benefit us and Earth.

The geometric codes within our bodies are activated and amplified when reinforced by our surroundings. We're part of the whole and everything we do either reinforces that wholeness and builds harmony or disrupts it. The thirteen meditations are designed with sacred geometry to activate the sacred geometric codes within us. Sacred geometry is specifically used in Chapters 17 and 19.

Geomancy

Geomancy is a name for designing human activity in relation to the flows of Earth energy. The essence of geomancy is right relationship to Earth. How we use Earth's resources, how we walk on the land, how we position ourselves in relation to Earth energies, what we connect with, and what we transmit, all impact the flow of energy and vibration of the planet.

As with feng shui, geomancy often focuses on placing or arranging buildings or other sites to increase their favorability and to increase the effects of our spiritual intentions. In its highest form, the use of geomancy harmonizes human activity with nature to cause the least disruption to natural flows. Geomancy responds to nature on visible and invisible levels, taking into account spiritual and elemental beings—the Devas and Nature Spirits that reside on the planet with us. When we work in balance with Earth, all life prospers.

Many people feel called to assist in the cleansing of Earth's energy structures and grid system. The Pyramid Purification meditation on page 47 is specially designed for this use. Discerning energy flows can be accomplished through intuition, kinesthetic body awareness, inner sight, or using devices such as dowsing rods and pendulums. The Five-Hearts Open meditation on page 33 helps sensitize our awareness to Earth energy, allowing us to feel flows more clearly. There are exercises for how to position our homes, gardens, and activities in Chapter 14.

Nature or Earth Spirits

Everything in nature has a biological, interactive intelligence we can name Spirit. Humans have a long history of awareness of and occasional cooperation with Nature Spirits. Most visible today are the intentional communities of Findhorn in Scotland and Perelandra in the United States.

The Findhorn community was founded in the early 1960s in Northern Scotland by Eileen and Peter Caddy and Dorothy Maclean. During meditation, Dorothy began to receive inner information encouraging her to sense and connect with the forces of nature. Her daily explorations guided the community in cocreating with Nature Spirits.

Using meditation as the forum for communication, they contacted and worked with the "over-lighting" beings of different plant species. The result of their efforts was the ability to grow forty-pound cabbages and other exceptional garden feats in the rocky soil of an inhospitable climate. Findhorn has spearheaded the resurgence of interest in and cooperation with the spiritual essence of nature. You can learn more at *Findhorn.org*.

Perelandra was founded in Virginia by Machaelle Small Wright in the 1970s. Perelandra is a nature research center and seeks to empower individuals by providing the tools to cooperatively engage the intelligence in nature. Wright believes that in cocreating with nature, we will find the solutions to reverse the ecological damage to the planet. She also believes in the power of one; each individual can create dynamic and purposeful change. She willingly shares her techniques to communicate with Nature Spirits in her books and workshops and makes flower essences for healing and spiritual growth. If you are interested, her essences and work can be found at *perelandra-ltd.com*.

Nature Spirits are powerful guides and allies. They exist in many different forms with many different functions, from the elementals that maintain physical forms to the Devas who hold the over-lighting spiritual blueprint of the species. Like subtle energy, the existence of Nature Spirits has been acknowledged in most cultures. According to the website *crystalinks.com*, in Jewish literature they were called Shedim. The Egyptians called them Afries, Africans called them Yowahoos, the Irish called them Little Folk, English called them fairies, and the Persians called them Devas.

The term *Deva* comes from Sanskrit and means the "radiant ones," or "beings of brilliant light." Although conversing with Nature Spirits was fairly commonplace in many societies, today people are surprised when cooperation with the spiritual essence within nature results in the ability to grow phenomenal crops and solve ecological problems.

Fundamentally, within the forms of nature is a spiritual essence that has consciousness and with which we can interact. Connecting with this intelligence through meditation and intent with respect is important and empowering. Inviting their support in our energy practice can enliven our ability and create more successful outcomes. Some exercises for connecting with Nature Spirits can be found in Chapter 14.

Celestial Energies

The Earth is in constant exchange with other bodies in the solar system and galaxy, providing a mosaic of energy influences. An example on a physical level is the Northern Light phenomenon, which occurs when the Earth receives boosts of energy from the sun in electromagnetic waves. The influx is received and dispersed along the Van Allen belt, a torus-shaped path of energetically charged particles held in place by Earth's magnetic field.

Of course we're all aware of the effect the moon has on tidal waters and our moods. Less obvious are the effects of the movement of planets in our solar system, the path of the constellations across the sky, and our solar system's orientation to the center of the galaxy. Each celestial influence interacts across the entire range of physical to energetic reality, and every physical expression has a corresponding energetic manifestation affecting emotions, psychic abilities, levels of awareness, and so forth.

The ancient Maya provide a unique and magical perspective into the cosmos. Looking through the lens left behind in the codices they wrote, we see a world where everything is connected by lines of force—where planets move across the sky magnetizing conditions on Earth as they pass. Alignments between celestial bodies open portals allowing energy to flow from one place to another, and the human body is intimately linked to the cosmos.

Spiritual energy received through the Third Eye and Crown Chakras is often thought of as related to the heavens and residing among the stars. Though this is a useful metaphor, it's a misnomer to call higher spiritual energies "celestial." We probably do so because the word higher takes us upward. It's more appropriate to eliminate the word higher altogether and call them multidimensional energies. These energies don't exist "up there"; they exist right here. Personal guides, angels, ascended masters, departed loved ones, and any number of unseen beings exist alongside us, vibrating at a different rate and sharing our world. We interact with them on a daily basis, often without realizing it.

Although all the meditations assist in interacting with Spirit, Mystic Triangle on page 44, Pyramid Purification on page 47, and The Living Matrix on page 50 are specifically designed to access higher frequency and provide connection to dimensional consciousness. Chapter 20 has more detailed information and exercises.

Chapter 9

Deciphering the Language of Subtle Energy

The body is the link to our subconscious mind where we sense and interpret internal and external flows of energy. We sense energy all the time, just below the level of our conscious awareness. Energy received through the aura is translated by the chakras into messages experienced in the body. Paying attention to and understanding energy messages are skills we know but may have forgotten. This chapter is a guide to remembering the tools of energy awareness.

Felt-Senses

Our senses are geared to receive information along a range of frequencies. Physical senses of sight, sound, smell, taste, kinesthetic feeling, and emotions can be stimulated by subtle energy. Because they happen in the body, these tools are often called felt energy senses or felt-senses.

The essence of energy awareness is listening to our felt-senses and using what we learn in creating our circumstances. The chakra level where an impulse is received determines what senses are activated. Physical sensations, gut feelings, and emotions are the most accessible of our felt energy senses. Others include inner visions, inner knowing, shifts in moods and perception, and direct intuition. All of these modes, or any combination of them, may be activated when encountering energy. We can all feel the "vibe" of a situation when walking into a room; now we're becoming aware of how.

Physical or Kinesthetic Sensations

The translations of energy information in the chakras produce physical sensations that often coincide with other modes of awareness, acting as confirmation of the information we perceive. Physical sensations without a discernible physical cause are often the first sign of subtle energy interactions. Tingling, vibration, warmth, cold, excitation, goose bumps, hair standing on end, skin crawling, pain, burning, the sensation of air moving across our skin, nausea, butterflies in the stomach, a sense of being dropped, heart racing, and more can all be indicators of encounters with subtle energy.

Identifying the specific signals the body sends in different situations becomes the dictionary of our personal energy language. For example, imagine crossing a ley line and feeling your hair stand on end, or receiving intuitive information and noticing a wave of tingles from head to foot, validating the truth of what you're hearing, or perhaps your frequency changes and you notice a strong vibration as old patterns are disrupted. By taking note, we learn to decipher the language of energy.

When sensations occur without a discernible physical cause, notice any coinciding thoughts, emotions, or gut instincts. These are clues to an energy interaction.

Changes in Perception

Receiving energy information can cause a shift in perspective. The scenery may suddenly seem far away, or one object may enlarge as everything else fades into the background. Sounds may become tunneled or faint, and be accompanied with a heightened sense of knowing, focus, or mental acuity. With other sounds muted, we may hear inner messages from Spirit or musical tones of extraordinary clarity. We may suddenly see colors around people or streaming light between them. We may see flashes of light, movement in the corner of our eye, or misty outlines of shapes and scenes.

Always ensure the changes are from energy shifts and not indicators of physical ailments. Check any distortions with a health expert.

Gut Feelings and Intuition

The vibe we get from a person or place, the sudden, instinctive knowing of something we can't logically deduce, is based on the internal processing of energy information. What's unique about gut feelings and intuition is our certainty of their validity. There's a sudden, immediate awareness of truth that will not be silenced, with no rational way of knowing why.

Gut feelings and intuition are often accompanied by strong emotions and/or physical sensations that are unrelated to what's happening around us. For example, we may experience a strong attraction or repulsion to a person or place for no discernible reason. We may recognize a place without having been there, and even know what will be around the corner before we turn.

Gut feelings and intuition can be at odds with our mind, causing us to choose between our instinct and rationale. For example, you may want to enter a business arrangement that makes good sense, but feel agitated and reluctant to move forward. Your gut instinct may be telling you to take a closer look at the details before committing, or check the feasibility of the timeline. Conversely, a goal you really want may look impossible, yet you feel compelled forward and are met with odd synchronicity and flow.

Sometimes, it can be difficult to know the difference between intuition and wishful thinking. One way to discern is to identify where in the body the certainty is coming from and how many additional indicators are present. Do you feel compelled due to mental determination, or due to an excitation deep within that's accompanied by physical sensations that validate your feelings?

Moods and Emotions

It's not a coincidence that the chakras and meridians correlate to specific emotions. Emotions are the body's way of decoding energy information for conscious processing. Although the majority of energy information is underneath conscious perception, emotions bring it into direct awareness. Emotions are often thought of as being either good or bad, but actually all emotions, when listened to, have function. They rise to provide information and recede when the information is received. If we are stuck in an emotional state, it's because we haven't received and/or acted on the information. We don't need to avoid or pursue emotions; we need to accept, listen, learn, and act accordingly.

Energy information may stimulate mood changes that seemingly have no correlation to what's happening. We may suddenly feel calm and peaceful in the face of difficulty or, conversely, feel apprehensive with no cause. Changes in mood that correspond with physical sensations alert us to shifts in energy states.

Inner Vision and Inner Knowing

Images that form in the mind's eye are called clairvoyance and are a direct translation of energy information. When images arise as we're sensing energy, they're usually telling us something important. As with intuition, it's sometimes hard to decide if what we're seeing is a vision or "just our imagination." Here are some tips:

- True visions are rarely what we're inclined to imagine. They're surprising in their content, with details we've never considered.
- When we imagine, we decide what will happen next. In a vision, what occurs is outside of our control.
- Ask yourself: Are you feeling a connection in your body to what you see in your mind's eye? Does the image come with physical sensations like goose bumps? Is it surprising to you, and if not, are you in some way controlling it?

Inner knowing, or gnosis, is similar to gut feelings except more related to thoughts than instincts. An inner knowing might be a thought that says, I need to go, while a gut instinct might be a feeling that is so uncomfortable you must move. With an inner knowing, we have mental knowledge as opposed to a compulsion. As with all energy intuition, other modes of awareness validate the information. With practice, which means learning through mistakes, we develop the discernment needed to distinguish truth from wishful thinking and further develop our library of energy translations.

Dreams

Messages, symbols, feelings, and metaphors in our dreams often reveal our energy reality. Especially communicative are vivid, lucid dreams that feel as real as waking awareness and recurring dreams or themes within our dreams. With practice we can use dreams as direct communication with our subconscious awareness. We can plan assignations during dreamtime with our inner wisdom and spiritual guides, or travel to dimensions of higher knowledge.

To promote this mode of awareness, keep a journal by your bed and write down whatever you remember from your dreams. Set an intention before bed to receive information. Go to sleep while focusing on this intention.

Emotions: Translations of Energy

Emotions are the key to translating energy. They're a direct link between the body, mind, and energy processed in our chakras. Emotions have two essential functions: they provide information and the motivation to do something with it.

The first person to articulate this link between emotions, the body, and energy was psychoanalyst Dr. Wilhelm Reich, the father of body-centered psychotherapy. Through his work and those who followed him, we understand that every emotion provides direct and immediate information. It's either telling us what's happening around us right now or replaying something in the past that we didn't fully process. Then it provides the physical energy to act.

For example, a man walking in the jungle is attacked by a tiger. Before he's consciously aware, his energy field transmits information about the danger and he feels sudden fear. His muscles tighten; he's on high alert, ready to fight or flee. Slowed down, the Root Chakra that deals with survival processed the information and generated the emotion of fear, which stimulated the release of adrenalin.

In this example, the emotion provided information in response to an event in the present moment. But if the man doesn't process the experience, the next time he walks in the jungle, an entirely new set of events takes place.

Unprocessed emotions from this trauma will cause the man to be afraid at every sound and sudden movement. His emotion will no longer alert him to present danger, but tell him where he got stuck in the past. Until he processes the event, he'll continue to experience fear over non-threatening stimulation. Trying to suppress it through avoidance or even trying to "release it" will only drive it deeper into his psyche. There it will link with other fears and become a fear-based thought-form. What started as fear that the jungle isn't safe becomes a thought-form that life isn't safe, and, suddenly, it won't be.

Not processing this trauma originally may reflect an even deeper block. Restimulating the trauma offers an opportunity to heal. The situation could, for example, trigger unresolved issues around death. Thoughts about his mortality, what happens after death, and how prepared he is to die may be activated and linked to his current experience. While daunting, the original event provides access to the unknown inner block. Resolving it is a grand opportunity for growth.

Importantly, beyond teaching us where we're stuck, this type of experience also tells us the encounter wasn't an accident. It was a wake-up call. Whenever past issues link to an event in the present, we're being given an opportunity to heal. And if we say no thanks and keep on going, events will continue to be drawn toward us to stimulate this block until we take care of it.

Individual emotions that provide information about our immediate environment are different from our emotional constitution, or predominant emotional response to life. Maybe you're an optimist or a pessimist, believing that the universe conspires on your behalf or that the world is against you. Whatever your belief, if you don't like the emotional lens you view the world through, it's time to change. Accept what you feel, explore how the feeling directs your life, and determine the underlying experience that created your lens. Then ask: is the belief created from this experience true or is it a distortion from a wounded ego?

The Body's Revelations

Being awake in the present moment is achieved through body awareness and by embracing our emotions and listening to their message. The problem is that not all emotions are comfortable and we don't like being uncomfortable.

Difficult emotions are judged as unworthy. We think they mean we're unenlightened, seeped in low-frequency energy. Consequently, instead of learning about the energy our emotions are translating, we tend to suppress and avoid feeling them. How this is accomplished is quite fascinating.

When an emotion is uncomfortable, the body tightens around it, creating an armor of tension. This stops the flow of energy into the tightened area, dampening the emotion. Areas of armor happen in body segments that were identified by Wilhelm Reich. Segments are horizontal rings of muscles that contract front, back, and sides to constrict the flow of energy into an area.

Segments contract without involving muscles in the segments above or below them. Here's an example: try tightening the front of your chest without tightening your back at the same level. You can't. This is the chest segment. But you can tighten the chest segment without tightening the neck segment above it or the abdominal segment below it.

The segments are ocular, oral, neck, chest, upper abdomen, lower abdomen, and pelvis. Each segment correlates to specific emotions and corresponds to the location of specific chakras. (See the Emotional Associations chart on page 104.)

Avoiding uncomfortable emotions by tightening the muscles in the corresponding segment not only decreases the flow of energy, but it also decreases nerve conduction, circulation, and organ function. This is a big price to pay, and the cost isn't over. Not only do we shut off the uncomfortable emotion, we impede all emotions generated in the segment, even the pleasant ones.[1] If the chest segment limits grief, it also limits joy. Without the full range of emotions, life loses meaning.

Side effects of emotional armoring include:

- No longer feeling any of the emotions generated in a specific segment, including enjoyable emotions.
- Pain and physical dysfunction in the segment due to muscle tension, trigger points, and organ discomfort.
- Isolation from vital energy, blood, and therefore nourishment.
- Inability to live in the present; living in past trauma, recreating the same scene again and again.
- Hypervigilance and excessive emotional control.
- Flat-lined emotions with lower mountains and shallower valleys.
- Lack of spontaneity and joy.

When we avoid experiencing our emotions, we lose the capacity to feel. The messages our emotions provide are lost. We're no longer awake, aware, and alive in the present moment. Uncovering repressed emotions requires releasing muscle tension and feeling the emotional content they hold. This is where skilled bodywork can be invaluable.

When Wilhelm Reich originally proposed that emotions are generated in the body, it created a great deal of controversy. Even though most people agree that emotions are felt in the body, the assumption was that they are the result of chemical reactions in the brain. The work of Dr. Candice Pert, explained in her book *Molecules of Emotion*, substantiated the idea that emotions are body events.[2] The Chakra Clarity meditation on page 21 helps access the emotional content of body segments.

Although everyone is different, this chart of Emotional Associations provides correlations for deciphering energy. If this information is interesting, enjoy my book *The Path of Emotions: Transform Emotions into Energy to Achieve Your Greatest Potential*.

Emotional Associations

Emotion	Surface Message	Chakra and Segment
Anger	Your boundaries have been breached. There is obstruction in your path.	• Solar Plexus Chakra • Upper abdominal segment
Healthy Pride	You have grown and developed. You belong.	• Solar Plexus Chakra • Upper abdominal segment
Fear	You are not safe.	• Root Chakra • Pelvic segment
Shame	You have interfered in a significant way in someone else's path. You have disregarded your own boundaries.	• Second Chakra • Lower abdomen segment
Guilt	You have breached someone else's boundaries.	• Heart Chakra • Chest segment
Joy	You are part of a bigger purpose.	• Heart Chakra • Chest segment
Sadness	You have lost something of value.	• Heart Chakra • Chest segment
Grief	The configuration of energy in your life is incomplete.	• Heart Chakra • Chest segment
Jealousy	You have undervalued some part of your life, you don't value yourself, or you don't know your own worth.	• Solar Plexus and Second Chakras, mixed • Upper and lower abdominal segments
Satisfaction	You know that you have stretched and grown.	• Both Solar Plexus and Heart Chakras • Upper abdominal and chest segments
Embarrassment	You are locked in judgment.	• Whole body event
Love	This is a self-transcendent emotion. You are complete, whole, where you're supposed to be, and part of an intentional universe.	• Heart Chakra • Chest segment • To a lesser extent, all chakras and segments
Ecstasy	This is another self-transcendent emotion. You are one with the universe.	• Both Crown and Third Eye Chakras • Orbital segment • To a lesser extent, all chakras and segments

Chronic Pain and Illness

Chronic pain and illness can be communications from the body-mind. Long-term unresolved emotions and associated muscle tension can disrupt energy flow resulting in chronic pain and illness, alerting us to the need for processing a hidden trauma or for making a change. This does not mean that all illness has an emotional or energetic cause; it means that all illness has an emotional component relating to an energetic reality.

There is survival benefit in using body tension to contain emotion, especially when related to trauma. Some events are so traumatic that without protection from their full impact we would simply crumble. Using muscle tension to dampen emotional intensity provides time to process slowly. The protection creates a problem only if it becomes a way of life rather than a respite.

We always need to be sure we're not using metaphysical explanations to avoid medical treatment. Case in point: A friend went through early menopause in her thirties. She didn't get a medical checkup because her mother had recently died and she believed she was moving into the role of matriarch for her family, which was true. Thirteen years later she learned she had a tumor in her pituitary gland, the reason for her early menopause. Although the changing of her family role triggered events, there was also a treatable condition.

No one knows what another person's path is, what his/her traumas are, and what her/his muscle tension or illness means. It's an exploration. If someone's pushing you to heal faster than you're comfortable with, remember: this is your path and no one besides you knows what you need to learn or what you need to do to heal. Don't let anyone shame you into rushing. There's no judgment in your pain. We're on this journey together, learning as we go. The only thing that's utterly true is that we're here to learn and grow and support each other on the way.

Emotions and Thought-forms

Emotions can be tricky. We can be overcome with anger, jealousy, and fear, missing the meanings within. Many of us also know the unintended consequences of jumping into a situation too quickly due to the imbalance of over-joy. When emotions get entwined with repetitive thoughts, they become even trickier. Emotional management turns out to be less about what happens to us, and more about what we believe about ourselves and the world.

Before we have a thought, we make an unconscious decision to think it. Our beliefs and expectations about the world generate the thoughts we give room to in our head. Once we have a thought, if we then invest it with emotional energy and choose it over other thoughts, it becomes a thought-form. Thought-forms live in our energy field as independent entities, directing our mental focus and attracting our experiences as discussed in Chapter 12.

Queen Nefertiti's Headdress on page 36 is excellent for discharging the energy enlivening the thought-forms in our aura.

Putting It All Together

The language of subtle energy is personal. We create it with information received through various modes of perception that include body sensations, emotions, intuition, and so forth that each of us assemble into our energy language. Each of us learns through experience how to combine the words of our language into sentences with context and meaning. In the beginning, we're just creating the dictionary.

When we start using our energy language to discern reality, it's possible to lose our mooring. Sometimes we're confused, other times, self-impressed. Sometimes we think our language is the only or best one and all people should speak it, or our perceptions are universally true for everyone.

Working with energy requires humility. Not the type of humility that's actually inverted arrogance, the humility that downplays our essence. The humility required for energy awareness is that of knowing we are all part of the hologram and, like it or not, every perception is valid. Like the famous parable of a group of ants looking at an elephant, each of us sees only part of the whole. What we see and know is not what's true for everyone. The entire picture becomes clear when we put all our perceptions together.

Part III

Empowering Your Life

Awareness of the flows of energy that sustain and direct life is the first step in consciously using energy to solve personal and planetary problems. This section of the book provides suggestions for using energy awareness in developing inner resources.

The exercises in each chapter are based on the thirteen meditations in Chapter 3. The exercises are not recipes. They're not the only way to use energy skills, and they may not be the best way for you. Each chapter offers a step-by-step process to provide ideas and generate insight. They are possibilities only. Use them as they are, incorporate them into techniques you already use, modify them to fit your beliefs, or discard them altogether. Only you know what is right for you.

Each exercise begins with activating one or more of the thirteen patterns and ends with closing the activation. To activate a pattern, simply visualize it in its completed form. You don't need to go through the original steps. If you've activated the pattern once, your body will remember it; all you need do is visualize it. To close an activated pattern, simply imagine the pattern dissolving.

Each exercise also starts and ends with grounding, centering, and establishing boundaries—skills taught in Chapter 10. Opening this way shifts your awareness internally, marshalling your resources so that you can act with power. Ending this way makes sure that you leave the altered state of your meditation and are fully present in everyday reality.

Approach this practice as a grand adventure. Open yourself to change, surrender old concepts and ideas, and be willing to step into something new. Allow rich vistas to open with unimaginable rewards!

Chapter 10

Developing Personal Power: Grounding, Centering, Creating Boundaries

Personal power is not about having authority over other people. It's not the power of self-importance used to intimidate or manipulate others. It isn't even about getting everything we want in life. Personal power is the ability to live authentically. It's standing in the integrity of our essence before any circumstance and holding our intention with clarity, to remain calm, compassionate, and resolute, regardless of opposition. Personal power is the key to creating a life of meaning and joy.

There are four basic components to building personal power: grounding, centering, presence, and maintaining boundaries. As we become better with these skills, we become more successful at using energy. The three most useful meditations are the Spiral Pillar of Light, Earth and Sky, and Circle of Life. Engaging these activations on a daily basis will increase all four elements of personal power. More importantly, activating them when feeling challenged can be life changing.

As you progress through this book, if the energy practices are not creating the changes you want, come back to this chapter and practice building personal power. It's the key to energy mastery.

Grounding

Grounding is being connected to Earth. This connection increases stability and strength, and helps us maintain a balanced approach to life. When our attention is on the ground, that's where our energy flows. As we connect, Earth's energy flows back into us.

Walking is a good example of how this happens. It may feel that gravity weighs us down and only muscle strength allows us to move forward. However, the ability to move depends on pushing off from the ground. A solid base acts like a spring board. Anyone who has gotten caught in quicksand or walked through a bog knows that the strength of our muscles isn't enough to move us forward. Earth is the other half of the equation.

Signs of being ungrounded include lack of confidence, worry and anxiety, lack of mental focus, difficulty making decisions, inability to manifest ideas into reality, and even physical pain and fatigue. Sometimes we're so ungrounded we trip over things, bump into doorways, and feel spacey.

Grounding :

- Stabilizes our energy field and helps us manage energy surges. It releases excess charge in our energy field in the same manner that grounding wires discharge electricity in an electrical circuit.
- Restores energy when we're depleted. Much in the same way that the roots of a plant bring nourishment to the leaves, grounding restores vitality and replenishes our energy field.
- Creates strength and flexibility. Roots stabilize plants against wind and erosion, and grounding stabilizes us, helping us maintain calm, flexible strength no matter the circumstances.
- Encourages growth. The deeper our root system, the higher we can grow. When we develop our energy sensitivity faster than our ability to ground, we're likely to topple in the first big wind, or become overcharged and unable to dissipate excess energy.
- Calms our emotions and prevents burnout.
- Releases negatively charged energy. While energy itself is neutral, it can be a carrier wave for harmful thoughts, intentions, and desires. Sending this energy into Earth is one way of clearing our energy field. Once energy is released from its harmful intention, it returns to pure light.
- Improves body awareness, connects mind and body. The body is the vehicle of our consciousness in this 4-D reality. When we're fully present and embodied, we have more access to our inner wisdom and physical signs of energy.

In short, grounding helps us be more connected, responsive, engaged, energized, strong, stable, and present. Grounding is essential for working with energy, and Earth is a powerful ally for empowerment.

The best grounding exercise is the Earth and Sky meditation on page 19 and here is a simple addition.

ACTIVATE THE EARTH AND SKY MEDITATION

Place one hand over your head or heart and focus your attention on your feet, encouraging a downward flow of energy.

Exhale, and shift your attention from your feet to the center of Earth.

Visualize the center of Earth as pure spiritual light.

Inhale energy from Earth back into your feet, then exhale it up to your head.

Imagine the connection as two sides of a highway going straight up and down the Hara-line.

Use your breath and attention to maintain the flow and connection.

Once the connection with Earth has been felt, it's easy to return to it when we notice we're ungrounded. Just placing a hand on the top of our head and remembering the feeling will bring us back "down to Earth."

Centering

Centering brings our attention into the core of our being and connects the spiritual center in our heart with the physical center in our lower abdomen. When we're centered, we're able to be ourselves, resolved and compassionate in the face of obstacles.

In Traditional Chinese Medicine (TCM), the heart is where our Spirit resides. It's sacred space where we connect with our path, purpose, and spiritual source. The Heart Chakra helps us know our true self.

Our physical center is below the belly button and above the pubic bone, in the Second Chakra, and is called the Tan Dien or Hara in TCM. It's where the "Sea of Chi" resides, the storage area for vitality. The Tan Dien is the source of unassailable intent that enables us to pursue the direction of our heart. When we're physically centered, like the Weeble toy, we may wobble, but we won't fall down.

Centering is making a connection between our spiritual center and physical center through the Solar Plexus Chakra, bringing all three into alignment. Maintaining this alignment ignites a brilliant light in the lower sternum, just under the Heart Chakra and above the Solar Plexus Chakra. This is our true center. When you're centered, there's no mistaking it. Free of the developmental issues of the chakras, being centered is our North Star.

SIMPLE CORE CENTERING EXERCISE

Put your right hand over your Tan Dien below the belly button and your left hand over your Heart Chakra in the middle of the chest bone.

If you wish, activate the Winged Disk pattern.

As you inhale:

Imagine light from your spiritual Source entering the top of your head and collecting in your heart, filling it with brilliance.

On the same inhalation, imagine Earth energy flowing into your Base Chakra and collecting in your Tan Dien, filling it with light.

As you exhale, visualize the energy from the two centers moving together and merging.

With each inhalation, draw energy from Earth and sky into your Tan Dien and Heart Chakra, building energy in these centers.

With each exhalation, let the energy between the two centers merge.

Continue this breathing pattern, placing your awareness on the lower part of your chest bone, below the heart chakra and above the solar plexus. As you come into your center, a light will emerge and grow, spreading the clear, calming effect of being centered. This light often takes the shape of a star.

Once the light of our center has been established, it's easy to reestablish when life knocks us off balance. Just focusing awareness on the lower chest bone and remembering the feeling restores us to center.

Creating Boundaries

Our energetic boundary is the place where we end and another begins. It marks our emotional, physical, and energetic space. Having a boundary protects our center. For many, their boundary encompasses their entire aura. For others, it encompasses the strongest layer of the aura, which is usually the third layer. Healthy boundaries provide independence of thought and action, allowing us to be in exchange with others without losing our personal identity, uniqueness, or autonomy.

There's a profound dichotomy in working with energy. On the one hand, we're all interlinked. We feel each others' energy and influence each others' energy flow. On the other hand, we're separate individuals with our own distinct energy, patterned according to our vision, intent, and emotion. The quandary is how to stay connected and flowing with others while maintaining our distinction. We can think of the energy boundary as a semipermeable membrane, opening to the energy experiences we want and closing to the ones we don't want.

When doing energy work, a boundary ensures that we don't take on another person's energetic condition or fall under someone else's influence. At the same time, it minimizes our projections so that we don't unfairly influence another. Healthy boundaries demonstrate that we trust and respect other people's path, purpose, and contribution because we know who we are and are confident in our connection to Source.

The demarcation of a person's aura in someone with poor boundaries might appear either very weak or very rigid. Weak boundaries make it difficult for us, to hold our space and be authentic. We allow other people to influence us and the fibers of our chakras may become tangled with theirs. We may conform to ideals and beliefs we don't hold as true. Sometimes when we give our power away, we play victim and unload the consequences of our choices on the stronger influences around us.

Rigid boundaries are overly protective and detached. The aura becomes hard and impenetrable, and the energy fibers are often coiled in the chakras. We lose connection, support, and exchange of energy from our surroundings. Flow is essential to health, and without it, we become isolated. Isolation can cause physical, emotional, spiritual, and mental health issues. Overly rigid boundaries give the illusion of personal power, yet are as disabling as not having any boundaries at all.

Rigid or weak, poor boundaries cause us to disconnect from our body, especially if we feel powerless to change. Once disconnected, we no longer receive energy information through our senses. This impacts our centeredness, grounding, and presence, diminishing our personal power. In this state, effectively working with energy becomes difficult, if not dangerous.

Activations to help define your boundary are the Spiral Pillar of Light on page 17 and the Circle of Life on page 22. Here's a simple exercise.

CREATING YOUR BOUNDARIES EXERCISE

Ground and center.

Spread your arms straight out from your body and swing from side to side, demarking your personal space. Twist, bend, and explore the area around you. This is your space.

Activate the Spiral Pillar of Light pattern by inhaling and visualizing a pillar of light coming down into, through, and around you to Earth, encompassing you in safety and peace.

In your mind's eye:

- Create an image of the perfect boundary for you. Perhaps it's a cell membrane with receptors for what you want to bring in, and ports for what you want to put out. Perhaps it's the radiant light of an ascended master. Or maybe it's a zippered cloak you can open and close at will.
- Take your time; try on several different types of boundaries. How do you feel inside each one?
- Choose the image that feels most like you.
- Direct everything that isn't for your highest good to leave. Imagine a whirlwind or cleansing force. Try Queen Nefertiti's Headdress.
- Intend that everything inside your boundary is your sacred space and only the highest good is allowed inside.

Draw on this image anytime you feel your inner space needs support.

Presence

Our personal emanation—the projection of self into the world—is what we call presence. Our presence is our ambassador to the world. It communicates our intent and opens or closes the doors that cocreate our circumstances.

Our presence conveys the vibrational quality of our energy and reflects how our energy follows our attention. If our mind is frenzied and our attention is jumping from one thing to another, our energy will be scattered and our presence insubstantial. If our mind is focused, our energy will be coherent and our presence masterful.

Where we place our attention is where our energy flows. Presence grows with the ability to maintain focused attention on our center and ground, simultaneously with events in the outer world. This dual attention is a master skill we can use in maintaining awareness of both intuition and reason, of inner feelings and external events. Focused attention develops our energy awareness and opens our perceptions, turning our presence into a powerful ally.

Presence activates our personal power. The point of power is always in the present moment and the ability to be engaged in the present is a reflection of our presence. Being with someone who has true presence is profoundly comforting. It's the difference between being listened to and being heard, between being in someone's company and being welcomed.

Ground, center, and establish your boundary.

Open the Spiral Pillar of Light.

Imagine that the space inside the Pillar, all the way into the center of your core and out to the edge of your boundary, is your magic garden.

Add flowers, trees, cliffs, waterfalls, meadows, seascapes, whatever adds to your vibration and makes you feel complete. Be sure to include a place for you to sit.

Breathe into your core and expand your brilliance, filling your garden with light.

Expand with self-transcendent feelings of love, compassion, wonder, awe, kindness, and respect.

Invite your highest self to live within this magical landscape.

Carry this image and feeling with you in your daily activities.

Being Powerful

When we're grounded and centered with healthy boundaries, expansive spiritual energy flows into our Crown and Root Chakras and is integrated into our energy structures. The emanation that we radiate through our presence is bright, clear, and strong. We have a definable, but fluid exchange of energy with our surroundings and our fibers are flowing and curious. We balance energy intuition with reason and are free to explore life fearlessly.

This is personal power. In this state, what we create in our relationships and circumstances reflects who we truly are. We let go of past conditioning and embrace our wounded ego. Even when we don't have a clear idea of path and purpose, we feel intentional, and life has meaning.

Using the techniques in this chapter is the best way to master them. Practice grounding and centering every time you feel unfocused, confused, or overwhelmed. When in conflict, move into your personal power. Start every day with a short meditation; even five minutes is enough.

Every exercise in subsequent chapters will begin and end with grounding, centering, and establishing boundaries. When you open meditations this way, your personal power will be brought into each exercise. Closing will disengage the activation and bring you back into present time, fully engaged for daily action.

Chapter 11

Sensing Subtle Energy

The human body is continuously sensing and interacting with subtle energy. The dialogue we're engaged in is largely subconscious, and the hints of it in our emotions, sensations, and other modes of awareness are easily dismissed. Becoming conscious is taking part in the conversation and creatively participating in the grand and beautiful mystery of life.

Success in sensing subtle energy often depends on releasing expectations. When we have trouble feeling our energy senses, or suddenly feel closed down, we're likely overinvested. We're invested in a certain outcome, either for our self or someone else, and our sense of importance has gotten involved. Letting go of investment requires taking a step back, breathing, and simply enjoying our energy senses.

Discouragement and elation are constant companions when developing or fine-tuning a skill. Don't rely on either as guides to your progress. Sometimes, we overfocus on the signs of energy in Chapter 9 and are discouraged when we don't feel them. Other times, it all seems too easy to be real. Remember the ability to sense energy is innate; everyone perceives uniquely and awareness awakens naturally. Pay attention, have fun, be patient, and play.

Felt-Perceptions

While felt-senses refer to the modes through which the body receives energy information, felt-perceptions are how the brain conceptually interprets the body's reading of energy. Felt-perceptions combine information received through multiple modes of awareness and converts it into understandable messages. The messages are communicated through three simultaneous components: physical sensations to get your attention, emotions to motivate action, and spontaneous thoughts that inform your action. The thoughts are short, mental insights that consist of a single phrase. Here's an example:

In my early twenties, I worked in the Toronto Greenpeace office. Early one morning, after a night-long surveillance, a colleague and I parked on the side of the road alongside a phone booth. Our surveillance had failed and we needed to call the home office. My colleague, Kai, got out of the car to make the call.

I closed my eyes, exhausted and discouraged, and within a few minutes fell into a light sleep. I was woken by uncomfortable twitches in my legs. At the same time, I became irrationally irritated and the thought flashed into my mind, "Get out of the car." I ignored it and tried to go back to sleep. Immediately the twitching turned into electric shocks, the irritation became anger, and the thought returned, much stronger. Again, I ignored the message. Suddenly, the shocks became intense agitation, I became extremely angry, and I was compelled to get out of the car. I simply couldn't stay inside.

I jumped out and strode toward Kai. As I rounded the back of the car and approached the phone booth, Kai looked over my shoulder, his mouth dropped open, and he pointed toward the road. I turned in time to see a van slam into the back of our car at about fifty miles an hour, tossing it across the street. Fortunately, no one in the van was hurt.

I was stunned. What happened? Later, I understood that my body had felt the energy bow wave of the coming car accident. In his book *Entangled Minds: Extrasensory Experiences in a Quantum Reality*, scientist Dean Radin demonstrates through double-blind experiments that upcoming events are preceded by a bow wave that our body can perceive. The stronger the emotion the upcoming event has the potential to generate, the greater the amplitude of the bow wave.[1]

We all feel the bow wave of upcoming events, but usually, the physical sensations and emotional content aren't strong enough to get our attention. Over time, we learn to tune in at even the slightest indication of the triad of physical sensations, emotion, and an unreasoned thought. This requires whole body listening, which means our body, mind, and spirit must be in present time to receive and understand the communications. As we become more present and aware, communications and energy shifts become clearer and our responses more assured.

Discernment

Reading energy requires sensitivity and is further challenged by the bias of our personal lens. Everybody, no exception, is influenced by past experiences, traumas, and personal development. This may be why all spiritual practices begin with the dictum "Know thyself." As we learn to sense energy, we must constantly question whether the information is filtered through our bias or is clear insight.

One way to discern whether information is biased or not is to ask. For example, to know if an insight is related to present-time events or flavored by past patterns, simply stop and ask: Is this information about the current situation, or stored information about the past? Ask the question and then pause and wait for an answer. Pay attention to gut feelings, stray thoughts, inner knowing, and so forth. Breathe, be still, and be patient.

This practice seems deceptively simple; nevertheless, internally we know the answer. Within a few minutes we either receive an insight about our energy encounter or realize that the emotional content is terribly familiar. Techniques for clearing old emotional patterns are found in Chapter 19.

Active Engagement

At this point, sensing energy may seem a passive pursuit, as though we simply wait to receive energy impulses. When we're learning, this is often true. However, sensing energy becomes more dynamic when we extend our awareness to actively engage energy domains. This level of engagement is predominate in all upcoming chapters.

Actively sensing energy is the result of energy flowing in the direction of our attention. Where we put our attention is where our energy flows. However, just as awareness requires whole-body listening, attention requires whole-body engagement. We send our attention complete with the free fibers of the chakras to explore and connect with the energy world around us. The fibers act as antennae, and we listen with our entire body to the communication they bring home.

The best meditations to explore how our attention directs our energy are Chakra Fibers on page 28 and Five-Hearts Open on page 33.

Here's an exercise using Chakra Fibers to get you started.

EXTENDING AWARENESS EXERCISE

Ground, center, and establish boundaries.

Quickly clear your mind and energy with three chakra breaths, inhaling through Root and Crown Chakras and exhaling through the front and back of chakras two through six.

Inhale light; exhale everything you no longer need.

When you are still and clear, allow a location, person, or situation that is close to your heart to rise in your mind. Ask for permission to resonate with and explore this image.

With a gentle, soft focus, align your whole being to this intention. Shift your frequency to resonate with what you're focusing on.

Allow your chakra fibers to explore. Imagine sending them out as sounding lines.

While your fibers explore, pay attention to the sensations in the chakras and your entire body. You may feel tension, pulsations, flow, magnetism, vibration.

As you pay attention to the sensations, notice any emotions. Observe any thoughts that arise.

When you're finished, send light through your fibers, give thanks, and call your fibers home.

Assess what you've learned and journal it.

Ground, center, and relax.

You can use this technique to explore anything. Practice by making the focus something you enjoy in nature. Create the picture in your mind and send your unattached fibers to explore; allow thoughts and inspiration to flow to you. Imagine having a spiritual guide and notice the light connections between you. Be open to receiving insight.

Palpating Energy

The biggest impediment to feeling the subtle energy of another person, animal, or plant is that we describe energy as an isolated substance contained in defined structures. Truthfully, energy doesn't flow in little tubes in the body, and it isn't constrained into separate containers. Energies are separated by their individual vibrations.

Consider different currents in a stream: it's all water, just moving more or less quickly, depending on the forces driving it. Energy flow in the body is like a wave passing through an ocean. When we visualize energy as motion, it's easier to feel. Instead of trying to find a structure, we're locating a vibration, or flow.

When starting to palpate energy, it's easiest to feel it with our hands as the field around them is especially sensitive. Often, the first thing we notice is pressure. It can feel as though we're trying to push two same poles of a magnet together. Alternately, we can feel magnetically drawn into an area that needs balancing. While sensing with our hands, we also receive information from our body, emotions, and thoughts. We might notice sensations in our chakras and feelings of internal flow. Essentially, hands are antennae and the body the receiver.

Physical sensations themselves are only indicators of movement, like seeing a twig traveling in a stream. Whether a twig is there or not, the stream is still flowing. Don't become discouraged if you don't feel anything physically. Try not to overfocus on needing proof of feeling energy. Each person is unique with their own library of experience as their guide.

The best meditations for helping to feel energy are Five-Hearts Open on page 33 and Winged Disk on page 38. Here's a sample exercise.

SENSING EXTERNAL ENERGY EXERCISE

Ground, center, and establish boundaries.

Activate the Winged Disk pattern and Five-Hearts Open pattern. Inhale light into your heart, hands, and feet, filling them with energy.

Bring your attention to your Heart Chakra and inhale conscious, living light through your Crown, down your Hara-line, and into your Heart Chakra. Let your Heart Chakra become an extension of light.

Focus on your palms, filling them with light from your heart. You may notice your palms tingling and/or becoming hot.

Hold your hands with your palms facing each other about three inches apart.

- Pulse them toward each other. Feel for them to push against each other as you pulse.
- Pull them apart to about eight inches and pulse them. Push them together and pull them apart until it feels as if you are stretching taffy or Silly Putty between your hands.
- Compress the energy into a ball and follow the contours of the ball with your hands.

Do the same exercise with a partner.
- Start with each of you facing your two right palms.
- Move your hands toward and away from each other as though compressing the energy between them. You may notice a magnetic repulsion/attraction between your and your friend's hands.
- Repeat using a left and right hand. Explore and notice what feels different.

Do the same exercise over your friend's entire body. This is easiest with your friend lying down.

- With light-filled hands, explore the area three inches to three feet away from the person's body.
- Pulse toward and away, feeling for the contour and layers of the aura.
- Try and feel the concentrations of energy vibration that mark the chakras.

In all three exercises, notice changes inside your chakras as you connect, including body sensations, emotions, gut reactions, intuitions, visions, or insights.

When you're finished, close the activation, ground, center, and establish boundaries.

Physically Seeing Energy

Most people see energy in their mind's eye rather than with their physical eyes. However, some people are natural clairvoyants and see energy as easily as they see color or light. Children often have this capacity, typically losing their ability between the ages of three and eight. This is partly due to the pressure of socialization, but losing the ability is also protective. Being able to see and interact on an energy level without guidance is potentially dangerous to the development of a healthy psyche. Many people who lose the ability in childhood regain it later in life.

The easiest way to see energy is to train our mind to shift perception. Holographic images are a great training tool. The book series *The Magic Eye* by N. E. Thing Enterprises[2] is a set of books with pictures that look like random lines or simple drawings. Changing our focus, like applying coherent light, causes the random lines to burst into complex, three-dimensional pictures. Magic Eye shifts perception and trains the brain to be more coherent.

Seeing the 3-D images requires looking slightly before or beyond the picture while softening the gaze. With practice, eventually the brain makes new patterns. When the three-dimensional image forms, it's accompanied by a sense of centering in the body and a distinct feeling in the brain as our perception shifts. The same is true when looking at subtle energy.

EXERCISE FOR SEEING ENERGY

Ground, center, and establish boundaries.

Open the Third Eye Chakra using the Mystic Triangle meditation.

Gaze at a person, plant, or animal, looking slightly beyond them with softened eyes. It helps if they're against a background that's appreciably darker or lighter than the person.

Try to reproduce the feeling in the brain experienced when looking at *The Magic Eye* pictures to guide you.

At first, you may see only a clear space around the person. It might look as though there are heat waves coming off their body. Don't shift your focus to look directly at this area; remain looking beyond or before the person.

Let your mind empty. Don't try, just relax.

Continue to observe this way, noticing whatever arises for 10 to 15 minutes.

Repeat for short periods often.

Ground, center, and relax.

This takes time, so don't give up. As with everything, practice and patience are key. Make practice sessions short and often. Use different people, trees, animals, and so forth. Most importantly, relax and enjoy the practice!

Chapter 12

Energy Protection

Protection is the last of the foundational skills needed to negotiate energy terrain with clarity, safety, and intent. The majority of people who come to me for energy work do so for one of two reasons. They want either healing support or help getting free of harmful energy influences.

Ultimately, protection lies in having our own frequency so clarified that other frequencies simply have no purchase in our field. Truthfully, though, none of us is completely clear at all times. When needed, energy protection helps us maintain personal power, disengage energy projections, and dispel energy attacks. Protection can be especially important when we're new to negotiating the energy terrain.

Protection is the primary use of energy defense techniques; however, these practices also help us contain our own harmful impulses. In day-to-day living, these practices help us stay centered and aligned to higher purpose, especially when we're uncertain or in conflict. The Spiral Pillar of Light pattern on page 17 is useful anytime we feel stressed, confused, or manipulated.

For ease of discussion, we can classify harmful external energies into disruptive energy, manipulative energy, and energy attack. Before we look at harmful energy, however, let's look at energy protection.

What Is Energy Protection?

Energy protection isn't a matter of creating an impenetrable shield; it's about shifting vibration. We become susceptible to harmful energy when some part of us resonates with it. The resonating part is where our unhealed emotional pain or trauma is stored. Unhealed emotions in the energy field create highly charged areas that are receptor sites, or docking ports, for harmful energy. Any part of us that works against our higher path and purpose can become a receptor site, including poor self-esteem, fear, anger, isolating beliefs and attitudes, addictions, and limiting thought-forms.

Receptor sites can also be called attractors that pull in harmful events. Over time, we can become attached to our receptor sites and the energy they attract. They become part of our identity. They're comfortable and known and, more importantly, provide hidden benefits. Some common benefits of being available for harmful engagements with energy include increasing our sense of self-importance, gaining energy from the emotional charge of fighting, avoiding unresolved issues, and providing an excuse for lack of progress.

Essentially, protection is the act of aligning with our spiritual Source or higher ideal. It can be done by shifting our frequency with transcendent emotions as discussed in Chapter 2. When aligned with higher truth, our vibration is heightened. Grounding, centering, and establishing boundaries are keys to maintaining alignment. When we feel unable to shift frequency due to fear, anger, or other causes, energy protection techniques are called on. The Celtic Cross pattern on page 41 is especially designed for protection during such times.

However, long term, we need to remove the attachment sites that make us vulnerable. Working to clear attachment sites is powerful, life-affirming work that improves all aspects of our life.

REMOVING RECEPTOR SITES EXERCISE

Ground, center, and establish boundaries.

Activate the Spiral Pillar of Light pattern.

Scan your energy field and locate your receptor sites. They may feel like empty spots, dark or sticky areas, or blocks in your field, reflect as painful areas in your body, or simply draw your attention.

Explore one or two of these areas. How big are they, how dense, what is the texture? What do you gain by being available for harmful attachments?

Activate the Queen Nefertiti's Headdress pattern on page 36.

Connect your Heart Chakra to the headdress. Inhale light into your heart, letting it expand with uplifting awareness. Exhale pure light out the front and back of the Heart Chakra, into the aura.

Visualize the layers of the headdress aligning to the layers of your aura. Inhale light into the layers through the headdress.

Visualize the receptor sites in your aura vibrating at faster and faster rates until they break apart and return to pure light. Exhale white light out through the headdress.

Intend to maintain this higher vibrational rate.

Ground, center, and establish boundaries.

What Is Disruptive Energy?

Harmful energy from external sources can disrupt the body's energy flow and damage energy structures. Disruptors include excessive, uncontrolled increases in energy, drugs, dissonant energy, and generational miasms. Sometimes even spiritual energy practices can be disruptive by bringing in too much energy too quickly. Signs that disruptive energy is impacting our energy field include:

- An inability to attain goals, coinciding with an inability to stay grounded and centered.
- Depletion, often from an inability to maintain a coherent energy field, possibly due to holes in the aura.
- An inability to integrate experiences and learn from the past. Usually related to distortions in one or more chakras.
- A loss of confidence or trust in one's inner wisdom, often due to chakra damage.
- An inability to see oneself truthfully; either overvaluing (delusions of grandeur) or undervaluing (inferiority complex) one's contribution.
- Nerve pain, psychotic breaks, uncontrollable vibration, and emotional instability also occur, usually from encountering too much energy of too high a vibration, too quickly.

Generally, our natural defenses protect us from energy disruption, yet, as with our immune system, there are times we need extra support. When we're feeling extra vulnerable, the Spiral Pillar of Light pattern is an excellent daily protection.

Some common causes of energy disruption are geopathic stress, drug use, Kundalini rising, and generational miasms.

Geopathic Stress: Three common conditions in which Earth energy disrupts human energy are when:

- Earth energy accumulates with more charge than the human system can manage.
- Ley lines cross and generate dissonant interference patterns.

- Earth energy contains emotional imprints from extreme traumatic events such as human and/or animal massacres, concentration camps, scorched-earth clearing, and so forth.

Drug Use: Under certain circumstances, hallucinogenic or psychedelic drugs can violently open the Third Eye and Crown Chakras beyond what an untrained system is capable of managing. This can result in the closing down of these chakras and/or a disruption of mental function.

Kundalini Rising: When Kundalini rises prematurely, an unprepared nervous system can be damaged as energy circuits overload. Unresolved developmental issues in the chakras are activated, creating psychological stress and even psychosis.

Generational Energy Miasms: A generational energetic miasm is an energy pattern passed down through families. Patterns are repeated through the generations unrelated to the natural passing of family traits or skills and occur outside of the control of the family that's living the pattern. Some patterns are simply curious, like all the girls in a family being born at the same hour. Other patterns involve families living the same tragedies generation after generation. When a miasm activates, often a feeling of confusion and brain fog become present. Shifting a miasm can shift generations of dysfunction.

While shifting our frequency is the best protection we have, when out of balance or under stress, activating protective techniques can help maintain our energy field. At the first sign of feeling disrupted, ground, center, establish boundaries, and activate the Spiral Pillar of Light pattern on page 17.

Energy Manipulations

Although subtle energy is essentially life-affirming, it can consciously be imprinted to hurt or manipulate, as with a psychic attack. However, not all energy that's misdirected is done so knowingly. Having hate-filled thoughts about another, for example, is rarely intended to have an impact. Some misdirected energy is completely unconscious, as in transferring limiting thought-forms from parent to child.

When we're being energetically manipulated, we can feel the impact without necessarily understanding it. It can feel like being pulled in a direction we don't want to go, an obligation to a group without knowing why, or simply being unable to shake an association no longer wanted. Manipulation can create brain fog, causing us to make unexplainable decisions.

If we know the manipulator, we might start thinking of the person obsessively, dreaming of them, or seeing their face when our eyes are closed. We may suspect we're being manipulated, yet still have difficulty extracting the person from our mind. We may dislike the person, yet feel unable to detach. In fact, the more energy we put into resistance, the more stuck we feel.

The three most prominent forms of energy manipulation are thought-forms, projections, and hooks. These can be initiated by one person or a group, such as a family, organization, or institution.

Thought-forms, projections, and hooks can attach to the aura.

Thought Forms
Thought-forms are intentions powered with emotion that live in our aura. They're structured geometric constructs and are part of the attractive force that generates our experiences, as discussed in Chapter 7. Many thought-forms are self-created, others are adopted. We might consciously create a thought-form for manifestation, for example, or unconsciously create a thought-form out of our limiting beliefs. We adopt thought-forms belonging to other people through socialization.

Self-generated thought-forms are different from our daily thoughts in that they don't require our continued attention to exist. Once created, they're independent with a life of their own. Seeking to fulfill their programming, they grow by finding resonant energy and become more powerful. In doing so, they attract toward us the people and events that fulfill their program and our unconscious beliefs.

Thought-forms can also be projected into our field by others. This happens anytime another person uses fear, guilt, or shame to make us believe what they believe, regardless of whether or not it fits our path. Thought-forms that we absorb from other people are meant to manipulate us to do, say, think, or believe as the other person wants.

Children are easily manipulated with thought-forms, and part of growing up is clearing the ones that don't fit. As adults, anytime we give our power away to someone else, we're joining our thought-forms with theirs. Larger constructs are formed and reinforced through the news, teachers, religious authority, governments, and so forth. When a limiting thought-form is deconstructed, negativity is transformed back to pure light. This also frees us from everyone else who was linked into the thought-form with us.

A curse is a type of thought-form intentionally constructed and placed in another person's field to purposefully destabilize and control them. Curses are programmed to stay through time and may activate under specific conditions. For example, a curse from an old lover placed on your love life activates when you're establishing a relationship. Curses are difficult to see, yet can be easy to get rid of. The power they have is given to them by our own fear. The exercise to remove attachments reduces our susceptibility.

Projections

Projections are directives and desires intentionally or unintentionally projected into another person's energy field. To some degree everyone is under the influence of other people's projections. Children try to live up to their parents' projections of what they should do or be in the world; spouses are influenced by their partners' projections of what they want in a partnership, and so forth. Many of the negative self-images we carry are the result of a conflict between our true self and someone else's idea of what we should be.

Projections don't direct our thoughts as much as they direct our emotions. They keep our thoughts moving in a circle we can't break free of by manipulating us emotionally. We feel we're not good enough before we think it—feel we're not capable, worthy, or attractive enough before our mind agrees.

Surprisingly, projections are often used to keep people connected. When we receive someone's projection, we're connected to them as long as the projection is in our field. For some, this connection is better than none and the reason we give them so much power. Consider a child agreeing with family limitations so as not to abandon those they love.

Each of us has received projections, and certainly sent them as well. Every time we judge someone or think we know what's best for another, we're sending an energy projection. If there's a receptor site for it in the other person, they're susceptible to our influence.

In order to grow, we need to remove the projections in our field and also reclaim those of ours embedded in another. This allows us to form relationships based on equality and trust.

RECLAIMING PROJECTIONS EXERCISE

Ground, center, and establish boundaries.

Activate the Mystic Triangle pattern with the palms of your hands holding the two corners of the base of the triangle. Have the triangle lie in the horizontal plane with the apex falling away from you.

Call to mind a person you would like to have peace with. You must genuinely want a resolution.

Ask permission, then invite this person to join you in a healing exchange. Imagine them sitting in the apex of the triangle with a violet flame in the center between you.

If you wish, invite a guide or spiritual being to be present for each of you.

Take a moment and scan the other person for your projections. What do they look like? Where in the other person's energy field are they embedded?

Sincerely apologize for any harm you've caused the person, and ask to have your projections back.

Visualize the person extracting your projections and handing them back to you. As you take them, give thanks, bundle them up, and bury them, burn them, dissolve them, or hand them to your spiritual guide and transform them into light.

Tell the person you're returning their projections, as well. Find the projections in your field, forgive the person, and return their projections with grace.

When you have returned all of their projections and reclaimed all of your projections, notice how you feel.

Allow light to flow between you. When you're ready and the exchange is complete, close the activation by collapsing the triangle.

Ground, center, and establish your boundaries as you end the exercise.

Hooks

A hook is created from someone's desire that's crafted into an intentional thought-form. It's hooked into your energy field to pull you in a specific direction. This happens most often in unrequited love, but also in business partnerships or any type of relationship where one person wants to covertly maneuver the other.

Hooks are insidious because they're based on desire and, often, affection. The person sending them rationalizes that they are acting for the other person's "best interest." Hooks prey on the part of us that wants to please others. Nobody likes to disappoint someone, especially if we care about them. Hooks manipulate that feeling. (How this relates to patterns of codependence is found in Chapter 16.)

Couples often have hooks in each other as part of an unconscious agreement. Each person accepts the other's hook and maintains the receptor site that receives it. People do this to fill empty parts of self and avoid having to grow, as in relationships where one person provides the discipline and the other the nurturing. At its core, this is a codependent arrangement.

The difficulty with romantic hooks is that they're often mistaken for love. However, unlike actual love, hooks always have an agenda. With a hook, the person wants something: your commitment, agreement to join a project, or simply your approval. Every time this person thinks of you, the hook becomes stronger. This can be particularly devastating when disrupting an existing partnership or marriage.

A hook can't take hold in our field without us opening to the person sending it. Just giving someone our attention with an extra sparkle can be enough. Once received, a hook can be reinforced without our participation. When someone is hooking into us, every phone conversation, e-mail, or text message is reinforcement. Closing the receptor sites and eliminating the hooks are essential in order to be free.

Hooks can show as feeling obligated to respond to another person, feeling unduly influenced by someone, an inability to make decisions without the other person's input, or continually feeling responsible for another's happiness.

If you feel you need a specific person to fulfill your purpose, yet feel off your path, you're probably hooked. A particularly strong hook will leave you feeling confused, depleted, and frightened whenever you try to break it.

Any unfulfilled part within, any unhealed wound, can be a receptor site for a hook. Any time we feel vulnerable and are looking for a savior, we're open to being hooked. This is the basis for many advertising campaigns and political messaging. Populists hook people by identifying mass vulnerability, telling the masses their failures aren't their fault, throwing stones at an identified villain, and assuring everyone that they, and only they, can save the situation. The line is cast and the fish hooked. It works every time.

The best protection against hooks and projections is to "know thyself." Because hooks rarely augment our true path, if we're in alignment, we can't be hooked. If you think you have a hook, use the Removing Receptor Sites exercise at the beginning of this chapter and the exercise for removing low-level entities and hooks further in this chapter. Also, review Chapter 10 and practice grounding, centering, and creating boundaries.

Attachments and Influences

Energy attachments are people or entities that have attached themselves to us, as with a hook, for the sole purpose of using our energy. They don't want us to pursue a particular course of action or join them in an endeavor; they simply want our energy. Attachments have no power other than that which we give them. Every time we engage an energy attachment with fear or anger, we feed it and make the person or entity more powerful. Directly attacking the attachment can also fuel the person's hold. The best approach is to eliminate receptor sites, which eliminates the ability to attach. Use the Removing Receptor Sites exercise earlier in this chapter to do this.

Energy Vampires

Drugs, trauma, loss, and psychic attack can tear holes in a person's aura, making it difficult for them to hold energy. Over time, this person becomes depleted and unable to maintain enthusiasm or direction in life. They may fear being left behind and seek to hold on to those who are moving forward. To increase vitality, they latch into a chakra of another person with their energy fibers, then use the other person's subtle energy as fuel. Those who attach to another are called energy vampires.

An energy vampire comes alive when latched into a susceptible person and collapses when separated. It's an interesting dynamic to watch: the vampire expands energetically as the person they are draining deflates. Once someone is latched into another, they can draw energy anytime. The connection doesn't have to be in person as time and space don't inhibit entanglement. Energy is most available through strong emotions, and energy vampires might purposefully inspire anger or fear in their victim simply for the boost. For this reason, energy vampires are generally found attached to the lower three chakras where fear and anger are generated.

If you know someone who drains you every time you see or talk with them on the phone, this person may have energy fibers latched into you. The first thing to do is remove your attachment sites, then detach the person's energy fibers. To eliminate, use the Removing Energy Attachments exercise that follows. You might want to do the Removing Receptor Sites exercise first.

If you, or someone you know, has become an energy vampire, two things are required to heal. You need to repair the hole in your aura and remember your connection to Earth and Source, the only places you can receive an unlimited supply of energy. (An exercise to repair your aura can be found in Chapter 19.)

REMOVING ENERGY ATTACHMENTS EXERCISE

Ground, center, and establish your boundaries.

Activate the Spiral Pillar of Light pattern and stand inside its protective boundary. Use your breath and attention to expand your light and shift your frequency as you ask for your spiritual guides and guardians to be present.

Scan your chakras for energy attachments. You may simply be drawn to a chakra for no discernible reason or you might feel heaviness, see dark areas, or feel empty and drained in this chakra.

Visualize the chakra and ask to see any energy fibers that are attached. Allow an image to form in your mind's eye. If you're having difficulty, activate your Third Eye Chakra with the Mystic Triangle.

Set the intention that any energy fibers or attachments, seen or unseen, felt or unfelt, known or unknown, be returned to light.

Then gently, but firmly, extract all energy fibers by increasing the light in your chakras and pushing out anything that is not you. If you feel so directed, energetically grab hold of the attachments and pull them out. If you're having trouble, ask your spirit guides for assistance.

Once the attachments are out, with kindness, send them back to whomever they belong to.

Clear your field three times by inhaling through your Crown and Root Chakras and exhaling through the front and back of chakras two through six.

Fill your aura with light.

Ground, center, and establish boundaries.

Low-Level Entities

It would be nice to think that only beneficent energy beings exist, such as guides, angels, and Nature Spirits. Unfortunately, low-level entities also exist. Sometimes these are simply destructive thought-forms that have become independent from their original source and are looking for more energy. Other times they are entities looking for emotional fuel. They seek people with unresolved issues who throw around a lot of emotional energy, attach to their biofield, and feed off the emotional outbursts.

When first encountered, these entities seem relatively benign, using only the emotional energy being freely expressed. As they get stronger and as their host gets used to their presence, the entities begin to manipulate their host into damaging behavior in order to feed off the emotional turmoil. Such entities are commonly associated with alcohol and drug addiction.

These types of entities are like parasites and get stronger from anger, greed, fear, lust, jealousy, desire, and hatred. If you have receptor sites, these entities can be picked up in gambling facilities, prisons, mental institutions, and other places where people are either vulnerable or their destructive impulses are unchecked.

As with other types of attachments, low-level entities can't impact us unless we're available. This exercise to remove them can also be used for hooks and thought-forms. It involves eliminating the receptor sites and vibrating at a higher rate. Before using the exercise to remove entities, first eliminate your receptor sites.

REMOVING LOW-LEVEL ENTITIES, HOOKS, AND THOUGHT-FORMS EXERCISE

Ground, center, and establish your boundaries.

Activate the Spiral Pillar of Light pattern and stand inside its protective boundary. Use your breath and attention to fill your personal space with light as you ask your spiritual guides and guardians to be present.

Scan your aura for energetic parasites, hooks, or thought-forms. You may be drawn to an area or feel unusual sensations, see lumps or moving areas, or simply know.

Set the intention that any energy parasites, seen or unseen, felt or unfelt, known or unknown, be returned to light.

Visualize your aura merging with the coiling energy of the Spiral Pillar and being electrified with high-energy light. Imagine the low-level entities and other attachments being short-circuited, detaching from your energy field, and returning to the pure white light of their origin.

Clear your field with three breaths, inhaling through your Crown and Root Chakras, and exhaling through the front and back of the rest of the chakras.

Fill your aura with light as you close the Spiral Pillar.

Ground, center, and establish boundaries.

Taking command of our energetic space is essential to maintaining the personal power to consciously create our life. Keeping as clear as possible requires the inner resolve to take responsibility for what we carry. Start each day grounding, centering, and establishing boundaries. Maintain light, gratitude, and humility with a heart-centered approach to life.

Psychic Attack

Psychic attack is an attempt by one person, or group of people, to inflict harm on another using energy to disrupt their emotional, mental, physical, or spiritual state. The more intentional and focused the attack, and the more emotional energy it's fueled with, the more harm it can cause. Jealousy, envy, hurt, grief, revenge, fear, and desire for power are common motivations for a psychic attack.

Psychic attack can cause a person's life to suddenly fall apart. Hard-fought goals, without reason, slip away. Relationships are disrupted with no understanding of why. Motivation and direction may founder, causing depression. Suicidal tendencies can be amplified. Physical exhaustion, body aches, and heart palpitations are common. A severe attack can even feel like a heart attack.

Psychically attacking someone is a narcissistic act, and the perpetrator often wants to be known. Recognition cements their feeling of power. Consequently, the attacker may project his or her image into the mind of the target, causing frightening dreams and appearing in the mind during meditations or when falling asleep at night or waking in the morning. The person's face may appear large with a cruel expression. Thoughts of this person can become obsessive, taking control of the target's mind. All of this is part of the control the attacker is exerting in attempts to disrupt the target's life.

It's actually not too difficult to stop an attack. When someone resorts to terrorizing another, it's a sign of weakness. Acknowledging the attack without fear disempowers it. If you are under psychic attack, the first step is to control your own emotional energy. A psychic attack turns your mind and energy against you, so short-circuit the attempt. Let go of fear and laugh. When the attacker's image enters your mind, replace it with light. Shift your frequency, align with your spiritual Source, and trust that there are spiritual laws you can call on. No one can energetically harm you unless, somehow, you agree. Take your power back by using your mind and emotions on your own behalf.

Directly confronting your attacker with the desire to overpower them doesn't work. It's what they're hoping you will do as they can use your energy to make you fight yourself. As soon as you engage on this level, you become a perpetrator of energy misuse yourself and damage your spiritual connection. Instead, exercise your rights as a spiritual citizen and arrest your attacker in the name of spiritual law.

DISABLING A PSYCHIC ATTACK EXERCISE

Ground, center, and establish your boundaries. Open the Spiral Pillar and merge the boundary of your aura with the Pillar. Fill your space with light, connect with your spiritual Source, and ask for your guides and guardians to be present.

Open the Celtic Cross pattern and stand firmly inside its spinning field of energy. Acknowledge that a psychic attack is under way.

If you know who is attacking you, use his or her name as you form your intention. Firmly state the following or something similar: I, (state your name), call back my power. I am in command of my space and being. I turn this perpetrator, (state the name if you know it), over to those who maintain spiritual law.

Focus on the Spiral Pillar of Light and visualize any harmful energy directed at you being transformed by the Pillar into love and/or light and returned to the attacker.

Clearly state that you are not available for any future attack and that all energy sent to you by the attacker is transformed to love and/or light and returned.

Fill your field with light.

Love is the only true force. There is nothing more powerful. Emanate love.

Ground, center, and establish boundaries.

If you feel any ongoing attempts to breach your energy field, form the Celtic Cross pattern around you, your family, and your property. Start every morning and end every day by grounding, centering, and establishing boundaries.

A psychic attack has a lot to teach. Unknowingly, you may be using the attack to feel important. Stop and ask, what are you gaining from this experience? Beyond what you gain, an energy attack is a concentrated opportunity to practice mental discipline and find your inner power. Sometimes a psychic attack is an initiation that pushes you into a higher level of awareness. This doesn't excuse the attack, and the attacker will still face karmic backlash, but was some part of you wanting to test your energy prowess with a worthy opponent? If so, take your success to heart. You are a worthy spiritual warrior, up to the tasks that need to be fulfilled at this time.

Karmic Backlash

Misusing subtle energy comes with consequences. Psychically attacking another results in the eventual return of our own energy, called a karmic backlash. This often feels like psychic retaliation as light bulbs explode, computers break down, and other challenges emerge, however, this is only the return of our own intent.

When we use our energy skills and personal power to manipulate and influence a person or set of circumstances to favor us at the expense of another, we lack awareness of our own wholeness. Feeling incomplete allows fear to drive us. This is not a judgment; it's a natural part of developing genuine power and awareness. We do, however, have to transmute the karma in order to grow.

Consciously attacking someone with psychic energy empowers the undeveloped parts of self, turning these parts into external realities that we have to face. The only way forward is to reclaim our shadow parts and integrate them.

None of us can avoid the ultimate purpose of life—to grow more than we can avoid the laws of nature that determine that we are born, grow, and die. Whatever we put out will return as we must meet the results of our actions.

OVERCOMING KARMIC BACKLASH EXERCISE

Ground, center, and establish boundaries.

Give thanks and invite spiritual helpers to be present. Activate the Mystic Triangle pattern.

Imagine the triangle inscribed on the ground with you sitting in one corner, a guide sitting in another corner, and leave the third corner open.

Intending the highest and best good for all, call in someone you have harmed and invite him or her to sit in the third corner. Invite the person's spiritual guides to be present.

Honor the divine within the other person.

Give an accurate detail of all the ways you've harmed this person and offer a sincere apology.

Ask the person to give you your projections back.

When you have your projections, give thanks and acknowledge what you've learned from the situation and how you've changed.

Forgive yourself, the other person, and anyone else in the situation.

Release this person from any further karma between you.

Imagine ropes around you being unbound as you are freed of this continued karmic pattern.

Send love and light to the other person and, when it feels complete, disconnect.

If the other person did not return your projections or did not receive your apology, forgiveness, and love, then respect their choice. State that you release the person from any further karma with you.

Give thanks to your spiritual helpers and close the activations.

Ground, center, and establish boundaries.

Chapter 13

Clearing
Space

Keeping homes, offices, cars, and land clear of energetic debris is as important as keeping our mind and psyche clear. The energy in a house or specific geographic area can be imprinted by impressions left behind from previous events. Clarity of energy can leave positive feelings, just as arguments, worry, and stress can create a sense of disquiet. Keeping our space clean allows fresh input rather than being overshadowed by the ambiance of previous events.

The strength of an imprint is determined by the emotional intensity of the event, as well as repetitive input. We can make intentional imprints by purposefully inputting refined, uplifting frequency, as in the creation of sacred space. Sadly, tragedy generally generates more emotion than celebration and carries stronger imprints. Also, it's worth considering that even positive imprints can carry an agenda. For example, the spiritual energy in a church, synagogue, or mosque can be both uplifting and controlling. The bottom line is that we want our space to carry intentional imprints that are free of unconscious past programming.

Since emotional intensity creates high-amplitude imprints in the land, battlefields, mental institutions, murder sites, hospitals, and other such places often carry strong energy imprints. Sensitive people living in houses built over these sites often report disruptions such as the inability to sleep, confusion, and anxiety. Such houses are often considered to be haunted.

Fortunately, nature has mechanisms to cleanse imprints and restore natural vitality. The elements of wind, rain, and sun restore the electromagnetic clarity of land, and we can use the same principles to clear and transform our living space. When clearing space and eliminating imprints, whatever is holding back the movement of energy is transformed and released into the etheric space as creative, life-enhancing energy.

Clearing the Aura

Clearing space begins with clearing our personal energy. The aura has a magnetic quality and collects energy and emotional imprints as do houses and land. The imprints might entangle with our existing thought-forms, increasing their strength, or become energy critters adhering to our field as discussed in Chapter 12.

Clearing the aura before doing energy work is a basic practice that can be accomplished with the Spiral Pillar of Light pattern on page 17. It's a good idea to clear our field on a daily basis, just as we clean our body. This can be done by visualizing Queen Nefertiti's Headdress pattern on page 36. In addition, the grounding, centering, and creating boundaries exercises in Chapter 10 also clarify our energy field.

The following exercise includes a number of clearing activations. Use them all, or only the ones you need or are drawn to.

DAILY ENERGY-CLEARING EXERCISE

Ground, center, and establish your boundaries.

Activate the Spiral Pillar of Light pattern and allow your aura to expand in light.

Further energize your field with the strength of the Earth and the freedom of the sky by activating the Earth and Sky pattern.

Do three deep chakra clearing breaths, inhaling through the Crown and Root Chakras and exhaling through the front and back of chakras two through six.

Activate the Queen Nefertiti's Headdress pattern to clear any attachments or imprints in the aura.

When your energy feels clear and free of imprints, close the activations.

Ground, center, and establish boundaries.

Before doing spiritual work, you may want a deeper cleanse. Here's an effective technique you can use alone or in combination with the previous activation.

DEEP CLEARING OF YOUR FIELD EXERCISE

Ground, center, and establish boundaries.

Shake a rattle through your entire energy field, moving it all around your body. The rattle moves stagnant energy, loosens attachments, and shifts thought-forms.

Light a cleansing herb, incense, or tree resin such as sage, sweetgrass, or copal, and scoop the smoke into your hands, then wash it through your aura.

Inhale, visualizing light entering your Crown and Root Chakras to fill your central core, then exhale light through the front and back of chakras two through six.

Establish a higher frequency with sound. Chant "Aum" or ring a singing bowl or tuning fork.

Fill yourself with self-transcendent emotions such as awe, gratitude, appreciation, and so forth.

When you feel complete, ground, center, and establish boundaries.

Energetic Detoxification

Toxicity is a serious and often-unrecognized health hazard that can cause major health issues. The primary source is pollution, from both physical poisons and low-level energy emissions. Heavy metals, pesticides, insecticides, and plastic residues are better-known poisons; however, the list is long and distressing. Toxins that overload the liver's clearing capability are collected and stored in tissue, where they eventually cause damage. Most people benefit from detoxification protocols that use saunas, supplements, and diet. Adding an energy detox into the protocol can dramatically improve results and decrease side effects.

On an energetic level, toxins generate a magnetic attraction that accumulates vital energy. Locked in place, the energy stagnates, losing its vitality and becoming part of the energetic foci that attract more toxic residue. The charge in these sites attracts imprints of emotional trauma as well. When we move energy through our system, we encourage energy foci to release their toxic load, physically and energetically.

Adding this energy detoxifier to your physical protocol can be highly beneficial. Naturally, this exercise does not take the place of appropriate medical care.

ENERGY DETOXIFYING EXERCISE

Ground, center, and establish your boundaries.

Activate the Pyramid Purification pattern and visualize supportive Earth energy entering the corners of the pyramid base and coalescing in the center where you sit.

Imagine the energy spiraling up a violet flame in your Hara-line. Be with this image for a few minutes, feeling its effect.

Observe that the violet flame magnetizes the energetic and physical toxins in your body, drawing them into the Hara-line.

Visualize the toxins meeting the flame and incinerating. The transformed energy is released to spiral upward, through your Crown Chakra, and out the top of the pyramid.

Maintain your awareness on the violet flame until the flow stops.

Bring your awareness back into present time and close the activation.

Ground, center, and establish your boundaries.

Clearing Houses and Other Spaces

Clearing our house, office, or meditation rooms regularly helps maintain a beneficial ambiance. One way to clear space is to simply activate the Pyramid Purification pattern and let it go to work. The following method can be used to clear rooms, gardens, barns, and outdoor areas. To clear larger areas of land, use the Earth-clearing exercises in Chapter 14. Many people set a schedule for clearing space, such as once a week, month, season, or every time they clean house. Clearing our space is also a great addition to decluttering. To maintain the clean atmosphere and promote energy flow, open windows for at least a short time every day.

CLEARING SPACE EXERCISE

Ground, center, and establish boundaries. Open the Spiral Pillar of Light pattern.

Activate the Five-Hearts Open pattern and spend a few minutes flowing energy through your hands and fingers.

Disrupt the energetic dust bunnies and stagnant thought-forms collecting in the corners of the room.

- Use a rattle or shake your hand with loose fingers into the corners while imagining stirring everything up.

- Move systematically around the room, pausing and giving more attention to areas that seem dense or sticky.

Disperse the energy that's been loosened by sweeping the air with a feather or with the energy projections from your fingers. Walk around the space or stand in the center of the room and sweep from top to bottom, turning in a 360-degree circle to cover all the space.

End the clearing by smudging the room with burning sage, sweetgrass, resins, or other herbs. Walk around the room sweeping the cleansing smoke into the corners and all the nooks and crannies.

Establish a new harmonic to raise the vibration of energy. Stand in the center of the room with your arms lifted sideways slightly away from your side and open the Mystic Triangle pattern between your hands and third eye. Radiate love from your Heart Chakra through the triangle.

Add sound vibration with Tibetan bells, singing bowls, chimes, or chant "Aum."

Seal the cleansing by enclosing the room in the Spiral Pillar of Light.

Close all the activations except the Spiral Pillar of Light.

Ground, center, and establish boundaries.

Creating Sacred Space and Sanctuary

Clearing techniques are useful when creating sacred space and sanctuary for spiritual practice. Sacred space promotes reverence and connection with spirit. A sanctuary is the holiest part of a sacred space, a place of refuge for the soul. More than physical places, sacred space and sanctuary are states of mind and heart. Any place can be sacred space and provide sanctuary if we intend it and treat it with reverence.

Sacred space promotes safe energy practice and generates an ambiance of upliftment. Keeping space clear of imprints and tuned to higher vibrations means we don't have to start from scratch each time we meditate. The connection to spirit is palpable and tangible, enhancing our ability to quickly enter deep meditation and increasing the effectiveness of our energy work.

Creating sacred space is a matter of intention. In order to protect the space from energy imprints, the location needs to be designated for spiritual purposes and not used for daily activities. The designated space doesn't have to be a room or even a corner of a room. It can be a special chair, window seat, or single altar shelf in a bookcase. Once declared, respect the space, keep it clear, and build its energy. In other words, don't set your laundry on your meditation chair or put your keys on your altar.

Once designated, bring in pictures, candles, crystals, a prayer shawl, or any items that help focus your intent. Keep the space simple, comfortable, and meaningful. Use the clearing techniques in this chapter to raise the energy and seal it using the Spiral Pillar of Light. As you regularly use the space for spiritual work, it will increase in energy and focus, deepening your spiritual practice.

Chapter 14

Earth Alignment

Living in today's technological world has dulled our awareness of nature. All around is a source of energy so powerful it provides for all our needs. This is true physically as the Earth supplies food, water, and the power to run our technology, and spiritually as Earth maintains our energy structures and fuels our intentions. In addition, as explained in Chapter 8, Earth's aura modulates frequency input from other dimensions, affecting the evolution of consciousness on the planet.

Learning to connect with Earth helps us clarify what's important. The connection magnifies our ability to sense and feel energy and to perceive with higher levels of awareness. At the same time, connection provides us with vital life-force and grounding for the full experience of being human. Earth is a spiritual being who is our Mother.

Aligning with Earth Energy

Aligning with Earth is a call to use our spiritual power with the intelligence of nature to repair the environmental damage of the planet. When we do, we take our place as stewards of Earth. Throughout time, there have been Indigenous people who maintain this stewardship of Earth. The Tibetan Monks of the Himalayan Mountains, the Kogi, Arhuaco, and Wiwa tribes of the Sierra Nevada Mountains in Colombia, the Aborigines of Australia, and the First Nations of America maintain a continued practice of harmonizing the planet. Through ancient practices of prayer and meditation, they hold sacred space for Earth.

Exploring our connection with nature is enhanced using the Five-Hearts Open pattern on page 33 and the Dancing with the Elements exercise on page 53. These two practices open our feeling senses to link with the powerful flows moving through, into, and around the planet. Other ways include establishing a personal power spot and connecting with Nature Spirits.

Personal Power Spots

Power spots, vortices, or sacred sites refer to the Earth's many energy sites described in Chapter 8. A power spot links us with Earth energy, amplifying and transforming our energy. These sites often occur in relation to converging ley lines and are areas of rejuvenation and spiritual upliftment.

Heightened energy also accumulates in places where nature is left undisturbed. Waterfalls, mountains, lakes, forests, rock ledges, and caves all have unique energetic properties. Typically, power spots are associated with areas of extremes of nature, as in the Grand Canyon or Victoria Falls.

The idea of power places and sacred sites is common in most traditions. They are able to amplify and intensify intention, so whatever is brought—both good and bad—is magnified. Meditating, praying, or performing manifestation in these locations can profoundly impact the desired result. Consequently, power spots are chosen as the sites of temples, monuments, and places of worship, such as Stonehenge and the Great Pyramid. Aligned to planetary and celestial events at specific times of the year, the natural energy of the location is enhanced through influx from planetary alignments. The configuration of the stones also incorporates sacred geometry so that Earth energy combines with celestial energy in the alignment. The result is a site capable of generating creative energy.

To create your own sacred site, identify or choose a power spot. Any place can accumulate energy with the right intention. Choose a place you feel connected with, one that gives you a sense of belonging. You can leave it exactly as it is, or enhance its effect by placing stones in a geometric pattern. You might create a single circle with four points for each direction, or a Flower of Life mandala. Align the pattern with stones that designate the rising sun at the solstices and equinoxes. If you live in a place where you can't get outside, make a power spot in a room in your house. Reach into Earth and draw a ley line to you. Here's a simple yet powerful exercise.

SELECTING AND CREATING A
POWER SPOT EXERCISE

Ground, center, and establish your boundaries.

Take a walk outside, or inside if need be, and notice how you feel in different areas. You may already have a favorite spot or be drawn to a particular location. You will know when you've found the right place by heightened feelings of connection, opening, or inspiration.

Ask permission to designate this as your power spot. You will know if you're received by feelings of flow, upliftment, and openness. If granted, stand or sit in the center of the space.

If you did not receive permission, give thanks and, with respect, move on to a location with better resonance for you.

Activate the Spiral Pillar of Light pattern and bring the cone of power down, into, through, and around the chosen area, creating a circle of peace, safety, and healing.

If you feel drawn, incorporate sacred geometry into the creation of your power spot like so:

- Inscribe a circle inside a triangle in your power spot. The circle and the triangle are transformative shapes in sacred geometry and can be used separately or together to magnify connection and spiritual continuity.
- Design with any geometry to which you're drawn.
- Place markers around the perimeter of the geometric shape you're using. You can use crystals, stones, poles, or even mounds of dirt to mark the space.
- Place large markers for the four directions and smaller markers where they feel right.

Use your inner sense to guide you. If it doesn't feel right, change the arrangement until it does.

Use the clearing practices in Chapter 13 to cleanse the area of any psychic imprints.

Invite the Nature Spirits of the location along with your spiritual guides to enjoy the space. Spend several minutes transmitting love.

Declare your space a sanctuary for peace.

Use this place for spiritual activities: to meditate, vision, manifest, heal, ask for guidance, and so forth.

When entering and leaving, seal the boundaries by activating the Spiral Pillar of Light. When re-entering, check the markers and determine if any need to be shifted. Earth energy changes with the seasons, sky, and so on; your energy markers will shift as well.

Ground, center, and establish boundaries as you leave.

It's not always possible to be outside in nature, yet you can still connect with nature and create a power spot. Chapter 13 provides suggestions for creating a sanctuary inside your house; you can also create a sanctuary power spot inside yourself. Here's a simple exercise.

CREATING AN INNER GARDEN EXERCISE

Ground, center, and establish boundaries.

Take your awareness inside your body and make an intention to create an inner garden/power spot.

Ask which chakra would like to provide this anchor. Notice where your attention is drawn. Ask that this chakra be blessed.

Allow an image to form in your mind's eye of your power spot. Notice what naturally appears. Ask if there's anything that would augment the space, such as plants, flowers, a water feature, fire, rock, light, or vistas. If you try to add something and it doesn't want to stay, let it go. Allow your garden to extend into your aura. Make the energy here the first experience people have of you.

Create several seats: one for you, your guide, and any others you'd like to invite. If you're drawn to, arrange the seats in geometrically significant patterns such as a circle, a triangle, pyramid, star, or other pattern.

Dedicate your inner garden to a higher purpose.

Seal by activating the Spiral Pillar of Light pattern. Know that you carry this sacred space within yourself and can access wisdom here at any time.

Ground, center, and establish boundaries.

Connecting with Nature Spirits

Developing energy awareness alerts us to other energy beings we share the planet with. You may sense them by a smell such as fragrant flowers, or see a vision in your mind's eye while feeling tingles, rushes, or warmth. You may see a face, hear a voice, or feel a touch. You may receive an entire message, either as a complete knowing or a heard communication.

Learning to communicate with Nature Spirits requires listening to inner messages during meditation. Messages are usually coupled with a felt-sense that provides authenticity. Although connection to Nature Spirits is easiest in a natural setting, access is not limited by space. We're creatures of nature and carry the connection within. This exercise can be done in an outdoor power spot, a garden, or in a sanctuary created inside a house. It can also be accessed through an inner power spot.

The key to working with Nature Spirits is to give them due respect and not demand they perform. The truth is, we are in communication quite regularly, we just don't acknowledge where our insight has come from. Trust your instincts; they are from nature.

CONNECTING WITH NATURE SPIRITS EXERCISE

Go to your internal or external power spot, or indoor sanctuary.

Ground, center, and establish your boundaries.

Activate the Spiral Pillar of Light pattern and establish a cone of safety, healing, and connection.

Send out thoughts to the Nature Kingdom on a carrier wave of love. Acknowledge that they, not you, are in control of whether they choose to connect.

Activate the Earth and Sky pattern and feel the power of Earth flowing into your body. Feel the power of sky. Give thanks.

Gently broadcast your presence and give the Nature Spirits time to accept you and become curious.

Explain why you have come and what you want. Perhaps you want assistance planting a garden, making a flower essence, or knowing how to use an herb. Include a desire to assist them.

Follow what you feel and be thankful for any guidance you r eceive. You may need many meetings over a long period before trust is established.

Pay attention to the animals and insects that join you in your exercise; messages may come symbolically. Does a butterfly keep flying around your head? Is there a pattern in the cloud formations? Do you always see a hawk on the way to or from your meditation spot?

When you begin to receive information, ask questions. Present the Nature Spirits with problems and wait for solutions. Be sure to act on the information or explain why you can't. This is an important step in building trust. If you don't use what you're given, you won't be given more.

Nature Spirits will never ask you to do something harmful or wrong. If you receive a destructive request, question the source and do some clearing exercises. (See Chapters 12 and 13.)

Invite the Nature Spirits to join your daily energy practice, manifestation, healing, gardening, problem-solving, and so on. Be sure to ask if they need anything from you.

Release the connection and give thanks when they are ready to leave. You will know the door is closing by a drop in the vitality of the exchange.

Ground, center, and establish boundaries.

Powering Your Practice

Using the sanctuary of a power spot for subtle energy work deepens the practice, and connecting to ley lines can further boost intuition. Ley lines are Earth's supply pathways, distributing information and vitality that can empower our intentions. Ancient people used ley lines to transport their awareness across the planet. Through the energy pathways, they accessed information and sent information outward to harmonize the planet. The Tibetan monks and the Elders of the Sierra Mountains in Colombia still use this practice. Today, ley lines are used to transmit frequencies for planetary healing.

CONNECTING WITH LEY LINES EXERCISE

Ground, center, and establish boundaries.

Activate the Earth and Sky pattern.

Using your breath, feel the energy of Earth flow up into your body on the inhale. Send your energy down beneath the surface of the soil on the exhale.

Activate the Five-Hearts Open pattern. Feel the chakras of your feet come alive and penetrate the ground.

Picture the ley lines as energy highways traveling underneath the surface of Earth. Imagine the energy from your feet descending through the ground to meet this pathway. You may be able to go straight down, or you might have to weave your way. You will feel a sense of being "plugged in" when you find it. You may feel a surge of energy fill your feet, causing them to heat, tingle, and pulse.

Send love and light into the ley line and imagine it flowing around the planet, joining all others who are using love as a healing force.

Activate the Celtic Cross pattern and use it as a protective filter as you invite Earth energy from the ley lines into your body. The Celtic Cross will ensure that no other consciousness riding on the ley lines is invited inside your body.

Activate Weaving the Nadis pattern, and with your breath, pull energy up into your feet, into your Base Chakra, and upward through your body.

Focus your intent on healing, manifesting, or increasing psychic ability as follows:

- **For healing:** Activate the Winged Disk pattern and focus the energy from the ley lines into your heart. Allow the energy to cascade down your arms and into your hands.
- **For manifesting:** Using the manifestation practice in Chapter 17, focus the energy in your second, third, and fourth Chakras, letting it join the rainbow bridge surging into your future reality.
- **For psychic ability:** Activate the Mystic Triangle pattern and open the triangle in your Third Eye. Empower your intuition, remote viewing, or telepathic communication by focusing your attention on the Third Eye triangle as the energy in your feet travels along the ley lines. Pay attention to the images you receive in your mind's eye.

Close by sending love into Earth through the ley lines, intending it to go where it is needed most. Give thanks and express gratitude.

Inhale your energy back into your feet and Base Chakra. Close any activation patterns you used.

Ground, center, and establish boundaries.

Cleansing Earth Energy

As discussed in Chapter 13, locations can become repositories of low-level energy. Imprints from past traumatic events can create dead areas, impacting the health of the ecosystem. Plants may not grow well and animals may tend to avoid the site. People living in these areas tend toward depression. Unlike animals, people don't have the sense to move away.

The Earth has its own detoxification methods, however, human activity can interfere with them. Changing the meandering of streams, for example, decreases the vitality of the water. Some areas, such as the sites of devastating battles, carry so much emotional charge they attract low-level energy and can become repositories for lost spirits. This blocks the energy flow in the ley lines, forcing them to reroute around the site. Cleansing such areas transforms them and allows the return of nature, restoring the innate flow of the ley lines.

This exercise can cleanse ancient battlefields or graveyards, unblock Earth chakras, or cleanse the entire planet. It's an effective tool when used by one person and increases in power when people join together.

In her book *The Power of Eight*, Lynne McTaggart demonstrates that group intentions provide benefit not only to the target, but also to the senders.[1] We are all an interconnected whole. When we attend to each other, everyone benefits. When we attend to Earth, all life benefits, seen and unseen.

CLEANSING THE EARTH EXERCISE

Ground, center, and establish boundaries.

Activate the Spiral Pillar of Light pattern and surround the group with a column of safety, healing, and love.

Activate the Pyramid Purification pattern, aligning yourself and the people joining you, if any, in the pyramid as described on page 48.

Imagine the pyramid placed over the area you're cleansing with a violet flame in the center.

Invite the Nature Spirits to assist and ask if there is anything they would like to add.

Visualize all the pain, anger, fear, trapped souls, and trauma stored in the area flowing into the base of the pyramid via the ley lines, as well as streaming through Earth's aura. Imagine the pyramid acting as a vacuum, sucking up all the old imprints.

Focus on the violet flame.

Intend complete healing of all and visualize the imprints and emotional debris being consumed by the flame and transformed into rainbow-colored light. Watch the rainbow light flow out the apex of the pyramid as love, filling Earth's aura and releasing any trapped souls to the light.

Allow the process to continue until the flow ceases, then close the Pyramid Purification pattern.

Invite golden light to descend through the Spiral Pillar of Light to infuse the area, revitalizing Earth.

Imagine the area reconnecting with the ley lines and reentering the harmonic of the planet.

Give thanks to the Nature Spirits and close the activation.

Ground, center, and establish boundaries.

Chapter 15

Challenges and Limitations

The world is experiencing a paradigm shift that's changing the way people think, interact, and identify reality. Old ways of doing things no longer work to solve global problems—problems unlike any we've seen before. Personal and planetary solutions require flexible thinking, freedom from polarized emotions, compassion, open-minded wisdom, and the ability to stay balanced through wild fluctuations. It also requires being willing to feel and integrate our own shadow. The times we are in offer an unprecedented opportunity for using energy skills.

In many positive-thinking approaches, people in difficult situations are judged less spiritual than those with an easier life, as if the more spiritual a person is, the fewer problems they'll have. Truthfully, difficulties are not a measure of spirituality. They're not a punishment, a reward, or a reflection of a person's value. They represent a desire to grow. Sometimes, they're the road to achieve objectives best accomplished through challenge, or agreements made with others for everyone's learning.

Whatever challenge we face, we can choose to grow. We can choose to become more, rather than allow a challenge to make us less. The true measure of spirituality is how vulnerable we are willing to be and how much love we can carry into our challenges, not whether challenges exist.

Consider challenges a call to growth. Find the truth hidden in the situation and ask how you can express it. What quality or inner resource needs to be developed? Maybe it's a quality, such as courage, perseverance, forgiveness, compassion, unconditional love, or determination. Maybe it's flexible thinking, learning a new skill, or adapting an old skill to new uses.

This chapter engages the underlying energetic reality in the conditions we face, freeing us and our circumstances to change.

Obstacles and Limitations

Obstacles are interruptions in the flow of energy from one event to another. Energetically, we're connected to the people and situations around us in streams of energy forming ever-changing patterns. Ideally, the energy we feed into the pattern is magnified and returned. When it isn't, we encounter a limitation.

Sometimes limitations reflect karma, past decisions, childhood conditioning, or attitudes and beliefs. What needs to be learned from the past is embedded in the emotions we carry into the present. Emotions keep us connected to our growth edge and when we engage our feelings in making new choices, we change dynamics.

Limitations can be protective adaptations for survival. Although our spiritual essence can never be harmed, our mental and physical survival can require that we adapt our actions and attitudes to minimize external threat. Defense structures are often looked at as evidence of our mistakes, but in reality they were once lifesaving choices. We just don't need them anymore. Defense structures helped us survive, but they are not who we are.

Creating our identity based on our circumstances and defenses is what creates limitation. Rather than fighting our defenses, or endlessly analyzing them to find their meaning, thank them for their service and connect with your spiritual identity to let them go. An obvious example is growing up with an abusive parent. To survive, we might create or adopt beliefs such as "the world is not safe," "I'm worthless," "love is too painful," and so forth. These beliefs initially protect, but when the circumstance no longer exists, the beliefs perpetuate the abuse.

When facing an obstacle or limitation, ask, "Is this helping me or hindering me?" If it's helping you, is it protecting you from yourself or someone else? If it's hindering you, what inner resource do you need to develop to let it go? Just because an adaptation served us once, it doesn't mean we have to keep living it out. It was a choice, and we can choose differently.

Energetically, choosing a new path requires re-anchoring our fibers and clearing our energy field. Energy follows attention, so extracting deeply rooted energy fibers requires the ability to look for new perspectives. Then, send light fibers to anchor in the solution. This is like sending an emissary ahead to negotiate on our behalf. Once we detach our energy from limitation by affirming our spiritual essence, new possibilities appear. How this happens won't necessarily be how we imagine.

If limitations are pushing you to develop new resources, look at your situation and ask what inner resource will help overcome this challenge. Do you need a new skill, courage, belief? We sometimes think limitations are keeping us from being the person we want to be. Remembering that the person we want to be is an expression of a quality, not a circumstance, we can be that person right now. The best way to do this is to align with your new self. Who would you be if you had no limitations? How would you behave? What would be important to you? When you immerse yourself in being your new self, you open the door to becoming. Firmly attach your light fibers into the future and let your future be a magnet drawing you forward.

Consider this: In every religion and spiritual path, there is one prime directive: Love one another. It's so simple that we overlook that it is the point and purpose of being alive. That one sentence reduces everyone's purpose to the same thing: increase love in the world. Growth becomes clearing from within everything that resists love. How is your limitation an expression of a lack of love?

CLEARING LIMITATIONS EXERCISE

Ground, center, and establish boundaries.

Activate Queen Nefertiti's Headdress. Stream light through your aura and visualize the release of limiting patterns.

Activate the Chakra Fibers pattern. Picture a situation you want to change.

Observe the energy fibers connecting you to the situation. What chakra are they coming from? How thick are they? How much light is in them? What colors? How much energy and what is the quality of energy flowing through? Is it fast, slow, chaotic, focused?

Notice the quantity and quality of energy that flows from the situation back to you.

Ask your inner wisdom if this energy exchange represents your path and purpose. You don't need an answer; simply ask the question and notice how you feel.

Bring your attention to your core and the flow of energy along your Hara-line.

Invite the energy fibers to detach from the situation and coil them back into your chakra.

Thank the limitation/situation/pattern for the opportunity and assert that its job is done and you no longer need it.

Imagine yourself as the person you would be without limitation. Invite your energy fibers to explore this image and anchor into it. Feel energy flowing to you along energy fibers firmly linked to your new situation. Be the new you. See the new energy configuration, feel it, and send and receive energy through it.

Ground, center, and establish your boundaries as you go out into the day, renewed. Make choices throughout the day that support the flow of energy into your new situation.

Loss and Change

Even positive change is challenging. It requires withdrawing energy from one point of attachment and refocusing it somewhere else. Success happens when our fibers link to the new situation and an energy exchange occurs. Energy can flow only when we're in alignment with the situation, so the more congruent we are, the greater the flow and the deeper the energy connection.

Losing someone we love through death, divorce, or otherwise creates trauma to our energy structures. Fiber attachments can be violently severed, causing "energy bleeds" or leaks in our aura making it difficult to reattach elsewhere. The inability to maintain our energy causes depletion, depression, and loss of direction.

As difficult as grief is, it does have an energetic function. Its ravaging force travels along the damaged fibers cleansing and healing, preparing us to realign to the future. The fiery intensity of grief burns off old patterns and allows for reattaching to create new constellations of relationship.

Sometimes, however, we get stuck in grief. This can happen when grief becomes our way of keeping connected to a lost loved one. Instead of being cleansing, grief becomes an addiction. Moving on can feel like a betrayal as fear keeps us from moving forward. Focusing on old memories maintains an energy bridge to the past. However, we can choose another way of connecting. We can link to a person's spiritual essence in the present, whether the person is alive or has transitioned.

As harsh as it seems, holding on to grief is a choice, and mental discipline is required to direct our energy into a life-affirming connection. You can adjust the following exercise to reconfigure your energy in any situation. Instead of a person, you can release a situation or belief. Then, anchor to something new.

ASSISTING GRIEF, CLEARING FIBERS, AND RECONFIGURING ENERGY EXERCISE

Choose a time when you're not rushed with other constraints and settle inside a quiet, private, and sacred space. Use your power spot or personal sanctuary.

Add a memento of the person you're grieving (a picture, personal object, letter), or simply light a candle to represent the person's spirit.

Ground, center, and establish your boundaries.

Activate the Spiral Pillar of Light to create a protected circle of safety, healing, and light.

Ask the person to join you in spirit, knowing you're safe and protected at all times.

Notice the energy attachments that flow to the memory of this person. Feel his or her condition. Are the fibers strong and vibrant, or battered, tattered, and worn? Is there still an energy exchange occurring?

Let yourself feel your grief fully and completely. Don't hold back. Give yourself permission to fully embrace all of your feelings, the guilt, the loss, and the happiness. Don't be afraid of the depth of your feelings; you have time, the feelings will ebb, you will come back.

As you grieve, allow the pure fire of the pain to burn through any residual emotions you carry: longing, despair, resentment, envy, guilt, and so on. Let yourself feel with no judgment. You may be surprised to find many contradictions in the array of feelings you have. Simply allow them all.

Speak whatever words you need to this person.

Send a beam of light to this person and, with love, call your fibers back. Visualize light flowing into them, repairing the tears and stanching the bleeds.

Allow your light fibers to link with the spiritual essence of this person. You're never truly separated, even when the person you love is on the other side of the veil we call life; you are always connected.

Send love along your fibers to the spirit of this person. Receive his or her love in return. Love is never lost. No love you give or energy you spend is ever lost, regardless of how it appears on the physical level.

Ask for your partner's blessing in making new connections. Say goodbye to the way things were and give yourself permission to start the process of re-networking.

Ground, center, return to present, and establish your boundaries before ending.

Decision-Making

If life is an adventure and growth the purpose, then there are no truly right or wrong decisions. Thinking so is part of duality consciousness and weights each decision with judgment and fear of making a mistake. Duality consciousness is a function of the mind, so paying attention to the body offers another perspective. For example, we often feel resistance when making a choice. We either don't want to make a choice, or the direction we think we should choose doesn't match what we feel. If the body is resisting a decision, we might:

- Be encountering limiting beliefs or self-sabotage.
- Not have all the information needed.
- Have an unrealistic evaluation of our resources.
- Be encountering opposition we need to prepare for.
- Be feeling that going forward will damage our integrity.
- Not like any of the options.
- Feel our identity isn't reflected in the choices.

In all cases, our subconscious is joining in the decision-making process, showing us the arena of our growth. When we feel resistance, it's time to examine our feelings and listen. When we understand what our whole self is telling us, we will know what to do. Our resistance dissipates, we have ideas outside the box, we feel energized, and we sense flow. As we move forward, the path opens and synchronicity occurs.

CLARIFYING DECISIONS EXERCISE

Ground, center, and establish your boundaries.

Fully immerse yourself in the situation as it exists right now. Saturate yourself in the intricacies, frustrations, discomforts, hopes, motivations, and everything else that is part of the situation. When you've fully experienced where you're stuck, continue.

Physically move your closed eyes to the right and ask your past for permission to move forward. Notice what comes up.

Physically move your closed eyes to your left and ask your future for insight. Notice any images, impressions, and feelings.

Physically move your closed eyes straight ahead and put your options before you.

Fully immerse yourself in the first option. Send your energy fibers into the future and feel the situation you would be creating. Ask whether your fibers are flexibly anchored, fixed in one place, or floating without connection. Relax your mind and extend your senses. Open to what your life will be if you proceed along this path. Does it give you energy or take it away? Do you feel aligned or distanced?

Do the same with each subsequent option.

Which scenario gives you the greatest boost and sense of rightness? This is not necessarily the easiest path, but the one that mobilizes your internal energy and gives you the greatest sense of self.

If you are unclear, investigate what gets in the way. Are you afraid of loss, success, failure? Move beyond right and wrong. Make a decision and start the process. Action is better than stagnation because it gives you something to work with. You will soon see if you need to adjust your direction or even retreat. Rather than failure, this is reconnaissance.

If you're not connected to your spiritual essence, activate the Mystic Triangle to assist the connection.

Stand with your arms spread slightly away from your side, palms forward.

Imagine a triangle forming between your Third Eye and the palms of your hands.

Identify with your spiritual essence; let go of restriction.

Hold your situation gently in your mind's eye and allow new information, options, or insight to enter your awareness.

Return to present-time awareness. Ground, center, and establish boundaries.

Take a moment to write down whatever you have received and list the action steps you need to take.

Stress: Trauma, Drama, and Addiction

During stressful situations, the body is flooded with fight-or-flight chemicals. This allows fast, instinctive action. However, some people become addicted to the high-octane energy of stress. Initially, the energy boost that raises our blood pressure, activates our muscles, and sharpens our mind is lifesaving, but not if it becomes a long-term reaction.

We become stress addicts for two primary reasons. First, we need the adrenaline boost to feel alive. Relaxation feels like coming down. We get edgy, restless, and irritable as we look for or create the next adrenaline rush. We become workaholics or exercise junkies, engage in high risk activities, or create one emergency after another to keep the high going until, eventually, we crash.

The second reason for stress addiction is to avoid uncomfortable emotions. It's far easier to keep on running than to stop and discover that we have no joy in life or that our primary relationship has no real connection. Rather than put the energy into exploring how we feel and what we need, we stay busy.

Emotional addiction is a close cousin to stress addiction. In emotional addiction, drama is generated to provoke reactions that heighten energy. Getting energy this way turns us into high-drama junkies, always increasing the emotional trauma in order to stay fueled. Relationships become battlefields with few true connections. Trust is sacrificed as the people around us don't know when the next explosion and energy grab will happen.

Whether we're addicted to emotional drama, stress, alcohol, or drugs, the problem is essentially the same: we've replaced our spiritual connection as the source of our energy with a substitute. Overcoming this pattern takes mental and emotional discipline. As we restructure our energy, we must also change our actions. This exercise will help with energetic balance to support the counseling, addiction programs, and other healing actions.

RELEASING ADDICTION EXERCISE

Ground, center, and establish boundaries.

Imagine yourself engaged in your addictive behavior. Notice the energy rush you receive, as well as your conflicting emotions and negative aftereffects. Allow scene after scene to pass before your mind's eye. Let as many scenes flow through as come forward. When you feel fully saturated in both the rush and the harmful aftereffects, stop.

Where in your body do you receive the energy high? What part of you feels alive using this behavior? What do you lose by connecting to life this way?

Clear your addictive patterns by activating the Pyramid Purification pattern. Visualize all the old patterns being drawn into the pyramid and being transmuted in the violet flame in its center.

Activate Earth and Sky, pulling energy up into your core from the depths of the Earth and down into your core from your Star, your spiritual Source. Breathe through this pattern, sending energy through your body.

Imagine yourself engaging in an addictive pattern. Visualize pulling your energy fibers in, retracting your aura, and behaving calmly as you receive an energy boost from Earth and Sky.

Ground, center, and establish your boundaries.

Transmuting Karma

Karma is the spiritual law of cause and effect. The conditions in our life—where we're born, to what family, and in what situation—are determined by our past-life actions. However, karma is not a cosmic score card of retribution; it's a teaching tool. Once we've learned what we needed to learn, the situation is free to change.

Transmuting karma is done by recognizing and changing our harmful behavior then forgiving self and others. When we harm another, we're operating from the illusion that we're separate beings. Forgiveness is the bridge between the illusion of separation and the knowing that we are one—that one person's pain is everyone's pain. Simple forgiveness recognizes that despite how it may look, the people in our life are working in concert with us to provide opportunities for growth.

One of the misidentifications with the law of karma is judging another person by his or her circumstances. Circumstances do not define or reveal a person's soul. The quality of a person's spiritual path and what they offer isn't determined by material conditions. A person who manifested a BMW instead of a Ford is not spiritually more advanced. Wherever we are, we can carry light and create change for the good of all.

Karma is also misused when the suffering of others is ignored because "that's their karma." Ignoring someone's need teaches us a lot about our own spiritual condition, but nothing about the karma of the other person. To transmute karma, activate the Pyramid Purification pattern on page 47 and, as past actions are burned in the violet flame, release love, compassion, and forgiveness into the world.

Chapter 16

Dynamic Relationships

The moment we walk into a room full of people, we're in energetic exchange with everyone else. Imagine entering a party and looking for someone you know; your energy fibers are exploring, contacting, and assessing. What they find is fed into your chakras to become gut feelings and intuition. Although we're self-contained energy systems, we're connected to others and in perpetual exchange. The degree of exchange depends on the depth of relationship.

Relationships provide meaning and context to life. Through interacting with others, human and nonhuman, seen and unseen, we understand ourselves better. The information we receive through our subconscious energy connections is illustrated in our language. Metaphors describing emotional relationships also reflect energy interactions.

For example, when we're "attached" to someone, we're referring to an emotional bond that also describes being linked together through energy fibers. After an emotional trauma, we might say "my heart is broken" or "my heart is bleeding." The words reflect our emotional state and describe our energy state. Our Heart Chakra fibers may well be torn, broken, and bleeding (leaking energy). Emotions and energy speak with the same metaphors because emotions are the body's translation of energy reality. Becoming aware of the energy dynamics between our self and others is fascinating and helps create lasting and loving connections.

Energy Interactions

There are three primary ways people exchange energy. The first is simple resonance, also called correspondence, where one person raises or lowers another's vibration through the strength of their frequency. Being around people who raise our vibration is stimulating, exciting, and healing. If we let it, being around people who lower our vibration can be depleting. However, we can maintain high energy and bring our depleted friends up by connecting to self-transcendent emotions such as love, awe, compassion, and joy, or by connecting to the frequency of higher consciousness as discussed in Chapter 20.

The second type of energy exchange relates to the substance of subtle energy, occurring as streams that flow from one person to another. Barbara Brennan, author of *Light Emerging: The Journey of Personal Healing,* calls this exchange "bioplasmic streaming."[1] Essentially, any time you put your attention on another person, you're streaming energy to them whether that person is physically present or far away. This energy can be uplifting for the receiver, as when you think loving and supportive thoughts, or destructive, as when you project judgment and criticism as discussed in Chapter 12. Even loving thoughts can become hooks in another's field when sent with an agenda such as wanting the other person's love and attention beyond what he or she chooses to give.

The third type of exchange happens through the energy fibers that emerge from the chakras. They are sometimes referred to as cords, but it's important to remember that they're part of our energy anatomy. Links between two people's chakras are formed through strong connection and usually, although not always, occur between chakras of the same level; the Heart Chakra of one person links with the Heart Chakra of another, and so on. How many and which of the chakras are coupled depends on the type of connection. An employer and employee may have only one chakra tie, whereas a parent and infant are bonded through all their chakras.

Romantic Connections

When two people have a deep, loving union, all their chakras line up and link together. Their energy fields merge and their personal boundaries become more permeable, allowing for greater exchange. As the relationship grows, the couple's energy structures cojoin and their internal pathways of energy connect.

When two people with healthy boundaries and identities have a full energy linkup, they develop a depth of intimacy that has no comparison. It's as though they see through the same eyes and feel with the same nerve endings, sharing personal safety few people experience. Fully formed connections of this nature are rare and quite precious.

High-level romantic relationships are not luck or happenstance. They're painstakingly developed, if not in this life, then in a past life.

Although the energy spark happens naturally, the innate connection can be deepened using energy awareness exercises and meditation.

Energy-linking exercises can be used between friends as well as in romantic connections as long as the practice is approached with respect. As we explore our combined energy circuits, we're opening in very deep ways. Good boundaries ensure we maintain our individuality and don't absorb any harmful energy. Truthfully, every time we give someone our attention, an energy link is formed; the stronger our connection, the stronger and longer lasting the link. The exercises here are helping us become aware of what's already happening. However, if you're concerned you'll be harmed by consciously sharing energy, intend that your energy filters are strong and that nothing stays with you that isn't yours, and nothing within you is altered. Its also fine not to participate in these exercises.

The following three exercises progress in the degree of intimacy involved. The first and second can be comfortably explored with friends. The third is most comfortable with a primary partner. It may seem an oxymoron to establish boundaries before merging with another, but with strong, healthy boundaries you can choose what to open to and what not to. (Illustration of exercises can be found at *explorationsinenergy.com*.)

LINKING EXERCISE 1

Sit back-to-back with your partner on the floor in cross-legged position or on two stools. Feel the warmth of your partner spread into you as you lean in to each other.

Ground, center, and establish your boundaries.

Activate the Celtic Cross pattern to filter the energy moving between you.

Relax into each other and feel supported even as you're supporting your partner.

Let go of any tension and receive support.

Bring your attention into the back of your chakras. Notice the energy streaming between your chakras and your friend's.

Inhale together through your Crown Chakras, drawing energy into your Hara-line. Exhale, offering energy to your partner.

Synchronize your breathing to reflect this in-and-out flow of energy between your chakras. Play with breathing in while the other exhales and create a circle of energy.

Send love and light, and receive love and light.

Notice what you feel, see, and experience.

Gradually lean forward, away from your partner. Notice how far apart you are when you stop feeling the connection. Can you maintain awareness of the connection even across the room?

Draw your energy back into yourself, ground, center, and establish your boundaries as you close this exercise.

LINKING EXERCISE 2

Sit facing your partner in cross-legged position, or in chairs, with knees touching.

Ground, center, and establish your boundaries.

Greet your partner with a bow to honor the divine within.

Activate the Spiral Pillar of Light pattern or the Celtic Cross pattern to maintain a filter.

Each of you activate your own Circle of Life pattern using the internal energy flow of the pattern like this: Energy builds up your internal center line, spills out your Crown Chakra, and flows in a fountain over the top of your head, raining down all around to be collected under your torso and sent back up through your Base Chakra along your center line once again.

Once you've established the flow, with respect and in the utmost love, invite your energy to flow together.

As you and your partner come into sync, be with the energy flowing up the center line of both of you, out the Crown Chakra, down around you both, and then back up.

As energy flows along this pathway, notice how you feel in your body, what you see in your mind's eye, and what emotions you experience. Share this with your partner.

When the energy slows, let it return to individual flow patterns. Notice your energy flowing up your internal center line, out your chakra, forming a fountain over the top of your head, and so on.

When each of you feels complete with the exercise, bow to each other and offer thanks.

Close the activations.

Ground, center, and establish your boundaries as you disconnect. Share your experiences.

BUILDING INTIMACY EXERCISE

Sit facing your partner on a mat or on stools with your knees touching, or sit with arms and legs wrapped around each other.

Ground, center, and establish your boundaries.

To deepen the energy connection if you are on a mat with crossed legs, try sitting inside the circle of your partner's legs as he or she sits inside the circle of your legs. Wrap your arms around each other if not already sitting that way.

Touch foreheads and honor the divine within.

Individually activate the Circle of Life pattern using the external pathway of the body. The energy flows up your spine, over the top of your head, and down the center line of the front of your body, circling under your torso and rising up the spine again.

Merge your pathways. There are two variations for how this happens; the depth of your connection will determine which one is more natural for you.

Invite your energy flows to link. Energy rises along your spine, crosses over to your partner, and flows down his or her front center line, crossing back under you to rise up your spine. At the same time, your partner's energy is rising up his or her spine, crossing over the top of his or her head and flowing down your front center line. This pattern looks something like the Vesica Pisces symbol. A variation of this link is for the energy to flow up the spine of one partner and down the spine of the other partner.

The more intimate variation utilizes the inner pathway of the Circle of Life pattern. Invite energy to rise up the center line of one partner, out the Crown Chakra, and over the top of the head to the Crown Chakra of the second partner. The energy will then flow down the center line of the second person, out the Base Chakra, and into the Base Chakra of the first person. If the two partners are male and female, the energy usually flows up the female and down the male.

Once the circuit is flowing, activate the Chakra Fibers pattern and invite the fibers of your chakras to explore your partner's chakras as your partner explores yours. Notice how each of your chakras connects with your partner's chakra of the same level. Notice the strength and quality of each connection. Allow anything that needs to change to be adjusted.

Observe. Notice what you see in your mind's eye, feel in your body, and experience emotionally. Let creative impulse direct the energy.

When the energy flow subsides, share your experiences with your partner.

Close the activations.

Ground, center, and establish boundaries as you disconnect.

All of these exercises can be done at a distance. Time and space are pliable in the realm of energy, and distance is no object. Set an agreed time to do the exercises and imagine your partner sitting across from you as you explore the energy links between you. Write down what you experience and compare notes. You might be surprised that your experiences match.

Consciously connecting with another is not a practice that can be done without the other person's permission. If you have feelings for someone that are not returned, you must respect his or her boundaries. If you use your willpower and intent to create bonds that are not naturally part of a mutual attraction, your attention will become hooks and projections in the other person's field. In short, you will be engaged in a type of psychic attack, albeit unintentional. Prevent this by connecting with permission and awareness.

Imbalance in Relationships

Regardless of the type of association, a healthy relationship is characterized by each person giving and receiving equally. This is true in romantic partnerships, employer-employee relations, and everything in between. A fulfilling connection promotes personal growth for both people. Many relationships, however, are based on unequal input.

Losing balance almost always occurs as the result of uneven growth. Sometimes one aspect of a person grows at the expense of another, such as the intellect growing at the expense of the heart, causing difficulties in relating to others. Or in relationships, sometimes one partner grows when the other doesn't, or one partner's growth inhibits the other.

One way to rebalance a relationship is to shift the energy dynamics. This automatically alters our emotions and perceptions. Once we've initiated a change in energy flow, it becomes easier to address problems and find solutions. As with all things, moving the energy is only half the job. Making the necessary lifestyle adjustments is the other.

In any type of relationship, exploring the energy flow along the fibers that attach us is a powerful tool for rebalancing energy. This can be extremely effective, especially with life partners. Although not ideal, if one partner is unwilling or doesn't relate to subtle energy, the other partner can still work on balancing the energy between them by focusing on their end of the energy exchange. When one partner in the dance shifts, the dance itself shifts.

FIBER-BALANCING EXERCISE

Ground, center, and establish your boundaries.

If your partner is present, sit facing each other. If you're working at a distance or working alone, imagine your partner sitting across from you.

Bow to each other, or to their image, and acknowledge the divine within.

Activate the Celtic Cross pattern to filter the energy exchange.

Activate the Chakra Fibers pattern and visualize the fibers of energy that link the two of you. Look for the chakra(s) with the strongest connection; this often includes the Third Chakra.

Observe the condition of the fibers. First look at yours, then your partner's. Notice your first impressions and feelings, then look at specifics such as how thick the fibers are, how dense, rigid, flexible, or free. How firmly does your fiber attach to your partner? How firmly does your partner's fiber attach to you? Is this comfortable?

Observe the energy flow along your fibers. Is it slow or fast? Turbulent, free-flowing, or stagnant? A full stream or mere trickle? Notice how much it supports and feeds your partner. Then notice the same details about your partner's fibers that link with you. Are you both receiving what you need?

Assess whether the flow along both fibers is equal.

Assess whether or not you want to receive the other person's energy. You can't change the flow of energy the other person is sending; however, you can choose not to receive it. To do so, imagine placing a valve at the entry point that you can adjust. If you want, you can remove the attachment altogether. You can change what you receive; what you can't do is take more than is being offered, or seek to change the other person. Stay with this image until the flow is smooth.

Decide if the flow of energy from you to your partner is as you want it. If you're sending more than you want to send, slow it down. If you want to increase the flow, do so, but don't demand the other person receive it. Stay in the flow until the flow is smooth and balanced.

If you're working with your partner, share your impressions. Try not to force your observations or be influenced away from your own impressions; just let each person's experience be part of the picture.

Focus on unconditional love for yourself and your partner while holding the intention of balance. Observe changes in your fibers and the flow and quality of energy. Continue until you both feel the flow is equal and stable.

Take note of what you feel, see, and experience.

Bow to your partner, or the image of your partner, and give thanks for the exchange.

Close the activations.

Ground, center, and establish your boundaries as you end this exercise.

Performing this practice can't ensure that your relationship will become more balanced or even survive long-term. It will make clear what needs to change and allow you to decide whether it's possible to do so or not. If you and your partner decide to do the work to reestablish a solid relationship, doing this exercise on a regular basis can support your intentions.

Codependence

Codependence happens when two people are drawn together to complete each other's imbalances. One person in the relationship operates strongly where the other is weak, and vice versa. In the beginning, this is empowering as each partner "borrows" from the other and feels stronger, while at the same time each gives from an area he or she has an excess in. Ultimately, if both people don't develop their weak areas, the relationship becomes draining as each person loses his or her boundaries and the two become energetically enmeshed.

A common codependent imbalance happens to people connected through the First Chakra of physical safety and the Third Chakra of personal power. This imbalance can be part of a parent-child or employer-employee relationship as well as a marriage or partnership with traditional male/female roles. In this pattern, one person gives up the development of his or her personal power (Third Chakra) in exchange for safety (First Chakra). The other partner happily provides safety in exchange for feeling powerful. Ultimately, one feels underappreciated, the other feels used, and both feel victimized. In this arrangement, any attempt of one partner to grow happens at the expense of the other.

Another common codependent pattern in love relationships is a Second to Fourth Chakra imbalance where one partner provides the sexual energy of the Second Chakra (traditionally the male) and the other partner provides the heart-centered energy of the Fourth Chakra (traditionally the female). At first, each person feels complete, as his or her empty chakra is filled by the other, but eventually each feels drained. The heart-centered partner complains that the other "is unemotional and unfeeling" and she does all the caring. The Second Chakra partner complains that the other "has no sexual interest" and "it's all up to him." Each is drained by the other person drawing energy, the same exchange that was originally empowering.

Codependent relationships are based on avoidance. Not able to face the healing and growth that must take place in order to develop, the person avoids the problem by linking up with someone who can fill the missing element. Although each partner rescues the other, what's missing are equality and healthy boundaries; consequently the depth of connection suffers.

If you're in a codependent partnership, you can initiate change by developing your entire chakra system. Use the Fiber-Balancing Exercise (page 171) to assess which chakras are linked in dominant or weak patterns. Then use the Chakra Clarity meditation on page 24 to work with each of your chakras, developing your own inner resource and strength.

If we have a true connection with our partner, when we become more independent our partnership will strengthen. Then we can stay with each other and build our relationship out of joy, rather than need. On the other hand, if our partnership is based on need only, as we both grow we may realize that it's time to part. It's important to part with genuine care for the other person, knowing that he or she served a purpose in our growth, as we did in theirs. It's also possible that we may grow while our partner does not. In this case, the relationship will become harder and harder to sustain, and we will have to make a difficult choice of whether to stay and stagnate, or leave.

Enable versus Support

Another challenging imbalance happens when a partner, friend, business associate, or child is involved in self-destructive behavior that sabotages opportunity and growth. This behavior can be mild, as in being perpetually late for deadlines and thus losing jobs, or devastating, as in drug and alcohol abuse. In a relationship with a self-sabotaging person, it can be hard to know how to be supportive without enabling the destructive behavior.

A self-destructive person can fall into a downward spiral and lose the ability to maintain energy. As things degrade, the person becomes a vortex, drawing in other people and unintentionally ensnaring them. The person then lives off the energy field of those who help, becoming an energy vampire, as discussed in Chapter 12.

Support is growth-oriented. Enabling sustains the continuation of self-destructive behavior, allowing the person to avoid growth. Oftentimes the enabler is codependent, obtaining self-importance or purpose from helping. Energetically, the connection can look like hooks from the self-destructive person into the enabler and like projections with waves of streamed energy from the enabler to the self-destructive person. There may be a strong fiber link where the enabler is supplying energy through one or more chakras. Although a complete withdrawal of energy may cause the self-destructive person to spiral, a shift needs to happen or both people will collapse.

If we're enabling another, the protection exercises in Chapter 12, the Fiber-Balancing Exercise on page 171, and the Extracting Energy Fibers Exercise on page 175 can be helpful. Also, professional help may be necessary. This doesn't mean we withdraw our love and support. It means we develop our boundaries, practice protection, and learn to support the person in developing his or her own resources instead of loaning ours.

Growth-oriented support is clean, with no agenda other than love itself. The biggest gift we can give a person is to trust their path and support their essence. Every judgment and criticism adds weight to the person's problems. Don't imagine that the person doesn't see their own failures; they do. The best thing we can do is to screen our reactions with this question: Does this reaction help or hinder this person? If the answer is that it hinders, choose to focus on love.

Betrayal and Endings

Nothing is worse than a relationship ending through betrayal. The grief of loss is compounded by extensive damage to the chakra fibers that were once linked together. The damage is severe because energy fibers are literally ripped and severed, leaving tears in the aura and leaks in the torn appendages. Because these fibers contribute to stability and orientation, the sudden disruption can leave the person bewildered, confused, and disconnected. Physically, the person becomes drained and nutrient-deficient, often provoking underlying physical problems.

Techniques to repair chakra fibers were introduced in Chapter 15 (in the "Loss and Change" section) and are further covered in Chapter 19. However, even when using these techniques, damage can take years to heal, depending on how deep the connection was and how much of our identity was based on the connection. Without subtle energy work there can be permanent scars in the energy field and psyche. Damage of this nature needs to receive healing attention on all levels: energy healing, physical support such as nutritional balance and massage, and psychological-spiritual counseling.

One of the reasons overcoming betrayal can be so difficult is that energy fibers were never consciously disconnected and the person left behind may still have links to the person who moved on. Even though the quality of energy being exchanged may be characterized by anger and revenge, it still constitutes a connection. Consciously removing the energy links enhances healing efforts. This exercise can be used to finalize connection between ex-partners, regardless of how they parted.

EXTRACTING ENERGY FIBERS EXERCISE

Ground, center, and establish boundaries.

Activate the Celtic Cross pattern and invite your spirit guides to be present and help.

Bow to the image of your partner and recognize his or her inner divinity. Explain that you are releasing his or her energy fibers and retracting your own.

Activate the Chakra Fibers pattern and focus on your chakras. Where is your attention drawn?

Notice the fibers that connect you and your ex-partner. What is the condition of the fibers? What do they look like? How much energy is flowing toward you and away from you? How much hope does this connection have for you?

If there's anything you still need to say to your ex-partner, spend a few minutes visualizing your partner and looking into his or her eyes, and then tell him or her what you need to say.

Imagine letting go of your ex-partner's fibers, and visualize them being retracted and returned home.

Retrieve your fibers, visualizing them being recoiled like a hose being rewound.

Pull your fibers into your chakras and coil them into a nest of loving energy. Allow your spirit guides to fill this nest with healing light.

Consider the ways you've grown from this experience and acknowledge the necessity of your ex-partner's actions for this growth. Forgive this person, and be free. If you can't, put these feelings into a container, and ask your guides to hold them for you and help you come to forgiveness.

Thank your ex-partner, and acknowledge that you are both released and free. Then, close the activations.

Ground, center, and establish your boundaries.

Conflict Resolution

Resolving conflict can be very difficult, especially with the strong polarization going on today. This method works on bringing us into alignment with those we're in conflict with so that we can discuss our issues. It won't solve our problems; it will simply help reduce the charge in the discussion. This can be used during mediation, negotiations, divorce settlements, and so forth to clear unnecessary emotional charge.

CONFLICT RESOLUTION EXERCISE

Ground, center, and establish boundaries.

Imagine that your conflict with this person resides as a vibration in your aura. Using your intuition and energy senses, locate where in your aura your part of this conflict resides. You might feel it as a density, vibration, or color shimmering in one of the layers of your aura. Usually, you'll find it in your second, third, or fourth layer, or any place that draws your attention.

Using your energy senses, scan the other person's aura and locate the area holding the vibration of conflict. If you're not sure, trust your gut instinct or just pick a place.

Visualize the area in your aura being joined with the area in the other person's aura via an energy link.

Invite the two areas to find resonance with each other. No energy has to be exchanged; this is a change in vibration through resonance.

When you're finished, disconnect the link.

Ground, center, and establish boundaries.

Forgiveness and Relationship Healing

When two people are finished with their relationship, forgiveness is the final act of letting go. It releases anger and the desire for revenge, forces that appear to want closure but actually serve to maintain connection. In a state of forgiveness, the Extracting Energy Fibers Exercise on page 175 is very effective for closure.

When two people have been through difficulty and decide to stay together, forgiveness builds a bridge across the chasm of separation. One of the misconceptions of soul-mate or high-level relationships is that they have no problems. In truth, the closeness of these connections provides a depth of safety that allows the couple to work through deep karmic patterns and difficulties. No relationship is free from the need for growth, and these relationships are formed to allow both partners the opportunity.

Forgiveness and trust are not the same. Trust is built on a solid energetic connection. We can understand why someone hurt us, can forgive their actions, and still not trust that we won't be hurt again. Consider a wild animal in a cage: we can understand why it's behaving aggressively and feel compassion for the animal, yet wouldn't put our hand in the cage. A person becomes untrustworthy when they haven't integrated their unhealed shadow-side. Staying together may depend on whether both have a real desire to do the inner work necessary to be trustworthy.

If you and your partner are in conflict and want to stay together, there are two essential energy practices that can help, aside from the Conflict Resolution Exercise earlier in this chapter. First, create a sanctuary (as described in Chapter 13). Agree that in your sanctuary you're both safe. Neither will attack the other in word, deed, or attitude. Agree that while in this space you will not discuss your difficulties. You have all the rest of the world in which to talk about your problems; in your sanctuary, just be together in love. Let it be a place where you remember the true feelings that hold you together, not the difficulty that tears you apart. Respect this space and never violate it. If you find you can't maintain a sanctuary or that one of you doesn't want to create it, you may need to re-evaluate if you have the true desire to solve your issues.

Next, reframe the context of the issue. You and your partner need to be on the same side. It sounds contradictory to be on the same side with someone with whom you're in conflict, but both you and your partner want the same thing: a better, stronger, more loving, and fulfilling relationship. Be together in facing the issues that provoke separation. Instead of fighting with each other over an issue, stand together against the issue. This simple reframing reminds us that if both partners don't win, neither does.

RELATIONSHIP-HEALING EXERCISE

Create or enter your sanctuary.

Choose an item that represents the conflict you and your partner are having, or write down all the details of your differences on a piece of paper. Put them in a container such as a basket or bowl.

Sit next to each other and place the container across from you.

Ground, center, and establish your boundaries.

Bow to each other and acknowledge the divine within. Invite your spiritual guides to be present.

Start with each person making a statement of affirmation, such as "I believe there is a path we can walk where we both get what we need" or "Our health and happiness are increased when we both get what we need."

In a short statement, describe how you feel in the situation. Then listen to your partner describe how he or she feels. Don't interrupt each other. Even though you've both said how you've felt before, this time listen without judgment, reactivity, or guilt. You are speaking to each other's spirit.

Pretend you're the other person. Immerse yourself in the feelings your partner has expressed and, using empathy, be him or her in the situation. Imagine what you would need to get to the other side of the issue. Have your partner do the same.

Write down what you felt and understood when you pretended to be your partner, and put it in the container along with your partner.

Visualize light filling the container. Allow your energy to stream into the container. Turn the issue over to your highest selves.

When the flow is complete, leave it. Over time you will see/feel what has changed.

Ground, center, and establish boundaries.

Take a break from your issue. Wait a full twenty-four hours before talking about it on any level. During this time, take control of your thoughts and every time you find yourself thinking about the issue, replace your thought with this affirmation: "I release the situation to the highest and best good for all."

When you revisit the discussion, start by sharing how you felt when you walked in the other person's shoes.

Energy awareness can help rebuild a relationship that has broken down from neglect or betrayal. However, repairing a relationship isn't something one person can do for the other. Both people must want to rebuild.

Using energy awareness in relationships is exceptionally fulfilling. Partners who include this level of engagement delve into the deepest parts of each other and commit to a path of shared intent. However, as with all energy techniques, respect and permission are paramount.

In the midst of the hard work and self-development underway, take time to simply love and honor each other. The following exercise is a wonderful reconnection.

EXPANDING LOVE EXERCISE

Sit opposite your partner in chairs or in cross-legged position, or stand.

Ground, center, and establish boundaries.

Active the Spiral Pillar of Light pattern creating a circle of safety, healing, and light that surrounds and supports both of you.

Place your right hand on your partner's Heart Chakra while he or she does the same to you.

Cover your partner's right hand with your left hand.

Look into each other's eyes.

Activate the Winged Disk pattern and breathe light into your Heart Chakra. Feel it expand.

Send energy from your Heart Chakra down your right arm, through your hand, and into your partner's Heart Chakra.

Receive energy from your partner into your Heart Chakra.

Let the energy circulate and grow as your love expands and joy fills your entire being. If you are standing, feel free to dance.

Honor the divine within each of you. You may find yourselves laughing as you engage each other in this way.

When the flow slows and feels complete, remove your hands and close the activations.

Ground, center, and establish boundaries.

Chapter 17

Manifesting Your Vision

There's an inherent contradiction between knowing we create our own reality and doing so in concert with others. Using manifestation skills mobilizes our intentions and energy; however, creating our circumstances happens through interactions with more realms than those that we see and feel in the physical. We're engaged with other people and other dimensions and perceptions of reality. In this blending, our job is to protect our inner spiritual force from our own self-doubt and the outer criticisms of others.

Being alive is a creative process. Our visions and values are manifesting around us all the time. Manifestation in its most obvious form consists of having an idea, marshalling resources, and making the idea reality. This threefold principle of creation exists in everything, from making furniture to attracting life conditions. Subtle-energy principles also work in a threefold manner.

Some people think using energy skills to manifest is somehow manipulating spiritual forces. In fact, spiritual forces are never more present than in the synchronicity of how we create our ordinary life. Being aware of how and what we're creating is stepping into our spiritual identity and claiming the sovereignty of light in our life.

Tools of Manifestation

Changing external conditions starts on the inside. Manifestation of what we want to create must be preceded by an understanding of why we created our current situation. Otherwise, the same conditions will continue to be reproduced. The tools we have to work with are awareness, values, intention, and alignment, which together create correspondence with our dreams.

Creating something new requires awareness of how we energetically interact with the formative forces around us through thoughts and actions that align with our values. While our conditions don't reflect our spiritual worth or significance to society, they can reflect how well our inner beliefs and values align with our dreams. For example, buying a lottery ticket while believing that gambling is wrong presents a conflict. The alignment between our values, thoughts, and actions is projected via our presence, and it's through our presence that manifestation occurs.

The internal tools for creating change are synchronized with external manifestation through divine timing. The important thing about working with energy is to know that, like water, it can't be pushed. We can't "send" energy in the typical way we think of propelling something forward. Our attention goes first and opens the path for our energy to follow. It's an invitation. We can't force things; we offer a possibility and then match our frequency to what we wish for, creating a vibratory template that forms it. To be truly successful, what we want to manifest must be part of our soul purpose.

Correspondence

Drawing anything into our life, a miracle, new job, relationship, and so forth, occurs through correspondence. This happens when two objects, or systems, that vibrate within the same frequency range connect with each other. In the physical world, the frequencies of the two items synchronize with each other (remember the grandfather clocks) and increase each other's amplitude (remember the strings on the harp). In quantum physics, corresponding items become entangled, and are able to affect each other regardless of time or distance. In metaphysics, when synchronization occurs and the two objects vibrate as one, a flow of energy and information passes between them. Being as one with what we're visioning uses the correspondence method of manifestation.

Correspondence goes beyond creating a vision and wishing it into existence. It requires matching frequencies. Sometimes, we try to do this using high-octane emotion, such as joy or expectation, usually with mixed results. When we add a vision to our emotions, seeing and feeling our self in the outcome, we come closer and the results improve. However, correspondence is full immersion: vibrating at the same frequency, and becoming one with the essence of our dreams. Our ability to achieve correspondence starts with energy awareness.

Awareness

Energy awareness notices our own vibration and our interaction with the vibrating world around us. The thirteen meditations in this book are practices that help refine our awareness. They direct us to pay attention to how we feel in different vibratory experiences.

Awareness of vibration helps us understand the impact of our repetitive thoughts. These thoughts reflect deeper beliefs that are such a part of us, we can't always distinguish their impact on the quality of our life. By paying attention to our thoughts and how they affect our internal flows of energy, we can see/feel them as vibration in our aura. We can notice the correspondence between our inner life and outer world.

Everything around us is the result of a series of choices—ours and other people's. Each choice is the result of attitudes, beliefs, and thought patterns that create vibrations that interact with both the seen and unseen parts of reality. It's a circular situation; what we believe directs our choices, and what we choose is reflected in our conditions, which in turn supports our belief. Change requires imagination—the capacity to see beyond what we currently experience and become it.

Intention and Imagination

Intention is the directive of the heart. The heart is the seat of our spirit, the place where our true essence resides. Imagination is the canvas through which our essential self creates visions we aspire to manifest. Emotional connection fills the vision with energy and helps bring us into resonance with it. With awareness, we can assess where we resonate and where we don't, then determine what's getting in the way. As we remove dissonance, we come into correspondence.

Intention guides our choices, forming a bridge between what exists in the physical realm as conditions and what exists in the field of potential. Powerful intentions:

- Reflect our essence.
- Are fully formed, yet loosely held.
- Are available for creative interplay and evolution.
- Don't curtail future joy by limitations of current belief.
- Generate energy and engage our emotions.
- Are compelling enough to overcome the momentum of our current direction and any opposition that might arise.
- Excite, thrill, and satisfy.
- Are believable and consistent with our highest identity.

An intention that's unbelievable will create self-sabotage. This doesn't mean to settle for less; certainly, we should go for as much as we can energetically sustain and believe, and is aligned to our essence. But if we can't see our self there, we'll create our manifestation with a twist that reflects our disbelief. This is one of the main obstacles to success. When it happens, we move forward by reframing our intention to reflect the highest expression of our essence that we can believe in.

Alignment

Alignment is the fundamental nature of correspondence. To vibrate with a condition we want to manifest requires the vision to align with our path, including the contracts we made with self and others before incarnating. These contracts provide for our growth as well as those we contracted with. Intentions that undermine these contracts aren't in alignment with our path. In addition to our spiritual essence, path, and purpose, the intention must also align with our core beliefs and the unseen world around us. Difficulty creating a resonant intention might be impacted by:

- Not fully believing we deserve it.
- Feeling guilty for leaving other people behind.
- Identifying more with conditions we're in, than the one we want to manifest.
- Daily recycling of old thoughts.
- Responding with collapse to every obstacle. In other words, not being able to hold energy.
- Aligning with socially conditioned thinking.
- Listening to the voices of others rather than what we know inside is true.
- Wishful thinking that isn't grounded in world events.

Alignment removes the obstacles to our intentions. Like a combination lock, the gears of life click together around our intentions, bringing our vibration into resonance and opening the flow between us and the life we envision.

Divine Timing

No matter how perfectly formed and well aligned our intention, it can manifest only through divine timing. Timing is not based on a clock. It's based on synchronicity, the joining of events in response to our intention. Synchronicity works with a different dimension of time.

Not all cultures see time as a linear progression of measured increments where one event begets the next. The ancient Maya saw it as a relationship between cycles that carried specific qualities imparted to the events taking place within these periods. Synchronicity happens when different cycles overlap, opening portals between seemingly non-related events, increasing the flow of ideas, excitement, and opportunities.

Paying attention to synchronicity helps us see the links between actions and our intentions. The more synchronicity we notice, the more aware we are of how shifting our internal energy impacts external proceedings. We see how synchronicity reacts to our vibratory states of being, witnessing how our energy is cocreating opportunities and experiences. Manifesting anything requires that we learn to adjust our vibratory states.

The Principle of Three

The three steps of creating something in the physical world are having an idea, marshalling resources, and taking action. In the threefold principle of manifestation, we open for inspiration from Source, form and energize an intention, and take action. The following exercise can help shift our vibration to correspond with our desire.

THREEFOLD MANIFESTATION EXERCISE

Ground, center, and establish boundaries.

Activate the Spiral Pillar of Light pattern and connect to your personal Star, your doorway to your spiritual Source.

Activate the Earth and Sky pattern and breathe the light from your Star into your core, through your body to the Earth, and back again to the sky.

Activate the Mystic Triangle pattern, creating a triangle in your Third Eye Chakra, then stand with your hands pulled slightly away from your side, forming a triangle between your Third Eye Chakra and your two hands.

Invite your spiritual helpers to be present.

In your mind's eye, be open to the internal change and growth, known and unknown, that you need in order to manifest your intention. Invite spirit guides to assist you. Relax, open your mind, and wait for insight.

In your right hand, hold the situation as it currently exists. Fully immerse yourself in how things are at this time, seeing and feeling your condition. Move your eyes to the right, forgive any limitation in the past, and ask the past for permission to grow and create a different direction. Give yourself time to fully complete this.

Put your attention in your left hand, where you hold the vision of what you want to manifest. Move your eyes to the left and ask the future for permission and help in cocreating your dream. Fully immerse yourself in the vision of what you want. Feel it in your body.

Inhale light through your Crown Chakra and into your Third Eye and Heart Chakras. Envision your intention moving into the world through the triangle in a spiral of energy.

Relax and open your mind. Allow an image of what your fulfilled intention might look like, free of your own manipulation, five years in the future. What do you see? What do you look like? How do you feel?

Find the vibration of this future and shift your vibration into correspondence with it. Feel the flow of energy between past, present, and future. Give yourself permission to grow.

Maintain this flow of energy from your Source, into your heart, and through the triangular intention until the energy flow subsides.

Close the activations, and ground, center, and establish boundaries.

Partner Manifestations

When partners do manifestation work together their goals are magnified and their bond deepened. If you and a partner have a goal you wish to manifest, enjoy time before performing this exercise to fully create your intention. Combine your ideas until you have an intention you're both aligned with and committed to. Look for any resistance that pops up in your discussions and explore the message it carries. Take your time; the better aligned you are to each other and your goal, the more successful you'll be.

Essentially, the Partner Manifestations Exercise is the same as the exercise to manifest your goals, with a few modifications.

PARTNER MANIFESTATIONS EXERCISE

Sit or stand opposite your partner. If you are in separate physical locations, imagine yourselves opposite each other.

Ground, center, and establish boundaries.

Activate the Spiral Pillar of Light pattern and ask your spiritual Source to bless your intention.

Activate the Earth and Sky pattern to energize your bodies.

Invite the Nature Spirits, guides, and angels working for the highest and best good to be present.

Stand facing each other as you both imagine each of you has three small triangles: one in your Third Eye Chakra and one in each of your palms.

Place your intentions in your Third Eye. Feel it. Be it. Become the outcome you're wanting. Project your intention to a point that exists in the space between you and your partner. Allow the fibers from both of your Third Eye Chakras to weave together.

In your right palms, envision the situation as it has been.

- Acknowledge the fears and vulnerabilities that went into creating the situation as well as the learnings.
- Ask each other for forgiveness and permission to move forward.
- Face your right palms toward each other and pulse light between them.
- Acknowledge your shared path and purpose and beam light into it.
- In your left palms, see yourselves growing and changing to fit your intention.
- Acknowledge both your fears and excitements.
- Acknowledge Divine Timing and know that everything happens in relation to everything else.
- Face your left palms toward each other and pulse light between you.
- Vibrate with the frequency of your future.

When you feel complete, close the activations.

Ground, center, and establish your boundaries.

Group Intentions

When people join together in a circle of intention, the results are exponentially amplified. One of the most innovative group intention projects is led by Lynne McTaggart and described in her book *The Intention Experiment*. McTaggart is the author of several books, including the best-selling *The Field: The Quest for the Secret Force of the Universe*, *The Intention Experiment*, and *The Power of Eight*.[1] According to her website, she works with leading physicists and psychologists from the University of Arizona, Princeton University, the International Institute of Biophysics, Cambridge University, and the Institute of Noetic Sciences.

McTaggart's experiments in intention are not focused on making money or creating material gain. They focus on personal and planetary healing, including counteracting the effects of pollution and decreasing the prevalence of violence. We can call life itself an experiment in intention as we are all cocreating planetary conditions. To take part in McTaggart's experiments, visit her website at *lynnemctaggart.com*.

Be sure to clear your energy field before and after group meditations, not only to avoid taking something away, but also to avoid bringing something to the circle that might impact another. Using the Spiral Pillar of Light pattern will maintain your boundaries and the Celtic Cross pattern can act as a filter, if needed.

CREATING GROUP INTENTION EXERCISE

Ground, center, and establish boundaries. Spend several minutes in a guided meditation to ground and focus the group as a whole and clear each person's energy field.

State the agreed-upon intention and the period of time for the meditation.

Activate the Spiral Pillar of Light pattern and create a circle of safety and healing around the group.

Activate the Pyramid Purification pattern and create a side of the pyramid for each person in the group. Imagine each person sitting at a corner, as in the illustration on page 48.

Imagine a violet flame in the center of the pyramid.

Place the group intention in the flame.

Call in all the old, outmoded thought patterns that created the condition you want to change. Imagine the energy projections being pulled to the base of the flame where they're incinerated and transformed.

Envision the energy released from the violet flame as pure white light.

Focus on your new intention, sending it into the violet flame where it is empowered and released through the apex of the pyramid.

Focus the group on clearly seeing, feeling, and being the intention.

Imagine light from everyone feeding the strength of the violet flame.

Use a timer to stay focused for the agreed-upon period of time.

Close the activations.

Ground, center, and come back to present-time awareness.

Subtle Energy Work

Taking Action

Many people working on manifesting a change stop short of taking action. Instead, they wait for their vision to magically appear, believing this shows their faith. Nothing is further from the truth. Action and visioning complement each other. Just because we're moving energy on the etheric level doesn't mean we don't have to work on the physical level. The difference is that the actions we take are informed by our vision, and a path is created through the density of the material world through correspondence. So, if you're working on a manifestation, keep your frequency in tune with your vision, look for opportunity and synchronicity to take action, be flexible, and know your intention is unfolding exactly as it should for your growth and the highest good of all.

Chapter 18

Developing Your Intuition and Extrasensory Perception

Psychic ability and intuition are natural extensions of energy awareness. The terms extrasensory perception (ESP), intuition, and psi phenomena are often used interchangeably because all involve knowing information that is not obtained through the five senses or logical reasoning. I prefer to call this type of knowing full sensory perception. Here are some common forms:

Telepathy: the ability to pass information directly from the mind of one person to the mind of another.

Clairvoyance: the ability to see distant events (past, present, and future) through a combination of mental imaging and felt-senses.

Remote Viewing: directly knowing or seeing events in another location (past, present, and future) through mental imaging.

Clairaudience: the hearing of information or messages.

Precognition: seeing the future.

Mind-Matter Interaction, or Telekinesis: the ability to influence physical matter with mental intention.

Psychometry: the ability to uncover facts about an event or person by touching objects associated with that person or event.

If you're concerned that using these skills could invade another's privacy, that's good. Maintaining integrity is essential. Although it's unlikely that you will be able to see anything you aren't supposed to, when working with energy, integrity is key. At the very least, what you put out, you will get back. In all instances, use these skills with the utmost respect.

Mechanisms of Psi Phenomena

How telepathy and other extrasensory phenomena occur may not be as important as the effect they have in our life. Yet breakthroughs in scientific understanding often precede global changes in paradigm. How science reacts to psi phenomena helps or hinders our ability to accept our own high-strangeness experiences.

For decades, research into extrasensory phenomena was governed by the axiom "extraordinary claims require extraordinary proof." In other words, psi research is held to a higher standard of proof than other forms of scientific investigation. Interestingly, the advent of quantum physics is changing the conversation. What was once considered quackery is now in the realm of quantum mechanics as subatomic particles provide a model for paranormal mechanisms.

Let's review from Chapter 6 some of the primary principles in quantum mechanics that mirror our ESP abilities:

Resonance: two vibrating objects in the same frequency range come into phase and amplify each other. This is true in all systems, including biological. An example is human hearts that synchronize beats when people co-sleep.[1] Resonance is the basic mechanism of information exchanged through correspondence.

Nonlocality: subatomic particles that are connected can influence each other through space. Regardless of how far apart they are, the movement of one particle is instantaneously communicated to and reflected in the other. For psi phenomena, this means that time and space do not interfere with the transmission of information received through extrasensory perception.

Entanglement: the exchange between subatomic particles is not random. It requires pre-existing connection; the particles must have already "met" each other. Once they have met, they are forever connected and are able to transfer information from anywhere to anywhere. There's no limit to the number of particles that can be entangled, and an entire group can instantly receive information.

Holographic Consciousness: Stanford neurophysiologist Dr. Karl Pribram believes that the brain stores and retrieves information holographically.[2] For psi phenomena, this can align internally with the knowledge we want to receive from the hologram and bring it into awareness, and the brain has the ability to decode it.

Force Is Not Exchanged: Experiments conducted by Alain Aspect in 1982 at Paris University demonstrated that when subatomic particles affect each other across space, they do so without exchanging any apparent force, or energy.[3] Rather than a transfer of energy, there is a direct transfer of information. In essence, information is passed without a carrier wave to transmit it and exists in both places simultaneously. This has been supported by research into precognition conducted by Dr. Dean Radin.[4]

Energy awareness has trained us to use our body to feel shifts in energy and vibration, and to receive information carried on biological energy waves. However, psi phenomena teach us that our bodies are conveying information through more avenues than direct energy transmission. Although we have access to the entire hologram, what parts we are able to receive may relate to what we are entangled with. In short, the arena of research is wide open, exciting, and never what's expected.

Developing Your Skills

Psi abilities are natural and innate, although, some people have greater aptitude than others. Rather than forcing growth, the goal of expanding awareness is the organic unfolding of our abilities. The exercises in this chapter provide support for what's occurring all on its own.

A sound meditation practice is essential for success. Sinking into slower brain-wave states opens receptivity. The deeper we go within, the further our inner vision travels. Having difficulty with the exercises in this chapter usually indicates the need for a more regular meditation practice.

Other elements of success include:

A Clear Emotional Field: Energy perceptions rely on our body as an antenna, receiver, and transformer. Any charged areas in our energy field alter the type of information we resonate with, and how we interpret it. Practices of grounding, centering, and clearing are helpful. Useful patterns are the Spiral Pillar of Light, Earth and Sky, and Queen Nefertiti's Headdress.

Boundaries and Protection: Bringing in high-level information with clarity requires filtering out low-level input. Information that is overwhelming, confusing, contradictory, or potentially harmful isn't coming through a clear filter. First clear your own bias and projections using exercises in Chapter 12, then ensure your field is vibrating with high intention and a strong presence that will not attract low-level energy and will keep you protected. The Celtic Cross pattern serves both purposes.

Intention and Mindset: Intention is the road map for our experience, guiding the direction and determining what we resonate with. Our intention and motivations create the vibration that attracts the level of information we draw in. We can stay aligned by ending our intention with the axiom "for the highest and best good of all." Maintain a mindset of neutrality and non-judgment. As soon as we're invested in the information, we influence it.

Resonance with the target: Creating an energy connection with our target, whether it's a person, place, or answer, helps establish correspondence and attract useful information. Resonance can be found through transcendent emotions such as awe, love, joy, and so forth, or simply by finding the vibration of the target and matching our frequency.

Psi Methods

Most people have three main reasons for wanting to develop their abilities: to connect more deeply with other people, to better understand events and the forces behind them, and to receive guidance. Although there are many types of psi practices, the following exercises explore visioning, telepathy, remote viewing/sensing, lucid dreaming, and receiving a direct transmission.

Visioning and Journeying

Visioning is the practice of using altered states of mind, achieved through deep meditation for journeying into other realms. It's different from remote viewing, which seeks to mentally view an established target (location or object), and is different from astral projection, which seeks to project consciousness outside of the body. Visioning is an inner experience. It opens the inner eye of the Third Eye Chakra to unseen realms. We may watch events as an observer or navigate the terrain as though present. Visioning is easy and safe.

In this practice, energizing the Third Eye Chakra opens a portal to other realms. The Celtic Cross pattern can be used as a vehicle and as protection. Set an intention for the journey before starting. It can be as simple as, "What is the best way forward for me at this time?" Or, "What do I need to know in this situation?" Or you can ask to meet your power animal or guide. You can also have a complex intention, asking for insight into spiritual reality, to be shown information about the past or future, or asking for inspiration with a problem. The more you trust yourself and this process, the more complex your intention can become.

Ground, center, and establish boundaries.

Honor the spirits, give thanks, and make an offering of appreciation.

Active the Spiral Pillar of Light pattern to create a circle of safety and healing.

Activate the Mystic Triangle pattern and focus your attention on your Third Eye Chakra.

State your intention and invite your awareness to move further inward. If you feel moved to, activate the Celtic Cross pattern and intend it to be your vehicle for this journey. When you are inside, you are completely protected.

Imagine yourself moving into a dense mist. See and feel yourself surrounded by the white, swirling fog.

See a source of light and move toward it through the fog. As you move, feel yourself dropping deeper inside yourself.

Walk out the other side of the fog.

With no expectation, observe what you see, feel, hear, smell, and know.

Explore the terrain and interact with the beings, animals, and people you meet. Ask questions. Try not to analyze, direct, or dismiss the answers or any interaction you have.

You may be given messages and gifts. Receive them with thanks and gratitude.

Sit in the light, and absorb healing and insight.

Stay for as long as you feel energy, then give thanks and retreat back through the mist.

Emerge from the mist sitting in your meditation spot.

Close the activations.

Ground, center, and establish boundaries.

Telepathy: Person-to-Person Interaction

Dean Radin, author of *Entangled Minds: Extrasensory Experiences in a Quantum Reality*, defines telepathy as "feeling at a distance" the transfer of thoughts, feelings, or images directly from one person's mind to another's.[5] In general, it's easier to send and receive emotions than it is thoughts. Emotions are the most direct experience people have with nonlocal communication. When someone loves us, for example, we can feel the force of that person's emotion from across the room or across the country. Picking up the energy of emotions is familiar to everyone.

We all have considerable practice feeling the emotional space in both personal and professional environments.

When practicing telepathy, two processes make it more effective. First, make an energy link with the other person before sending the communication. Second, link the thought being sent with an image and a strong emotion. As with any skill, practice makes perfect. Practice with a friend or group of friends on a regular basis. When working with groups of people, remember to keep energy filters in place so as not to inadvertently take on someone else's thought-forms or projections. The Celtic Cross pattern (page 41) is an excellent filter for this type of work.

The more focused our mind is when we practice, the faster our abilities improve. However, it's important to avoid using willpower to send our message. Remember, energy can't be pushed, only drawn. Second, the force of our will can be perceived by the other person's body as aggression, which will block our connection. It's best to connect with love, by putting our attention on the other person, and presenting our message on the energy path that our attention creates.

This exercise can be performed with others in the same room or set up so that everyone tunes in and meditates together at the same time from different locations. A message can also be sent on and off throughout the day, checking in with each other in the evening to see if and when it was picked up. It's easiest to start by sending simple things like a basic shape in a primary color, or a playing card. Using energy activations to focus our intent creates a safe connection and augments our energy practice.

DEVELOPING TELEPATHY EXERCISE

Decide who's sending and who's receiving.

Ground, center, and establish your boundaries.

Establish any additional protection you may want, such as the Celtic Cross pattern.

Open the Mystic Triangle pattern and activate a triangle in your Third Eye Chakra.

Imagine a bridge of light flowing from your Third Eye to that of your partner's. Feel the love in your connection.

If you're sending:

- Build the image/thought in your mind's eye and invest it with as much emotion as you can generate.
- When the communication feels ready, imagine it flying along the energy bridge you created.

- When the message reaches the triangle in the other person's Third Eye, imagine it waiting patiently outside to be received.
- Try not to force any part of this. Simply focus your mind, feel the connection, and let the image be shared.

If you're receiving:

- Allow the bridge of light from your partner to join with your Third Eye Chakra.
- Open to receive the image/message on a blank screen.
- Pay attention to what you see, feel, and hear. Look for strong emotions, shapes, colors, and impressions.

When you feel the natural link begin to dissipate, let the bridge dissolve and close the activations.

Write down what you experienced and share with your friend.

Ground, center, and establish your boundaries.

HOLOGRAPHIC METHOD FOR DISTANCE COMMUNICATION

Decide whom you want to connect with.

Ground, center, and establish your boundaries.

Honor the other person and give thanks.

Establish any additional protection you may want, such as the Celtic Cross pattern.

Open the Mystic Triangle pattern and activate a larger triangle between your Third Eye Chakra and the palms of your hands. Drop the apex away from your Third Eye, until the triangle is horizontal (see illustration on page 45). This is now a portal. Invite the spirit of the person with whom you wish to communicate to sit in the apex of the triangle.

Deepen your meditation and move into the nothing behind your eyes, allowing yourself to relax even more fully.

Be with your partner. Feel, smell, and hear this person. Feel the frequency they emanate and match your frequency to theirs.

Focus on the message you wish to send, and/or open to the message you're receiving.

Notice what you see, feel, hear, and sense.

Do not force any part of this. Simply allow the sending or receiving.

When you feel the natural link begin to dissipate, come back into daily awareness.

Close activations.

Ground, center, and establish your boundaries as you disconnect.

This exercise can be done with three people as well. Follow the steps and, when you activate the Mystic Triangle, sit in one corner and invite the other people to sit in the other two corners. Come into resonance with each other. You might be surprised to find that you can have an entire verifiable conversation with the other two people.

Remote Viewing/Sensing

In its original form, remote viewing (RV) was developed at Stanford Research Institute and used in Central Intelligence Agency (CIA) programs. According to an article posted on the Military Remote Viewing website titled "CIA-Initiated Remote Viewing Program at Stanford Research Institute" by H. E. Puthoff, the CIA was involved for twenty years in researching and developing RV techniques. They used what they developed for intelligence gathering. The documents on how and why they used psi techniques were declassified and approved for release in 1995.[6]

RV techniques extend our awareness to touch other places and times on a screen in our mind's eye. We can see a target, watch events unfold, and ask limited questions, although it's primarily a passive technique. Often considered a form of clairvoyance, there are distinct differences. Clairvoyants receive vivid and clear pictures that are married to sensations that provide additional information. Remote-viewing techniques consider vivid pictures to be the product of the imagination, representing an alpha brain-wave level of awareness. The more intricate an RV, the more suspect the information it contains.

An RV experimenter seeks to use a delta or theta brain wave and looks for impressions, shapes, textures, and smells that together reveal a target. The point isn't to interpret information; it's to gather it. This technique is used with a blind control. The person looking at the target doesn't know ahead of time what they're viewing. They're simply given the target coordinates and asked to connect.

This technique is useful for developing confidence because there is direct and immediate feedback without an emotional overtone that you can misinterpret. People who have difficulty with visioning or telepathy find their confidence with RV. (To try an easy blind RV training exercise, go to the Greater Reality website at *greaterreality.com*.)

The following Remote Viewing/Sensing exercise is not a traditional RV format. It's also not a blind experiment. Pick a place and time you would like to see, or a piece of information you would like to understand better. The information you receive usually arrives very quickly and you won't need to spend more than a few minutes observing. Take the first images you receive, no matter how nonsensical they seem.

REMOTE VIEWING/SENSING EXERCISE

Ground, center, and establish boundaries.

Activate the Spiral Pillar of Light pattern and incorporate additional protection as desired.

Sit in a relaxed, comfortable, warm place where you won't be disturbed.

Activate the Mystic Triangle pattern and open a triangle in your Third Eye Chakra.

Visualize another triangle inscribing the place and time you want to see. Imagine that you sit in one corner of the triangle and that the other two corners are held by time and location.

Send energy from your Third Eye through the portal to the target, building an energy bridge.

Keeping your mind relaxed and alert, pay attention to the images you receive. Notice shapes, colors, relationships. Pay attention to any inner knowing or intuitive insight. If you see people or scenery, look at the details: What types of buttons are on the coat? What are the shoes like? Look at the trees, the grass, the furniture. Try to obtain as much small detail as possible.

As soon as the information starts to fade or feel stale, stop and write everything down. You may be able to move in and out of receiving and writing to refresh details.

When you're finished, close the activations, ground, center, and establish boundaries.

Direct Guidance

Some people are developing psi abilities in order to engage, receive, and hold higher frequency for the world. (It's such an important subject that receiving higher frequency is the focus of Chapter 21.) Many people want to channel higher beings, archangels, or aliens. Naturally you want to avoid dialing in a lower-level entity that doesn't have anything useful to offer. The Akashic Record is the name given to the hologram of Universal Consciousness from which you can channel direct guidance. The method is the same as for Remote Viewing/Sensing, only instead of connecting with a time and place, connect with your highest level of guidance in the Akashic Record hologram.

DIRECT GUIDANCE EXERCISE

Ground, center, and establish boundaries.

Open the Spiral Pillar of Light pattern and invite the guides and guardians of the Akashic Record to be present.

Honor the unseen world, your guides, and guardians. Make an offering of love.

Activate the Mystic Triangle pattern and open a triangle in your Third Eye Chakra.

Imagine you're sitting in a triangle that's a portal to higher consciousness.

Vibrate with the frequency of the highest love and come into correspondence with the higher consciousness of the Akashic Record. Allow a flow of energy; imagine yourself growing in light as you connect with the highest love.

Ask to channel guidance for yourself, another person or animal, Earth, or all life.

As information flows, ask questions. Stay engaged as long as there is an energy flow of light.

When you're finished, give thanks. Ask what you can give back.

Close the activations, ground, center, and establish your boundaries.

Lucid Dreaming

Lucid dreams are those in which we're aware that we're dreaming. These are very powerful states of mind and used by shamans to travel into other realms. Anything is possible in a dream; we can go anywhere, do anything, and have access to any truth. Dreams happen in delta brain states. (A delta brain state is a deep and highly connected state.)

Tibetan monks consciously dream, calling it Dream Yoga, which is a specific path of enlightenment. Awake or asleep, we create our reality. Shaping the elements in a dream creates a reflection in the physical. It also trains us to consciously shape the elements in our life.

Theosophists believe we travel in our dreams to meet with guides, to help souls cross over, and to attend etheric universities. Using lucid dreaming, we can meet with higher-dimensional beings, receive healing, and learn new skills and techniques, then remember it when we wake up.

Lucid dreams often happen spontaneously. We can be in the middle of a dream and suddenly become aware that we're dreaming. Typically when this happens, it's so surprising that people immediately wake up. The trick is to both induce the experience and then maintain it.

The first step to maintaining awareness in dreams is to improve our dream recall. It helps to keep a journal near the bed and make notes immediately on waking. More details often emerge as we write.

The subconscious mind alerts us in a lucid dream that we're dreaming by having something so odd occur that we suddenly recognize that we're dreaming. Flying is the most common cue, so the next time that happens, wake up in the dream and pay attention. To program yourself to lucid dream, simply place the intention as you go to sleep. Intend to immediately take control of the dream as soon as you're alerted to it being a dream. Using this practice every night helps induce the experience.

LUCID DREAM PROGRAMMING EXERCISE

Before going to sleep, activate the Spiral Pillar of Light pattern. Intend that it stay active and protective throughout the night.

Go to sleep with a threefold intention:

Program yourself to wake up in your dream. As you create the intention, imagine it happening. See a cue and imagine yourself waking up.

Program yourself to perform an action that will alert you to the fact that you have control. In his book *Don Juan: A Yaqui Way of Knowledge*, Carlos Castaneda suggests programming yourself to immediately look at your hands as soon as you realize that you're dreaming.[7] You will be surprised how hard this is to accomplish, but when you do it, you can become conscious in your dream.

Program yourself to wake up when the dream is over. If you wake up in the night, immediately write down what you remember even if you don't think you had a lucid dream. Theosophists say we have regular lucid dreams but simply don't remember. Writing may jog your memory.

Use the state of relaxed focus between waking and sleep to support your lucid dream program. This relaxed focus is called the hypnogogic state and is in the realm of theta and delta brain waves. This is a powerful time for visioning and will support maintaining your intention.

As you're falling asleep, imagine yourself having a lucid dream. See yourself in a dream; feel the wind, sun, or other elements. Smell where you are. Engage all of your senses. Repeat a phrase, such as, "Tonight I am lucid dreaming. Lucid dreaming is easy and effortless for me." Use recurring dreams as a focus for creating a lucid dream. As you go to sleep, review your recurring dream. Remember the dream in detail, and then at key points rewrite the outcome. This not only helps you take control, but it also programs you to wake up and become conscious when you have this dream.

This technique is great for taking control and transforming nightmares.

Write down your dreams first thing in the morning before you engage in any activity, even using the bathroom. If you have to get up, jot down keywords to help you remember when you sit back down.

Once you begin to lucid dream, add to your program the intention you want in your dream. Do you want to meet with masters or learn about a past life? Your dreams can take you anywhere you intend.

Start your day by grounding, centering, and establishing boundaries.

Practicing Discernment

Whatever method is used, it takes time and practice to get consistent, clear, and useful results. Trust the first hit; it's usually less contaminated by our inner critic and judge. Once doubt sets in, our mind in-fills with what it thinks should be happening, and our results more likely reflect our own bias. Always test results and fine-tune the approach.

As we start receiving intuitive information, it's important not to assume we know what's right for another person. Our insight might not be what that person needs in the moment. The other person is working on their own growth, and our input may or may not be helpful.

Chapter 19

Healing: Reconnect and Repair

The body is programmed with all the mechanisms needed to maintain and restore health. Healing work is not magic; it supports what the body does naturally. When the body has trouble recovering from an injury or illness, it's often because the processes of healing have been interrupted. There are three primary reasons why the body doesn't heal:

- The necessary ingredients needed for healing are missing or altered, such as diminished nutrients, sunlight, and exercise, or altered immune function and genetic mutation.
- Something is getting in the way of natural processes, such as toxins, medications, mechanical damage, or stored emotional trauma.
- From an energetic perspective, the illness may serve a purpose beyond what we can readily see.

Physical signs and symptoms can be a communication from the body-mind that some aspect of our life is out of balance (see Chapter 9). It's also possible we may be having difficulty managing the energy of spiritual expansion (see Chapter 20). Sorting this can be challenging, and complex matters are often oversimplified. An illness might have a surface message, such as we need better food and more exercise, along with a deeper more intricate message, such as we need to value our self more and make some serious lifestyle changes. Sometimes, an illness can be as simple as needing to take a rest.

Energetically, the body's functions are organized and maintained by a template in the aura. When the connection between the template and body is disturbed, the information flow is disrupted, creating a condition for illness. Regardless of whether an illness has an energetic cause, once it is physical it must be treated on both energetic and physical levels.

Anytime we use healing techniques on other people, we must have permission. As much as we want to help others, it's arrogant to imagine we know what someone else needs or wants. The patient is their own healer; the person acting as healer holds space for the healing and reflects for the person the road marks on their journey.

When doing energy work on another, it's more important than ever to ground, center, and establish boundaries before and after. Doing this before the session helps to keep our bias from impacting the session and our trauma from being triggered by the other person's issues, often called taking in negative energy. Doing this after the session assures we have fully separated.

Is There Science in Energy Healing?

There has been significant scientific study into the power of prayer in improving medical outcomes, but with mixed results. A meta analysis in 2009 concluded that the current scientific methods of "randomized controlled studies cannot be applied to the study of the efficacy of prayer in healing." The researchers determined the parameters cannot be fully identified or controlled for meaningful study.[1]

Self-healing using visualization techniques, however, has significant positive association with improvements in immune strength, reduction of stress, management of pain, and more. Visualization techniques are so successful they're now standard practice in palliative cancer care. Studies on visualization in sports demonstrate that imagining a sports practice is almost as effective in building coordination and improving skill as actual practice.[2] Recent breakthroughs in brain science have established the neuroplasticity of the brain is affected by visualization. As described by Norman Doidge, MD, visualization changes the brains neurocircuitry to overcome significant medical problems.[3]

Healing is often associated with our hands, and a mechanism to explain this was first investigated by Robert Becker, MD, when he discovered the health benefits of negative ionic fields. During research initiating limb regeneration in frogs and salamanders, he found the body establishes a negative electromagnetic field during healing. When he introduced a positive charge, the healing stopped.[4] Becker also found that the hands carry a greater negative ionic charge than other parts of the body. The natural instinct to hold an area that has been hurt seems to have a mechanism to explain the healing impact. Natural sites also generate negatively charged ions, especially areas of moving water, validating the experience of the healing power of nature.

Kirlian photography, a technology that purports to capture the human energy field on film, poses interesting questions on the role of the aura in healing. In a study called "The Phantom Leaf Experiment," Kirlian photographs taken of a leaf showed radiant light surrounding and infusing it. When the leaf was torn in half and rephotographed, the radiance followed the new contour of the torn leaf, but also continued to outline the original shape prior to being torn. The only difference was the missing piece had lesser brilliance.[5] From this, we surmise that damage to our physical body, through injury or illness, doesn't change the structure of the energy template, only its radiance and vitality. The aura itself and the information it contains related to our health remain intact.

Conditions for Healing

Subtle-energy healing seeks to create therapeutic effects by clearing the energy field, removing obstructions in the chakras and meridians, and establishing high-level healing frequencies. We facilitate this effect by creating safety with attitudes of non-judgment, compassion, and kindness. We keep our bias out of the process by establishing boundaries and eliminating goals. As soon as we want something specific, we put conditions on the process and inject our ego.

According to the Institute of Resonance Therapy (IRT) in Cappenberg, Germany, there are three fundamental requirements that are needed for healing. Throughout the 1990s, IRT used energy practices to restore damaged ecosystems throughout Europe. The three essential elements are information, vitality, and flow.[6] When doing healing energy work, we are increasing information in the form of light, increasing vitality, and assisting flow. After that, what happens is up to Spirit.

When using any healing practice, a key component is being able to shift our frequency while offering healing support. Chapter 2 provided the essentials of how to shift frequency. In addition, light is a good frequency shifter. Light holds the highest frequency we know next to pure energy. It is measured in terahertz, which is 10^{12} hertz. White light breaks into all colors of the rainbow, and adding color to our visualizations is a powerful way to shift frequency. Here are the frequencies of different colors:

Violet: 668-789 THz, corresponds to Third Eye Chakra
Blue: 606-668 THz, corresponds to Throat Chakra
Green: 526-606 THz, corresponds to Heart Chakra
Yellow: 508-526 THz, corresponds to Solar Plexus Chakra

Orange: 484-508 THz, corresponds to Sacral Chakra
Red: 400-484 THz, corresponds to Base Chakra

In the chakra system, the Crown Chakra is white or sometimes gold.

Sound is also a tool in shifting frequency, and nothing is more powerful than your own voice.

Information

Energetically, information that can guide healing resides in the first and fifth layers of the aura. The first layer holds the template for organizing the physical body and is directly related to the need for genetic and karmic programs. Just as genes represent our ancestral past, the first auric layer holds the imprints of our karmic past. Research into children's memories of past lives conducted by Dr. Ian Stevenson, former head of the department of psychiatry at the University of Virginia, demonstrates this connection. The children Dr. Stevenson researched remembered deaths in previous lives that seemed to correlate with birthmarks, deformities, and health issues in this life. The wounds the children remembered in their previous death were reflected in the physical conditions of their birth.[7]

The fifth layer of the aura maintains the template for our ideal health and can be used to inspire the first layer to a higher level of function. Profound healing is often associated with an influx of light into these auric layers.

Quantum physicist David Bohm stated in an interview with Renee Weber that light "is energy and it's also information-content, form and structure. It's the potential of everything."[8] In other words, light is encoded with information that interacts with the wisdom contained in the body, as well as the energy field of the body to promote healing.

Vitality

Vitality is the amount and quality of physical and subtle energy available for our well-being. Vitality enlivens the body and provides the force that initiates healing. Physically, vitality comes from nutrition, clean air, sunlight, water, and exercise and is impacted by toxins, pollution, and stress. Energetically, vitality comes from spiritual connection and is impacted by our thoughts, attitudes, beliefs, emotional trauma, unhealed wounds, and energy attachments.

Vitality can be improved with infusions of subtle energy through energy healing practices.

Flow

Health in body, mind, and spirit is a result of flow—the flow of energy and blood to each cell, the flow of nerve supply to tissue, the flow of emotion and energy between people, the flow to and from one's spiritual source. Isolation causes disease: cells isolated from blood flow die; tissues isolated from nerve supply atrophy; isolation within one's family, community, or spiritual Source causes mental suffering, emotional anguish, and physical decline. Babies deprived of touch die.

Physical, emotional, and subtle energy aspects of life are entwined, and supporting the flow of energy supports the health of all. Flow is the quality that connects vitality with information. Flow between people is one of the most important aspects of health. Flow between the layers of the aura and the body connects the body to healing information. Flow between the chakras allows for growth. Flow along the meridians keeps every cell connected to the whole. All in all, we can say the most common impairment to healing is an interruption in flow, which is often felt as an imbalance.

Energetically, flow is a function of alignment. As long as two systems are aligned with each other and no obstructions exist between them, there will be flow. This is true of spiritual energy flowing from Source to us, of energy flowing between people in relationships, and in the flow of healing energy. Flow, however, does not necessarily mean current. Flow can be an instantaneous transfer. It is the transfer itself that we think of as flow.

Energy Healing: Awareness as Medicine

Awareness is a force. The application of the force of our awareness is medicine. Applying awareness for self-healing is a simple thing. All we have to do is notice an imbalance, pain, dysfunction, emotional wound, and so forth, hold it impassively in our awareness without expectation, and raise our frequency. Then we leave it. Our awareness opens the door to resolution. We don't have to do anything more. By observing it in this manner, we create change.

In neuroplasticity, awareness is focused using a technique called see, say, and do as described in Chapter 2. See yourself healed, say an affirmation, and couple it with a physical action. For example, if you have a broken leg, visualize yourself with a fully healed leg performing an enjoyable activity, repeat a phrase that raises your frequency, and place your hand over the broken area. That's it. Nothing more is required other than repetition.

All the following exercises in which we're focusing our attention to create an exchange of information, vitality, and flow are using awareness as medicine. In most cases, we're doing much more than we need to. Whenever we're wondering if we should do more, most likely we should do less.

It's important to remember when we're doing energy work on others that the person needing healing is their own healer. We are the witness, and the healing is their process, not the end result. None of us knows the path and purpose of another. We facilitate by holding a container and creating a sacred space. We offer light to supply information and vitality, support flow, and act as witness. After that, we get out of the way. We remove judgment, bias, our ego, and personal goals to support the highest good.

Scanning the Energy Field

Interrupted flow and loss of vitality can be felt as an imbalance in the distribution of energy, so the first thing we want to do is scan the energy field.

In meridians, a block will cause an excess of energy to accumulate before an obstructed area, with a deficiency after it. The entire area beyond the block will show a deficiency of energy, possibly into the next meridian.

In chakras, a block appears as an over-function in one area and an under-function in another. The over-functioning chakra will be rigidly open and the radiance will be extended out from the body, as in an expanded chakra, but feel hard. The under-functioning chakra will be closed down without a very extended radiance. Consequently, perception and awareness will be skewed.

In the aura, charged areas influence mental, emotional, and physical function.

Although scanning requires whole-body perception, our hands are natural antennae. The increased negative charge creates attraction to the positively charged areas that need support. Using our hands has the added benefit of focusing our mind. Where our hands are placed attracts the mind, and where the attention goes, energy follows. We can bypass the use of hands and scan with the mind, visualizing the areas we're scanning and listening for felt-perceptions from our chakras. In the following exercises, hands or mental attention can be used to scan and balance energy.

Excess energy is often felt as a strong magnetic repulsion, intense vibration, roiling sensation, heat, fullness, hardness, and so forth. Deficiency is often felt as emptiness, coldness, and lack of movement or "deathly" stillness. The block itself has a magnetic attraction. Here is a simple scanning exercise.

ENERGY SCAN EXERCISE

To scan yourself, sit or lie comfortably. If you're scanning another person, have the person lie down on a massage table or couch. Make sure you're comfortable while sensing another to avoid being distracted.

Ground, center, and establish boundaries.

Ask the person for permission, open the Spiral Pillar, and create a circle of safety, healing, and light. Invite any spiritual helpers to be present.

Activate the Five-Hearts Open pattern.

Connect the energy beam from the soles of your feet into Earth and draw energy into your heart, then out into the palms of your hands. Stay grounded throughout.

If self-scanning, use your attention or hands where you can reach.

Meridians:

- Start scanning at the feet. Float your hands toward and away from the ankles, feeling for the resistance of the edge of the physical layer of the aura. If you don't feel it, hold your hands two to three inches above the body.
- Slowly glide your hands from the feet up the legs all the way to the top of the body.
- Notice any areas where you feel the signs of excess or deficiency.
- Notice any areas where your attention or hand is drawn to for any reason.

Chakras:

- If you're working on yourself, sit or lie down. If you're working on another person, stand on the right side of the table they're lying on.
- Place your right hand at the level of the person's knees around ten inches above the body, or where you feel the resistance of the body. Face your left palm toward the person's Base Chakra. If you're working on yourself, don't try to feel with your hands, just focus your attention on the Base Chakra.

- Keeping your right hand focused on the Base Chakra, place your left hand ten inches above the person's Second Chakra, between the pubic bone and the belly button. Notice what you feel between your two hands.
- Move your left hand to the Third Chakra between the breast bone and the belly button, and your right hand to the Second Chakra. Notice what you feel in your hands between these two chakras.
- Continue to move up the body one chakra at a time, noting where you feel excess, deficiency, and anything else to which your attention is drawn.
- Practice taking your hand further away and closer to the chakras to feel differences in resistance.

Aura:

- If you're exploring your own aura, extend your arms in front of you with palms facing inward or focus your attention. If you're exploring someone else, rest both hands in the air about two feet above your friend's body or where you feel resistance.
- Slowly bring your hands toward the body, then away, moving toward and away several times, as if compressing the energy between your hands and the body.
- Keep bouncing your hands and patting the air until you stabilize the resistance against your hands.
- The resistance is a plane of energy forming a layer; explore the contours of this layer all around the body.
- Try to find additional layers that lie further out and closer in; explore what you find. You may sense thickness, swirling, or other sensations along with mental images or sudden thoughts. Always pay attention to the triad of felt-perceptions.
- Take note of what you feel.

When you're finished, give thanks, close the activations, and ground, center, and establish boundaries.

Healing through Correspondence

Using the hands is only one way to assess someone else's energy field and offer healing energy. A person's state can also be assessed through empathic correspondence—the aligning of our frequency to another's, creating a flow of subtle energy. When this happens, there's a feeling of harmony between us and the other person, and we feel a reflection in our body of the other person's condition. We may experience the other person's sore joints, energy drain, or other state.

Correspondence is a natural phenomenon and many people, especially Empaths, use it as an effective diagnostic tool. It's also a natural part of healing. When two systems come into correspondence, the weaker system is strengthened, usually at no cost to the stronger system. Remember the unlit fluorescent light bulb in Chapter 6 that illuminates in the presence of a lighted bulb, not because it's taking energy, but because the resonance inspires the molecules to vibrate. As long as the stronger system is aligned with a more elevated frequency, it suffers no loss of vitality.

If you decide to diagnose using resonant correspondence, think of it as putting on someone else's clothes: You can wear them to see what it feels like, but they don't belong to you, so take them off when you have the information you need. If you have difficulty knowing which symptoms are yours and which belong to someone else, place your hand on your body where you feel the symptom and direct your body to release anything that isn't yours. If it's someone else's, it will go away.

Correspondence is achieved through our presence, and our presence is a reflection of the quantity and quality of energy we carry in our aura. The quality of energy is based on our frequency and that's determined by our choices: what we choose to think, feel, desire, and do. People who carry a heightened presence shift energy simply by walking into a room. They have turned their presence into powerful medicine.

EXERCISE FOR USING CORRESPONDENCE

Ground, center, and establish boundaries.

Open the Spiral Pillar of Light pattern and establish a circle of safety, healing, and light. Invite spiritual helpers to be present. Give thanks.

Clear your energy field using any of the patterns in Chapter 3 that are effective for you. Circle of Life and Queen Nefertiti's Headdress pattern are both excellent for this purpose. Keep your energy fibers nestled in your chakras.

Align with Source and shift your frequency. Visualize light entering and filling your system, chant or sing a healing tone ("Ohm" and "hallelujah" are always good), place your hands over your heart, and expand in love.

Picture yourself sitting next to a person needing upliftment. Ask permission to proceed. Place the person in your awareness and come into harmony or correspondence with them. Use your awareness as medicine, bringing the person into the frequency of pure white light.

Keep this connection until you feel the flow ebb, or that the transfer of frequency information is complete.

Bring your awareness fully back to your own energy field. Feel your auric boundary. Align with Source and allow your aura to vibrate with light.

Give thanks, ground, center, and establish boundaries.

Balancing Chi

The body is constantly employing homeostatic mechanisms to maintain balance and restore health. However, in an environment of stress, the process can be obstructed. When there are many demands at once, maintaining balance can lose priority to something more urgent. Then the body accommodates the imbalance. Once this happens, a new set point of normal is established. The new set point becomes familiar, and awareness of real normal is often forgotten.

Physical healing requires restoring balance. The process relies on light as the building block of matter. You can use the following exercise during your energy scan on the imbalanced areas you find, or on any physical illness. Remember that this does not replace professional help.

BALANCING CHI AND PHYSICAL
HEALING EXERCISE

Ground, center, and establish boundaries.

Ask for permission from your higher self to proceed. Open the Spiral Pillar of Light pattern and create a circle of safety, healing, and light. Invite spiritual helpers to be present.

Activate the Winged Disk pattern and allow your hands to fill with light.

After performing the body scan, simply connect an area of excess with an area of deficiency, and allow the body to reestablish balance. You can do this with your attention, or by placing one hand on the area of deficiency and the other on the area of excess, or simply hold both areas in your mind's eye.

If you have an illness, place both hands over the area involved.

You don't have to do anything to create balance and healing. Once you've brought the body's attention and energy to the imbalance, the body will decide what to do.

Offer light to the area.

You may feel a flow of energy into the area to be healed or between the imbalanced areas. When the flow stops, move on.

Repeat on as many areas as you feel called to. Include chakras and areas within the aura.

Don't limit the process to balancing chakra to chakra, or aura to aura. You can balance a chakra to an area in the aura or an area of the body, such as the Base Chakra to the feet. Explore. You can connect the area of illness in the body to a belief in the aura, and so forth. Explore.

Give thanks, close the activations, ground, center, and establish boundaries.

Repairing Energy Structures

In the challenges of daily living, energy structures can be damaged. Fibers can become psychically torn and tattered, as we saw in Chapter 16, and the aura can acquire holes or be compressed and unable to relay information. The meridians become blocked, and the flow to each cell interrupted. The following exercises offer a few gentle approaches.

BALANCING CHAKRAS AND REPAIRING
ENERGY FIBERS EXERCISE

Ground, center, and establish boundaries.

Ask for permission, then open the Spiral Pillar of Light pattern and create a circle of safety, healing, and light. Invite spiritual helpers to be present.

Activate the Chakra Fibers pattern.

Scan your chakras, and assess the size, spin, shape, vitality, and degree of openness. Assess the health of each of the chakra's fibers. Where is your attention drawn?

Activate the Weaving the Nadis pattern and weave Earth energy up and sky energy down along the Nadis.

As energy weaves back and forth along the Nadis, increase the vitality and spin in each chakra.

Visualize light streaming from the chakras and out through the associated fibers. Let the fibers come alive with vitality, shedding anything sticking to them that they don't need, letting go of unhelpful attachments, and repairing any damaged areas. Focus on any chakra whose fibers don't seem to respond, or that you know has sustained damage. Add color to your visualization.

Continue until the energy in the affected chakra is full and calm, and the fibers are radiating light. If you're drawn to, coil the chakras in their respective chakra.

Ground, center, and establish boundaries. Give thanks to your helpers.

RESTORING THE AURA EXERCISE

Ground, center, and establish boundaries.

Ask for permission and invite your spiritual helpers.

Activate the Spiral Pillar of Light pattern creating a circle of safety, healing, and light. Merge the Spiral Pillar of Light with your aura.

Activate the Earth and Sky pattern and fill your core with light.

Send the light that shines from your core into your aura.

Close your eyes and sense your boundary. What do you see/feel? If you have no image, what would it look/feel like if you did? How far does it radiate from your body? Is it the same all the way around? Is it weaker in some areas, or empty? Get a good, strong image of all aspects.

Observe your energy emanation. What is it like? Does it fill all the space within your boundary? Does it radiate beyond the perimeter? What does your emanation convey? How does it interact with your boundary? Do you see any thought-forms, projections, or hooks? These might look like dark areas. You might want to visit Chapter 12 if there are more than a few of these areas.

Now bring your attention to your center, the core that is home to your spiritual essence. Magnify your essence.

Use your imagination to energetically examine your aura with light fibers from your solar plexus. As you engage the edge of your field, you might feel resistance when your fibers push against the boundary. They may tingle or vibrate. You may have a vision in your mind's eye of the energetic grid that surrounds you. The overall feeling will be one of connectedness.

Ask to see/feel any holes and notice those places where your attention is drawn. Things you might feel when you engage a hole in the aura are emptiness, hollowness, extreme stillness, or an outflowing of energy. You may have visions of darkness and feel drained.

If you find a hole, envision it filling with light that weaves the boundary back together.

Send light to each area of aura that drew your attention and visualize the light reweaving the strands of your aura.

When you feel complete, inhale through the Earth and Sky pattern into your core; exhale your radiance into your aura, and shine your light.

Give thanks, close activations, ground, center, and establish boundaries.

REJUVENATING THE MERIDIANS EXERCISE

Ground, center, and establish boundaries.

Activate the Circle of Life pattern and use the external energy pathway of the Central Channel meridian; inhale energy up your spine and over the top of your head, and exhale energy down the front of your body and around under your torso.

As the energy circulates along this pathway, activate the Earth and Sky pattern, and fill your Central Channel with power and light.

Visualize light flowing from the central channel along all the meridians in the body.

Allow any blocked or stagnant energy to melt away and join the flow of life-force.

When you feel complete, close the Circle of Life pattern and collect the energy in your Tan Dien, or Hara, by placing your hands over your lower abdomen and breathing your energy into this area.

Give thanks, ground, center, and establish boundaries.

Healing Old Trauma

The aftereffects of trauma can live as unresolved emotions in our aura and body, causing blocks to the energy flow. Healing old traumas can often be done by using awareness techniques that allow us to give back another person's projections (see Chapter 12), or we can simply own and accept our emotions, allowing them to clear. Receiving help from a qualified therapist, energy worker, or counselor can be very supportive. The Chakra Clarity activation on page 25 can help retrieve the deeper information that was caught in our body and release it. This exercise should not be used in place of professional help.

TRAUMA-CLEARING EXERCISE

Ground, center, and establish boundaries.

Sit in a quiet, relaxed place, and activate the Spiral Pillar of Light and Earth and Sky patterns. Imagine yourself in a circle of safety and healing, surrounded by loving guidance. Actively invite any guides and angels you work with to join you.

When you feel grounded and centered, bring your attention to an old, emotional pattern that is limiting you. It can be anything: fear of mice, fear of intimacy, anger at injustice, grief over abandonment— anything that is limiting you.

In the circle of safety, allow yourself to fully feel the depth of emotion you carry on this issue. If you need to, imagine a time you felt this emotion very strongly. Recall every detail and grievance until you are completely in the throes of it. Accept it. Ask the past for permission to heal.

Notice where in your body you feel your emotion the most strongly. Is it in your heart? Your solar plexus? Your belly? You may feel the emotion as physical pain, heat, vibration, weakness, and so on.

Focus your attention on the chakra in the area where your physical sensation resides. If you feel an ache in your chest, take your attention to your Heart Chakra; if you feel butterflies in your stomach, take your attention to your Solar Plexus Chakra; and so on.

Observe the quality of energy in this chakra. Look at the color, texture, brightness, vibration, and so forth. If it were a room, what type of room would it be? If it were an animal, what animal would it be?

Thank the energy/room/animal/color for showing up and ask what it needs from you. Listen carefully, and provide what it needs if you feel comfortable doing so.

Ask the energy/room/animal/color if it has information for you. Be still and open to whatever comes to mind. Don't rush the process; just hold the question and jot thoughts in your journal.

When you feel you have an answer, or if you decide you aren't going to get one, ask what message and/or gift this energy/room/animal/color has for you.

When you're ready, ask the area that holds your pain what it would like to be different. What would this chakra like to look like? How would the room like to be decorated? What color would like to be present? Allow the area to morph into what it would most like to be. Notice how you feel as this occurs.

Put everything involved with the old situation into a sacred container: the people, the injury, trauma, hurt, and anger.

Make the container as beautiful as you can.

Forgive yourself and everyone involved.

Understand that everyone had something to learn here, including you.

Take back your projections (chapter 12) and accept the higher learning.

Release the container and everything inside. You can bury it and give it to Earth. You can burn it and send the smoke to the sky; you can pass it to your guides.

Now open your chakra to light and breathe in golden, dancing, living starlight. Let yourself expand.

Send the golden dancing stars to every cell in your body, and feel your aura expand. You can activate the Circle of Life pattern to facilitate this if you would like more pizzazz.

When you feel complete, give thanks, close the activations, ground, center, and establish boundaries.

Death and Dying

In this culture, we perceive death as failure: people succumb to death, give in to their disease, didn't have enough belief to heal, or didn't have a good enough doctor. Truthfully, death is the natural result of birth. There's no way around it. But death is not the end of consciousness. We were conscious before we were born, and our consciousness continues after we leave our body. People who have died and been brought back to life—an experience called a near-death experience, or NDE—all report a continuation of awareness during the time their physical body was declared dead. They all share a surprisingly similar chain of events. For the vast majority, the death experience is very positive; for a small minority it is distressing.

Positive experiences usually begin with the person leaving his or her body and seeing a tunnel of light that draws him or her inside. In the tunnel, the person is guided by friends and family who've already died. When the tunnel ends, the person is in a light-filled place, in a body made of light, with others they recognize and know.

Having a near-death experience changes a person. The fear of death is diminished, allowing the person to fully live. The priorities of life change. For more information, read the account of Dannion Brinkley in his book *Saved by the Light*, who has undergone several NDEs, one during which he was declared dead for a full hour and a half.[9]

People who have a negative experience often don't actually leave the body. While the body is dying they feel sucked out, often toward a dark tunnel, and struggle to stay in the physical body. It's a natural, programmed instinct to fight for life and certainly there is a powerful learning in this experience.

Caring for someone as they die is a beautiful experience, a unique opportunity to act in concert with those on the other side to assist someone's passage.

The following exercise can offer support if you're with another person during their death process. It can also be helpful if you're healthy but have a strong fear of dying. This exercise is not meant to take you to the other side; that will happen naturally in the right time, and you will have all the support you need in the process. This exercise is to help you feel your connection to the continuity of consciousness that exists through death.

AN EASING DEATH EXERCISE

Ground, center, and establish boundaries.

Open the Spiral Pillar of Light pattern.

Connect with your Star. Feel the love and energy from your spiritual Source surround you.

Imagine the faces of people you love who've already passed. Ask them for company and support when it's time for your passage. Feel their presence and know they will be with you when you're ready to go through the veil.

Imagine the faces of living people to whom you have a strong attachment. Let them know how much you love them and ask that they send you energy when it's your time to journey to the other side. Assure them that you will be there to assist their passage when it's time for their own journey.

If you need to make peace with anyone you're leaving behind or anyone you'll be seeing in the light, call the person's image to mind. Say what you need, and ask to be forgiven for any transgressions. Give forgiveness where needed.

Activate the Living Matrix pattern and feel yourself suspended in the matrix of a living universe. Feel your connection to Source and to the power of love.

Let the peace and love of your source fill you.

When you feel complete, give thanks, close the activations, ground, center, and establish boundaries.

Healing Events and Situations

Any situation can benefit from healing energy. Use the Mystic Triangle pattern and create a portal to whatever situation or event you would like healed—past, present, and future. Simply sit yourself in one corner, your guide in another, and whatever people are involved in the third corner. In the center, place the situation or event. Activate the Spiral Pillar of Light pattern all around the triangle and visualize healing rainbows of color flooding the situation with love. Affirm that the healing is for the highest and best good of all.

Chapter 20

Embodying Changing Consciousness

Right now, at this moment, there is an option to awaken. Inside, we have everything we need to experience expanded consciousness. When we do, we open to frequencies whose vibration will enliven our energy body and alter our physical structure. We become active participants in anchoring higher-dimensional frequency.

The frequencies we're receiving are not new. They've always been here, however never as accessible as they are today. Mystics foretold this period as one of a paradigm shift in which the separation between dimensions is thinned, making higher frequencies more accessible. The shift acknowledges that there is no separation between the seen and the unseen domains—between the material and the hidden forces that guide it. As ancient cultures have taught, the world is alive—all parts of it, animate and inanimate. Until now, we have been focused on the frequencies of material reality. Now we are awakening to the frequency of the unseen domains. It's important to remember that both are important, but we have been overly focused on the material. Now is the time for balance.

Many people are feeling that "time is speeding up." In other words, the vibration around us is quickening. One result of the quickening is that the amount of time between what we think and what our thoughts create is shortened, making it easier to see what our intentions create. It also teaches us to discipline our minds and consciously create the world.

Receiving higher frequencies and expanding consciousness instigate change in our physical and energetic bodies. Ever-increasing numbers of people are exhibiting signs and symptoms of this transformation. This chapter discusses the mechanisms involved, how it feels to receive higher frequency, and how to make the transition easier.

Due to the importance of the information in this chapter, current research is reviewed in detail. If you're more interested in the experience, simply turn to the end of the chapter and read the suggestions for embodying changing consciousness.

Perspective from the Maya

A compelling source of insight about the current changes comes from the prophecy related to the ancient Maya Long Count calendar, said to have ended in 2012.

The Maya astronomers were true mathematical scholars. Through continuous study and observation of the night sky, they developed knowledge of the mechanisms of the universe as they explored the depths of consciousness. Using mind-expanding techniques, they delved into the mysteries of time, energy, the interconnections of time and space, and synchronicity. Through their eyes, we experience being an integral part of natural cycles and connections.

The ancient Maya lived in what is now southern Mexico, the Yucatán Peninsula, Guatemala, and parts of Honduras and El Salvador. They left behind a legacy of flat-topped pyramids, cities, and astronomical observatories located throughout the jungle. The Maya were architectural, mathematical, and astronomical geniuses; their calendar system has proven to be as accurate as current time-keeping methods. They used more than seventeen different calendars that tracked short cycles, like the moon orbiting the Earth (a month) and the Earth orbiting the Sun (a year), as well as long cycles such as the approximate 26,000-year progression of constellations across the night sky called the Precession of the Equinoxes.

The Maya understood that astronomical and terrestrial cycles released energetic impulses that affected the spiritual energy they called k'ul. K'ul energy flows in pathways through the Earth and accumulates in specific places. The Maya structured life to coincide with this flow, harnessing accumulated energy to power ceremonies and structures. They observed that celestial alignments were like gates, injecting k'ul into Earth and influencing its movement from one accumulation spot to another.

Consequently, they tracked the stars, the progression of alignments, eclipses, and so on, using the information to plan their daily activities. They planted crops, performed ceremonies, built cities, and charted the course of war based on what was happening in the skies. Old buildings, temples, and pyramids were destroyed and new ones created to coincide with the ending of old cycles and the beginning of new ones.[1] This allowed the Maya to take advantage of the energy being brought onto the planet with each cosmic alignment the calendars marked. The present shift is no different.

The late John Major Jenkins, a renowned researcher and author of *Maya Cosmogenesis 2012: The True Meaning of the Maya Calendar End-Date,*[2] determined that the end of the Maya Long Count calendar in 2012 coincided with an alignment of our solar system with the center of the galaxy. In Maya cosmology the center of the galaxy is the home of Hunab Ku, the spiritual source of the universe. Consequently, the alignment opens the door to an influx of new spiritual energy heralding a transitional time of chaos followed by a Golden Age.

According to Jenkins, the end of the Long Count calendar coincides with the completion of a cycle of the Precession of the Equinoxes. This 26,000-year cycle was known to the Maya as an "Age" or "World," which was a very significant turning point in their creation myths. The end of an Age meant the destruction of the current way of doing things. The transition does not happen overnight, but occurs over a period of time. This is not the first Age to end for the Maya, but the fourth. Because the end of the Long Count calendar represents the end of a time period called a World, the mass media began heralding 2012 as the end of the world. This was never the case.

The *Popul Vuh,* written by the Quiche Maya, is one of five ancient Mayan books, or codices, that survived the Jesuit purging of documents in the 1500s. In it are details of the Maya creation myths, stories that tell how previous Ages began and ended. It also tells the story of how this present Age began and predicts how it will end. It describes the changing of the Ages as being marked by economic, social, and environmental collapse when "people distrust their government and religious leaders."[3] The old must crumble as new frequencies from the spiritual center of the universe provide the impetus for the new world we are creating.

Looking around today, no one can dispute that the social structures of religion, government, and finance are struggling. We are in an evolutionary bottleneck. Change is happening because it must; the way things have been cannot be sustained into the future.

This time period is an experiment. There are no guarantees. What happens as a result of this shift is determined by what each of us chooses to hold precious. As always, the choices we make will determine the world we will inhabit. The difference is that the choices we are making now will impact life on this planet for an entire Age to come.

Dimensionally Wired

Another way to look at expanding consciousness is becoming aware as a multidimensional being. Chapter 7 explains that each layer of the aura corresponds to a different level, or dimension, of reality. To experience different dimensions, we have to expand our energy senses.

Descriptions of subtle energy are simply constructs—ways of organizing information to be able to observe patterns. Constructs change as information and awareness change. The popular construct used to describe the human energy system comes from India, brought into Western thought through the Theosophists at the turn of the 20th century. Let's review this information from Chapter 7, keeping in mind that energy structures are changing:

- There are seven dimensional planes, or levels of reality.
- Each plane vibrates at a specific rate.
- Humans are connected to these dimensional levels through our own energy field, the aura.
- The aura is our personal energy field and also contains seven distinct layers.
- Each dimensional plane corresponds to a layer of the aura through which we receive information from these planes of reality.
- Each layer of the aura has a corresponding chakra, or energy center, that takes the information from the aura and steps it down to a level where it can be accessed by the body. The chakras are the aura's connection to the physical body.

In the past, expanding consciousness was viewed as rising through the chakras from the lower, more physical levels into the higher, more spiritual levels. Growth was a step-by-step progression with the assumption of a basic duality where spirit is good and material is not. Spiritual growth required transcending the lower physical planes.

Moving from duality consciousness into holographic consciousness reveals that being multidimensional means having the ability to encompass and inhabit all levels of reality simultaneously, to move freely between dimensions. This is the intention of the shift underway.

Rather than being a trap, the body is the anchor for us as spiritual, multidimensional beings to interact with the physical plane. We often overlook the gift of a physical body and identify this plane with pain, suffering, and ego. Some seek to escape through ascension into higher consciousness. In truth, we would not be in physical form if it didn't have meaning and purpose. Rather than escaping matter, we're here to help spiritualize matter, bringing the gifts of matter and spirit to bear on each other.

Spiritualizing matter is often mischaracterized as bringing spirit into matter. Of course, matter is already imbued with spirit; all life has spirit: human spirit, Nature Spirits, and so on. Matter is nothing more than the infusion of spirit into form. What is meant by spiritualizing matter is the introduction of higher frequency to expand the terrain of our awareness. Then, the illusion that matter is all there is loses its hold.

Receiving New Frequencies

New frequencies are instigating change by expanding our awareness, and change can be uncomfortable. As frequency increases in both rate and amplitude of vibration, it's received in our energy field and impacts our thinking and worldview as well as our physical body. Our perspectives, our beliefs, and even our relationships are all subject to shifting as we develop new patterns in our aura and energy structures. While ultimately the physical body undergoes healing, the process can be challenging with many uncomfortable signs and symptoms.

Socially, one of the most difficult aspects of this change is that people who have gained power through the material aspect of reality don't want the change that's coming. This is causing the strife, anger, and social unrest surrounding us as the old must give way to a more sustainable future.

As new frequencies come in, our job is to stay connected to the resonance of the physical, while expanding to bring in the frequencies of the unseen domains. Like trees, the higher we want to grow, the deeper we must anchor our roots.

Mechanisms of Change: Resonance and Kundalini

Higher frequencies influence the human aura through resonance. When the aura changes vibration, the step-down process increases the vibration through the body down to a cellular level. Cells, tissues, and organs vibrate with their own signature frequency, the basis of diagnostic procedures such as electroencephalograms (EEGs), which measure brain waves, or electrocardiograms (ECG/EKGs), which measure the electrical activity of the heart. Organs and body systems stay in sync with each other through vibration.[4] As higher frequency changes the vibration of the physical body, a series of physical and psycho-spiritual changes occur.

One of the changes occurring due to the increase in vibration is an activation of Kundalini, the dormant spiritual energy in the Base Chakra at the root of the spine. When Kundalini awakens, it lifts out of the Base Chakra and travels on the three Nadis that run along the spine and through the chakras. As it rises, it activates and awakens each chakra. When it reaches the Crown Chakra, Kundalini streams from the top of the head like a fountain and opens the person for mystical, divine union.

Advancing up the spine to the Crown Chakra doesn't usually happen in one sitting. The progression can take years or even lifetimes to complete, depending on the dedication of the person. However, in the current quickening Kundalini is being activated and is rising whether people are fully prepared or not. The awakening magnifies unresolved emotional issues in the chakras that may manifest as external events in order to be resolved. Consequently, people are coming face to face with multiple life lessons. This can be uncomfortable and disruptive. Ultimately, it is forcing each of us to find new solutions to lifelong problems.

Physical Interface

The frequency being transmitted is fed by the chakras into the body through the associated nerve plexus and endocrine organs. The nervous and endocrine systems are the first physical systems to receive subtle-energy information and are the master regulators, overseeing all body activities. The extremely high-powered energy of Kundalini can overwhelm the circuits of the nervous system, causing many uncomfortable symptoms.

Two organs of evolution, the pineal gland and amygdala area in the brain, are also at the forefront of the frequency shift. The more conditioned our neuroendocrine system is to higher frequency, the easier the transition is.

Pineal Activation

The pineal gland is about the size of a grain of rice, looks something like a pine cone, and sits in the back of the brain at the level of the root of the nose. The pineal gland receives and responds to light and electromagnetic energy. It produces the hormone melatonin and maintains our circadian rhythm, the biological rhythms that govern body functions in response to day/night, seasonal cycles, and the daily cycles in the Earth's magnetic fields. The activities of this gland can be disrupted by artificial light and magnetic fields.

The pineal gland is still one of the body's mysteries, releasing hormones in response to bioelectrical messages received through the eyes. Through the act of receiving light, this gland energizes the entire body.

Spiritually, the pineal gland is considered a portal to self-awareness, higher consciousness, and states of bliss by yogi masters including Paramahansa Yogananda, author of *Autobiography of a Yogi*.[5] In esoteric literature it corresponds to the Third Eye Chakra and, when activated, increases psychic ability, intuition, wisdom, and insight. It's considered a doorway for inter-dimensional experiences.

Given both its physical and spiritual functions, it's no surprise that the pineal gland is central to receiving higher frequencies. The energy activating this expansion is coded on light that triggers the gland to produce another substance called DMT, dimethyltryptamine.

DMT, a neuropeptide, acts as a natural hallucinogen and is associated with altered states of consciousness. It was first discovered in the human body in the 1950s but its function and role are still not completely understood. Dr. Rick Strassman, author of *DMT: The Spirit Molecule*, speculates that DMT is involved with dreaming and is found in high concentrations in the pineal gland during near-death and out-of-body experiences.[6] Today, more people are experiencing altered states and enhanced intuitive capability, possibly due to stimulation of the pineal gland.

Pineal Crystals

A strange anomaly has been discovered in the pineal gland within the past thirty years. A new type of crystal has been found forming in the glandular tissue. What it means is far from clear. However, the large amount of conjecture about it warrants a lengthy discussion.

The presence of crystals in the body is not new. Hydroxyapatite is a form of calcium phosphate that is found throughout the body in functional and nonfunctional placement. Functionally, it forms the crystal component of the bone's mineral matrix and is the basis of the otoconia crystals in the inner ear that promote balance. Nonfunctional hydroxyapatite crystals are observed in the pineal gland, called pineal sand, and are considered to be the product of poor nutrition. Hydroxyapatite crystals can appear in all age groups and have piezoelectric properties, meaning they can release electricity when placed under mechanical pressure.[7]

There is a new crystal found growing within the pineal gland that is not hydroxyapatite. The new crystal is calcite and is the focus of interest in relation to the spiritual unfolding underway. Colleen Behan of the Spirit of Light Wellness Studio (*thespiritoflight.org*) in Wallingford,

Connecticut, teaches Pineal Activation and Cranial Temple Activation to assist people in accommodating new frequencies. She believes the crystals are receiving higher frequencies and helping to uplift and spiritualize the human body. On the other hand, medical researchers wonder if the presence of the crystals is a pathological condition.

The calcite crystals are small, usually under twenty microns, which is truly microscopic (there are 25,400 microns in one inch). The crystals are formed with sharp edges and a rough surface. They were first reported in the late 1970s and early 1980s. The initial scientific studies concluded that they are aging artifacts, even though they were never seen before in older people. A study done in 1986 and reported in the *Journal of Neural Transmission* hypothesized that their presence is the result of the inability of aging cells to break down calcium.[8] A study done in Italy found the crystals occur more in women than men.[9]

In support of this assessment, during the thirty years since these crystals were discovered, people have been ingesting massive amounts of calcium supplementation to prevent osteoporosis, especially older women. At the same time there's an epidemic of Vitamin D deficiency. Vitamin D is a nutrient needed to metabolize calcium and incorporate it into bone tissue. It is obtained from the sun, and its deficiency is related to the fear of skin cancer, which has caused people to avoid sun exposure and use sunscreen. It's tempting to assume the presence of these crystals is related to over-calcification and Vitamin D deficiency. However, this might not be the full picture.

An Israeli study conducted in 2002 looked at the impact of this new form of crystallization with regard to the human biomagnetic field. The study states that the crystals are "the only known non-pathological occurrence of calcite in the human body" and theorizes that they are "biologically significant having a possible non-thermal interaction with external electromagnetic fields."[10] The study theorizes a functional interaction between the piezoelectric hydroxyapatite and the calcite crystals.

Crystals act as transmitters, receivers, and amplifiers of frequency, making them useful as components in watches and computer technology. Many people believe the new pineal crystals have developed to assist transformation, helping us receive and interact with the new frequencies.

Another viewpoint, developed through a study from the Ukraine, looks at the new phenomenon of calcite crystals showing up in the intercellular spaces in plants. The study, conducted in 2004, was able to initiate the production of calcium crystals in plants by placing them in a weak magnetic field. The study postulates that increased magnetic field exposure is responsible for the calcification.[11]

If the pineal crystals are not due to improper calcium metabolism, are they the result of electromagnetic pollution from cell phones, Wi-Fi, overhead power cables, and so forth? Or are they caused by changes in the Earth's electromagnetic field, or the result of new frequencies being received? Research may never be conclusive. We'll have to use our own intuitive capability to determine the importance, if any, of these crystals to the process underway.

Regardless of the presence of crystals, the pineal gland is an important player in spiritual expansion. This gland literally guides the enfoldment of light into the body, helping to activate our energy systems and expand our consciousness. Consider this comment made by physicist David Bohm in an interview with Renee Weber: "Light in its generalized sense (not just ordinary light) is the means by which the entire universe unfolds into itself."[12]

Brain Awakening

The amygdala is the part of the brain that deals with emotion and emotionally stored memory. The almond-shaped groups of nuclei are located deep within the temporal lobes of the brain as part of the limbic system. They are specifically involved in how we process and remember emotional reactions.[13] Their location is also home to the instinctual sensory system that allows prey to know when a predator is approaching, even without seeing, hearing, or smelling it.

Given the amygdala's function, many believe it's where we perceive paranormal experiences. A Canadian study published in *Brain and Cognition* journal in 1992 concluded that periods of intense meaningfulness, including sensing a spiritual presence and experiencing enhanced creativity, correlated with increased burst-firing in the hippocampus-amygdala complex.[14] Studies conducted by Russek and Schwartz demonstrated an ability of a subject to feel when someone is looking at the back of his or her head for an extended period. The study showed subjects had a 57.6 percent positive performance in knowing when they were being looked at from behind. The ability to perceive someone's eye contact increased with the belief in some type of spiritual reality.[15]

Given that the amygdala senses prey without any physical signals, can we suggest that the ability of subjects in the Russek and Schwartz experiments to sense subtle energy happens in the amygdala as well?

Signs and Symptoms of Change

Some of the effects of the changes we're going through are uplifting and gratifying; others are challenging. Essentially, the following signs and symptoms are instigated by the need to grow quickly. Of course, we must always be aware that each sign and symptom could be the result of a medical condition. A question for many people is how to discern whether a symptom is caused by an underlying physical problem or by an energy effect of expansion. The answer is that within every physical symptom are both an energetic and physical component, and both need to be addressed.

As you read through the lists of symptoms and identify those you are experiencing, remember that your symptoms can be reduced using the energy exercises throughout this book. There are additional exercises at the end of this chapter; however, you already have all the techniques you need.

Psycho-Spiritual Indicators
As the amygdala and pineal gland are stimulated you may experience:

- Being more open to sensing guides, angels, and feeling a beneficial presence.
- Sensing subtle energy.
- Noticing increased amounts of synchronicity and déjà vu.
- An increased ability to focus healing energy.
- Hearing voices and spiritual guidance.
- Higher levels of intuition and psychic ability, especially telepathy.
- Feeling more aware and in control of your own fate.

All these experiences are positive and beneficial; however, try not to get lost in them. It's easy to lose grounding, decreasing the ability to function on this plane. New frequencies influence change that can catapult us into new awareness, but also provide our ego with a lot of self-importance.

Some of the more challenging psycho-spiritual aspects are:

- Feeling overloaded.
- Overwhelming emotional responses.
- The reemergence of old emotional patterns.
- Being presented with life challenges at an accelerated rate.
- Depression, anxiety, psychosis.

Use Queen Nefertiti's Headdress (page 36), the Circle of Life (page 22), and the Chakra Clarity (page 25) patterns to ease the psycho-spiritual effects.

Interpersonal Dynamics

The first place the effects of change are often felt is in our personal relationships. The incoming frequencies are bringing everyone's issues to the surface. Relationships are a key arena in which we work out our issues, and so there is potential for interpersonal stress. In addition, as one person grows, the surrounding people must change. Some of them may not understand or be committed to what's happening. (Use the practices in Chapter 10 to keep your bearings.)

As with everything, effects can happen at both ends of the extremes. Here are some relationship impacts:

- New awareness of energy linkages between you and your partner.
- Stronger bonds based on deeper intimacy.
- Finding new ways to solve long-standing problems.
- Polarization with family members and friends as deep-seated beliefs surface, creating friction.
- Intolerance of differences.
- Distrust and fear-based thinking.

Try some of the practices in Chapter 16 to ease the challenges and expand the enjoyment in interpersonal expansion.

Physical Indicators

Physical signs and symptoms happen primarily though an excess of energy that overwhelms the body's circuits, or a frequency that is too high to be incorporated physically.

Nervous and endocrine system indicators include:

- Restless legs.
- Tingling.
- Trembling, shaking, vibrating sensations.
- Body jolts.
- Roving twitches.
- Memory and cognitive changes/brain fog, memory loss.

Sensory indicators include:

- Hearing voices.
- Sounds in the ear (clicking and high-pitched frequencies).
- Proprioceptive confusion (not knowing where you are in space).
- Sensations of pressure and heat racing through your body.

- Seeing light flashes.
- Seeing shadowy shapes out of the corner of your eyes.
- Seeing auras and color around people.

Miscellaneous indicators include:
- Multiple chemical sensitivities.
- Vivid dreaming.
- Temporal-spatial disorientation.
- Headaches.
- Waking between 3 a.m. and 5 a.m. (receiving downloads of information).
- Weight gain and loss.
- Extreme fatigue or manic levels of energy.
- Hot and cold flashes.

Easing the Transition

A list of symptoms doesn't describe how disconcerting some of these signs can be. For example, people report driving down the road and suddenly not knowing where they are or where they're going, even though they've driven that road hundreds of times before (temporal-spatial disorientation). Hearing voices or seeing shadows moving in corners can be scary for some, and many people report feeling as though they're going crazy and are afraid of losing control. It's a good idea to find other people going through these changes and form a support group for each other.

The best way to ease the transition is to use the changes in positive ways. For example, instead of worrying about how much sleep you're losing when you consistently wake at 3 a.m., use the time to actively interact with the information coming in. Sit with a journal and write. Meditate and connect with other realms. If you have hot flashes, see lights, and hear tapping noises, try to identify what's happening that may be triggering it. What else do you notice? What patterns can you discern? Use the signs as a wake-up to pay attention.

Added inputs of energy cause the body to function at a higher metabolic rate and burn more nutrients. A sound nutritional program with added supplementation can be helpful, as well as the basic meditations in Chapter 3. Weaving the Nadis assists in smoothing Kundalini and easing some of the nervous-system discomfort, and The Living Matrix helps the adjustment to living in higher frequency. Here are a few focused exercises.

Smoothing the Flow of Kundalini

Many of the signs and symptoms of expansion are caused by the rising of Kundalini with large influxes of energy. Preparing the pathways for Kundalini rising and grounding the excess energy help ease any stress. This is especially helpful in reducing the effects of restless legs.

EASING ENERGY OVERLOAD AND SMOOTHING KUNDALINI EXERCISE

If possible, go to your power spot. Sit in a chair or on a rock with your feet on the ground, or sit on the ground in cross-legged position.

Ground, center, and establish boundaries. Open the Spiral Pillar of Light and intend a circle of safety, healing, and light. Express gratitude.

Smooth Kundalini flow:

- Activate the Weaving the Nadis and the Earth and Sky patterns.
- As you inhale, imagine Earth energy flowing into your sacrum and up the two parallel pathways of the Nadis, weaving in one side of a chakra, out the other, and then up to the next.
- At the Crown Chakra, exhale and send the energy into the sky.
- Inhale and bring energy down from the sky through your crown and let it flow down the central line that corresponds to the Hara-line, through each chakra, to your sacrum. Exhale and send it down into the Earth.
- Continue breathing the Earth and Sky pattern through the Nadis.

Ground excess energy:

- Open the Circle of Life pattern.
- With your breath, circulate energy along the outer pathway.
- Inhale energy up the spine and then exhale energy down the front of your body for three complete rounds.
- Open your Base Chakra and, as energy circulates down your front, instead of sending it up your spine, imagine it flowing into Earth; imagine it being received by a ley line and streaming away.
- Continue until the excess energy subsides.

When you are done, give thanks, close the patterns, and ground, center, and establish boundaries.

ACTIVATING THE ETHERIC PINEAL GLAND
AND AMYGDALA EXERCISE

Activating your pineal gland and the amygdala area of the brain will help you open to new frequencies, receive heightened information, and adjust more easily to transformation. This is a complicated exercise, so be patient and practice. Illustrations can be found at *www.explorationsinenergy.com*

Ground, center, and establish boundaries.

Give thanks and open the Spiral Pillar of Light, creating a circle of safety, healing, and Light.

Activate the Pyramid Purification pattern and imagine two identically sized pyramids positioned so they are sharing one base. This creates an octahedron. Rotate one pyramid so that the corners of the two bases separate, forming an eight-pointed star. This geometry will assist in receiving new frequency.

Visualize this structure inside your head with the apex of one pyramid touching your Crown Chakra and the apex of the second anchoring in your Throat Chakra. The shared base stretches from the internal aspect of your Third Eye Chakra to the back of your head. The pineal gland sits in the center.

Imagine a beam of light coming from your Star, your personal Source, entering the apex of the pyramid through your Crown Chakra and focusing on your pineal gland (located in the center of your head at the level of the bridge of the nose).

Visualize an infinity sign forming in your head with the pineal gland in the center. The figure-eight pattern is horizontal. One edge hits the Third Eye and the back edge hits the back of the head.

As light continues to enter the top of the pyramid, imagine the infinity sign rotating counterclockwise. As it rotates it creates a torus of spinning energy around the pineal gland.

Rotate the octahedron in a clockwise direction. The pyramid and torus create two fields of energy, rotating in opposite directions.

Continue to focus on the rotating fields and see if they want to change direction. Notice what you feel throughout your body. Let the fields rotate back and forth in different directions until your brain and body feel awakened, energized, and balanced.

Affirm that your third eye is now activated and visualize your connection to spiritual impulses.

When you feel complete, close the activations, give thanks, ground, center, and establish boundaries.

Chapter 21

The Evolutionary Empath

We are in an evolutionary bottleneck, a transitional time during which humans are advancing to meet the challenges of elevating awareness. Bottlenecks are times of increased stress that drive the development of specific qualities needed for specific times. Right now, we're asked to understand and live our interconnectedness. Experiencing true connection involves feeling what other people feel, something we call empathy. The degree of empathy needed requires heightened energy sensitivity. People at the front end of this evolutionary wave are called Empaths.

The heightened sensitivity being developed ensures the emergence of transparency, truthfulness, and kindness built on intuition and authenticity. This sensitivity allows for deeper love. However, given the variety of the signs and symptoms of expansion covered in Chapter 20, Empaths can find themselves easily confused and overwhelmed. The specific coping skills Empaths need are rarely understood or taught. While most of this book is geared to feeling energy reality more deeply, this chapter helps the ultra-energy-sensitive Empaths integrate their abilities and thrive. Everyone has the qualities of an Empath to one degree or another; so ultimately, this chapter is for all of us.

Recently, I was sitting by an open window that overlooked the pasture where my horses grazed. A gentle rain was tapering to a drizzle and the sun sparkled on oak leaves dripping water. Through no act or intent of my own, and with no apparent shift in energy, I suddenly experienced my surroundings as though I had no skin. What I mean is that there was no distinction between inside and outside, between me and the oak leaf or the water dripping, or the sun reflecting prisms. This isn't to say I felt to be one with everything. Rather, I was physically experiencing sensations as though what I was viewing was happening to me. I distinctly thought, "This is what it is to be an Empath." In the same moment,

I realized that I had experienced the world this way before; that this was the natural state for me as a very young child. Like most child Empaths, I needed to fit into the "normal" world. I didn't stop being an Empath; I used my Empathic awareness to feel what other people wanted me to be, and then tried to be that.

Children always try to fit in and hide anything that's different. This is especially true of Empaths as their sensitivities are often dismissed as they're told to toughen up, to stop being a hypochondriac, and to stop complaining. Eventually, as they grow and accept their differences, they become the cage rattlers of the family, ensuring important issues aren't swept under the carpet. As teenagers, they're the rebels; as adults, black sheep. Through the discomfort they unintentionally create, they drive family dynamics into greater awareness. Sadly, they do so at a cost to themselves.

If you're an Empath, meeting the challenges and using the gifts of your sensitivity are part of your purpose. You're a pathfinder. Learning how to overcome the challenges of your sensitivity is your contribution to the evolution of the whole. This chapter is meant to help you feel safe in being your whole, authentic, human self.

Defining an Empath

There are four things about Empaths that explain their deepest challenges and gifts.

First, they experience the outside world through an extreme type of empathy. Empathy is defined as the ability to feel the emotions of another person and is a natural human ability that's essential in a highly functioning, emotionally intelligent society. However, Empaths experience this awareness more deeply than the average person.

Second, Empaths are almost more sensitive to other people's feelings—physical, emotional, and energetic—than they are to their own. Consequently, they put their own needs last on the list of concerns. This extreme sensitivity isn't limited to the needs of people they know; it extends to all of humanity and, for many, to animals, plants, trees, nature, and all of Earth. While this provides unique insight and connection, it also causes pain and confusion.

Third, Empaths have few, if any, boundaries. Dr. Judy Orloff, author of *The Empath's Survival Guide*, says, "Empaths have an extremely reactive neurological system. We don't have the same filters that other people do to block out stimulation. As a consequence, we absorb into our own bodies both the positive and stressful energies around us."[1]

It's important to understand, however, that Empaths are not designed to block stimulus from the outside world. They're meant to function just as they are: extremely sensitive, deeply perceptive, and concerned for the well-being of all. Unfortunately, these traits mean they absorb the physical ills, emotional pain and suffering, and even the self-imposed limiting beliefs of others. They're happy when others are happy, sad when others are sad, to the point that they feel responsible when people around them are unhappy. Not taking responsibility for other people's happiness is one of the greatest challenges for Empaths.

Fourth, while being an Empath increases their intuition, it doesn't change their human lessons. Actually, it gives them a few more. Using intuition, intelligence, and empathic awareness, Empaths usually know exactly what to do in most situations. However, they will often ignore their own wisdom, ceding the decisions to others even when knowing the outcome won't be good. Why? Simply to let the other person feel in charge, to gain that person's acceptance, and to feel like they belong. Belonging is another of the challenges Empaths face. The need for belonging is often greater than the need for authenticity. However, until they can be authentic, they never truly feel they belong.

Empaths are often identified as Highly Sensitive Persons (HSP), a term coined by psychologist Elaine Aron in the 1990s.[2] She describes HSPs as having a highly sensitive nervous system. Some people don't consider HSPs to be Empaths, citing that although they share the heightened sensitivity, they don't necessarily have extensive energy awareness. Personally, I've never met an HSP who wasn't an Empath. Certainly, no one needs to spend any effort deciding whether they are an HSP or an Empath; they should asume both. Knowing the term HSP only helps define empathic sensitivities to the medical community and to those who aren't energy aware.

To control the overwhelming stimulation they live with, many Empaths numb themselves. They learn to desert their bodies, block their emotions, and distance themselves from other people in order to survive within the confines of normal. This can happen at a very young age and includes using drugs, food, and self-harming to quiet the constant stimulation. The practices in this chapter are intended to help Empaths find comfortable, safe ways of using their abilities without being overwhelmed.

Characteristics of Empaths

Empaths display varying degrees of sensitivity and are often sensitive in specific areas; some are more sensitive physically, others emotionally, energetically, or spiritually. Few are equally sensitive in all areas, and none exhibit all the characteristics described here. In addition, Empaths resonate with specific life-forms. Some are attuned to humans, others to animals, even specific species, and others to plants, crystals, and nature.

It's tempting for an Empath to dismiss the gifts of this awareness and focus on the difficulties. Conversely, Empaths might feel the need to be special and declare that the only "real Empaths" are those who are highly sensitive. Be assured that whatever an Empath's degree of sensitivity, whether they notice changes in energy without being deeply affected, or can't leave the house for fear of being overwhelmed, they are Empaths. There's something specific to learn and contribute from exactly where every person is on this continuum. Each unique perspective is needed to create the entire picture and every person is born exactly the way they're supposed to be and where they're supposed to be, engaging the world with the faculties they're meant to master. Here's a simple truth for all Empaths: you are meant to be you.

The following empathic characteristics are divided into physical, mental/emotional, and spiritual/energetic.

Physical

Physically sensitive Empaths have a high degree of body awareness with access to deep levels of body wisdom. Their intuitive awareness is body-centered gut instinct. On the other hand, they have a difficult time staying embodied as they tend to pick up and manifest the ailments of people, animals, nature, and Earth. To avoid this, they abandon their body and lose their grounding.

Physically sensitive Empaths, especially children, are accused of being hypochondriacs. They absorb the symptoms of people around them, yet doctors find nothing wrong, so it's assumed they're attention seeking. Since physical Empaths feel the disruption to Earth of human activity, they sometimes manifest the ills of Earth in their own bodies. This makes them susceptible to disorders such as multiple chemical sensitivity disorder, sensory processing disorder, chronic fatigue, and other hard-to-define chronic issues that metaphysically reflect the condition of Earth.

An Empath's pain is real, even if the cause belongs to someone else. However, once the designation of being sick is discarded in favor of being energy sensitive, although the illness may still require treatment, the gifts within the challenge begin to emerge.

Physically sensitive Empaths are:

- Challenged by being:
  - Overstimulated by bright lights, strong smells, loud noises, chemicals, and electromagnetic fields (EMF), which often result in body pain.
  - Overwhelmed by large crowds, traffic, construction, action movies, office lights, and home appliances.
  - Prone to migraines, anxiety, or irritability when over-stimulated.
  - Reactive to medications, usually unable to tolerate even half a recommended dose.
  - Susceptible to taking on other people's pain and illness.
  - Unable to stay connected to their body and body wisdom without being overwhelmed.

- Gifted with:
  - The awareness of the physical needs of plants, trees, and/or animals.
  - The ability to identify another person's health issue, often by feeling it in their own body.
  - Often smelling pleasant odors such as flowers or perfumes that aren't physically present, alerting them to the presence of spirits from the other side.
  - Early warnings of danger, for example, feeling an impending traffic accident and getting off the highway beforehand or feeling the harmful impacts of toxins hidden in foods.
  - Feeling physical shifts in their bodies before earthquakes, volcanic eruptions, or other Earth events.

While physical sensitivity is uncomfortable, even disabling, most Empaths wouldn't trade their sensitivity to be pain-free if it meant giving up their gifts. Being connected is too important to them. Connection is the greatest gift of working through the challenges of physical sensitivity. Practices of grounding such as the Earth and Sky pattern on page 19, clearing as with the Circle of Life pattern on page 22, and the Discharging exercise at the end of this chapter can be very helpful in managing the physical discomfort.

Mental and Emotional

Since the energy field of the heart is the largest radiance in the body, larger even than the brain,[3] it's no surprise that Empaths are sensitive to mental and emotional impressions. Because they absorb so much, Empaths easily confuse other people's thoughts and feelings with their own, creating difficulty in identifying their own needs, desires, and path. They're susceptible to judgment, criticism, expectation, and dependency. Told they're too sensitive, they devalue themselves and get lost taking care of others.

Mentally and emotionally sensitive Empaths are:

- Challenged by:
    - Absorbing the emotional intensity of the people around them.
    - Taking on other people's thoughts and beliefs.
    - Becoming overwhelmed with anxiety, grief, or other strong emotion without having awareness that the feeling doesn't belong to them.
    - Having trouble making decisions even when they know the best choice.
    - Seeing all sides to a situation and losing sight of their own interest or rigidly holding on to their own perspective for fear of losing themself.
    - Having difficulty focusing on details or becoming overfocused to avoid the bigger picture.
    - Feeling guilty or responsible if everyone in a room isn't happy.
    - Craving harmony and trying to create it by people pleasing.
    - Overfocusing on their partners' needs in relationships.
    - Avoiding commitment out of fear of losing their identity.
    - Trying to gain self-acceptance through the acceptance of others.
    - Being rescuers, trying to save people from the consequences of their choices.

- Gifted with:
    - Being generous, kind, and nurturing.
    - Truly celebrating other people's success: they feel good when other people feel good.
    - Relating easily to other people so they are good listeners and spend time helping others.
    - Being intuitive, creative, and insightful.
    - Deep reservoirs of loyalty and love.

Children are especially susceptible to taking on responsibility for the feelings of those around them, particularly parents and siblings. When parents fight or divorce, all children feel it's because they did something wrong. When children are Empaths, in addition, they feel and process the emotions of the entire family. Child Empaths become the sponge and cleanup crew for everyone they care about, usually carrying this pattern into adulthood.

Mentally and emotionally, Empaths struggle with belonging as they isolate for protection from the onslaught of feelings, emotions, and thoughts. In the journey of learning what feelings are their own and what belong to others, they discover they belong to a group of kindred spirits who exchange on a deeper level. Empaths need safety to trust being different. Once they're safe to be themselves, they discover their unique value. They learn how to focus their mind and fuel their thoughts with emotions to create their reality. Because they care deeply about others, the reality they create is inherently kind.

Authenticity is the greatest gift of emotional and mental sensitivity. Practices of centering as in the Circle of Life pattern on page 22 and the Recharging exercise at the end of this chapter can be helpful.

Energetic and Spiritual

Empaths feel what's in other people's energy fields and in the energetic ambiance of Earth. They connect with the spiritual essence of what they encounter and use their own energy field and body to receive and transmit energy information. Empaths who are energy aware and connected to their own spiritual essence are good at the art of correspondence—the ability to link two similar things so that energy/light/information can flow between them. Correspondence allows an Empath to raise the vibration of those around them without others necessarily knowing it.

Energy-sensitive Empaths have difficulty letting go of old relationships, sometimes maintaining energetic connections that the recipient doesn't want. They can take on another's negative patterns by unconsciously configuring their own energy to match that of people they love. While this can be described as "taking on negative energy," since energy is neither positive nor negative, it's more correctly called transference of a limiting pattern.

Spiritually and energetically sensitive, Empaths are:

- Challenged by:
  - Becoming drained if they're invested in another person's process or attached to their outcomes.

- Becoming depressed by the disparity between spiritual reality and the physical world.
- Having difficulty clearing the energy imprints they pick up from others.
- Having deeply moving spiritual experiences that leave them unable to relate to everyday life.
- Becoming deeply depressed at world news and lose faith in humanity.
- Seeing people's highest potential but being blind to their human faults.
- Feeling energy blockages, emotional trauma, and automatic negative thoughts held in a person's energy field, often through their own body, and may have difficulty letting them go.

- Gifted with:
  - The ability to positively influence another's emotional and physical well-being simply by sitting next to them.
  - Feeling the presence of other beings such as guides, ascended masters, angels, and so forth.
  - Feeling the energetic imprints in specific locations of past events and the emotional atmosphere of world events.
  - Hearing messages from those who have passed and/or channeling information from spiritual guides.
  - Having a strong love for nature and a deep commitment to Mother Earth.
  - Being highly creative.
  - Making good energy healers, mediums, and medical intuitives.

Energy sensitive Empaths are challenged to maintain a coherent energy field. They can become attracted to the illusion of a dark force. Inwardly, they know that light is the true force and darkness is simply a lack of light, but continue the false impression of duality. Believing darkness is an independent force gives it power. The idea of a dark force becomes a repository for fear and unwanted emotions, turning the responsibility for our shadow self over to the dark force we envision. If you find yourself believing in darkness, connect with your source and shift your energetic pattern to shine more light. The Pyramid Purification pattern on page 47 is excellent for helping with this.

Being the forerunners in a time of chaos requires that Empaths work to the most expansive vision they can hold. The path through darkness reveals the true gift for the energy-sensitive Empath: the reality of their spiritual essence. Then connection with all life flourishes.

The Neurophysics of Empathic Ability

Mirror neurons in the brain probably explain the mechanism behind human empathy. Mirror neurons are a specific type of motor neuron. Motor neurons activate when we move or think about moving. Mirror neurons also activate when we see someone else moving. Of course, the body has a reality check. We know whether we are picking up a coffee cup or the person next to us is doing so through sensory neurons called proprioceptors. Proprioceptors tell the brain where we are in space. The mirror neuron says, lifting a cup, and the proprioceptors say, no not me, my hand is resting on the table.

Mirror neurons are critical for developing social skills.[4] We understand another's feelings because their facial expressions trigger resonant feelings in our own brain. Often, we engage in unconscious facial mimicry: understanding more deeply what someone else feels by mimicking their expression.[5] Is it surprising that people who lose the ability to make facial expressions also lose the ability to interpret them? [6] In other words, they lose their aptitude for empathy.

Mirror and motor neurons may explain the capacity for human empathy, but they don't explain the totality of being an Empath. Taking on another's illness or feeling the needs of a plant may best be understood through resonance. (See Chapter 6.) Resonance occurs between systems that share the same or close to the same natural frequency. A "system" may be another person, an animal, plant, etc. When we resonate with another system, barriers between us dissolve and our energy synchronizes with theirs, allowing information in the form of vibration to pass between us in a process called correspondence. This reflects quantum physics in that one system can influence another, even at a distance. Consequently, Empaths can feel the emotions of people they love even when they're half a world away.

Thriving as an Empath

No matter the degree of sensitivity, every Empath needs shielding from external stimuli in order to thrive, yet few Empaths can create boundaries to protect themselves. Through my career, I've tried to help Empath patients develop energetic boundaries. Without exception, they simply couldn't do it. Trying only made them feel like failures. I now understand that asking an Empath to create an energetic boundary is asking them not be who they are.

Empaths are designed without boundaries. It's not a mistake. Boundaries limit their abilities and the challenges they're here to find solutions for. To thrive, they need to learn another way to shield themselves. My experience with the oak tree helped me understand that instead of boundaries, Empaths need shelter. Shelter allows them to be who they are—to feel as they're designed to feel and still be safe.

When I first introduced the concept of shelter to patients, I was moved at the reception. Some people cried. They admitted that even the thought of creating a boundary made them feel disconnected. Empaths thrive in flow. Disconnection produces soul-destroying isolation.

What is shelter? Most people don't think about it, yet every person I asked had an immediate answer. For one, shelter was being within one of the mountain peaks in the Andes. For another, it was being inside a hollow in a tree. For others it was burrowing into Earth, standing under a canopy of leaves, being part of a constellation of stars, identifying with a guru or belief, being within the beam of one of the seven rays of light, hearing a musical chord or chant. The possibilities are endless. What all have in common is that shelter offers refuge while maintaining connection. It does not create a barrier, even the semipermeable barrier of a boundary.

When sheltered, impulses have less intensity. They're slower to arrive and are separated from each other so that they can be pulled apart— distinct chords in a symphony rather than a cacophony of sound. Shelter arrives through the reliance on being part of something bigger.

EXERCISE: SHELTERING

Shelter is a frequency. You can activate it anytime by visualizing your image of shelter and/or conjuring the feeling of shelter from connection with your source energy. If you don't have an image, this meditation may help you receive one.

Connect with your spiritual Source. You may see this as a star in the sky, a ray of light illuminating your aura, an Earth cave, or any image that gives you a feeling of safety and brings you into your heart center.

Activate the Winged Disk meditation by inhaling golden energy in through your Crown Chakra and filling your Heart Chakra. Exhale light from your Heart Chakra into your hands. Place your hands over your heart.

Take your awareness into your Heart Chakra with your breath. Ask your higher self/source energy to guide you in receiving shelter.

Sit quietly with no expectation. Notice any images, feelings, and awareness that come. Don't analyze, judge, ridicule, or dismiss anything you receive. Your image can be as unusual as sitting inside the mouth of a lion.

Once you have an image or awareness, immerse yourself in it. Imagine yourself facing your most frightening situation from inside your shelter. Notice what you feel.

When you're finished, give thanks and close the meditation.

Visit your image of shelter regularly and call on it anytime you're in situations where you habitually feel overwhelmed.

Thriving as an Empath requires being able to maintain a coherent energy field. Discharging what we've picked up from others is one aspect, recharging our field is another. Of course, the best way to discharge and recharge is in nature where our resonance to Earth frequencies is restored. Otherwise, this exercise helps discharge, and the next exercise helps recharge. They can be used together or separately.

EXERCISE: DISCHARGING WHAT ISN'T YOU

Discharge is the release of everything you carry that isn't yours. You don't need to identify the specifics, just be willing to release everything that isn't you. Queen Nefertiti's Headdress is the best activation to discharge the energy patterns, emotions, physical pain, and limiting thoughts and beliefs that you've absorbed from other people. Discharging requires connecting to your heart where your true self resides. One of the reasons many Empaths hold on to someone else's pattern is that they don't want to abandon the person. Remember: you can be most present for others when being the truest version of yourself.

Ground, center, and shelter.

Activate Queen Nefertiti's Headdress.

As you inhale light and high-frequency energy into the headdress, allow half of the energy you bring in to circulate along the striations of the headdress into the layers of your aura, causing your aura to vibrate with a very fine frequency. Allow the other half to descend into your Heart Chakra, filling it with light.

Hold your hands in prayer position in front of your Heart Chakra. Lightly press the fingertips together and separate the palms, forming a contained space between your hands. Rotate your hands so that your fingertips point outward, away from your body, and the heels of your palms are close to your body at the level of your Heart Chakra.

As the high-frequency energy circulates in your aura, call into your Heart Chakra everything that does not authentically belong to you: all borrowed beliefs, acquired limitations, physical pain, and emotional charges that aren't you. Consider them as young children needing comfort and transformation.

As you exhale, open your fingertips and exhale through your hands, comforting, blessing, and releasing the energy attachments into your vibrating aura where they are instantly transformed into light.

Close your fingertips and inhale, continuing to call the absorbed energy in your body that isn't you into your hands, and opening your fingertips as you exhale them into your aura to be transformed into light.

Continue until you feel clear, calm, and vibrating at a high frequency.

Close Queen Nefertiti's Headdress activation.

Sit and observe how you feel. You may continue to the recharging part of this process or stop at this point and return to present-time awareness with heightened clarity and inner freedom.

EXERCISE: RECHARGING YOUR ESSENCE

Whenever you absorb someone else's energy, you let go of or bury some aspect of yourself. Recharging is the calling back of who you are. You can do this independently of the preceding Discharge exercise or do them one after the other.

Ground, center, and shelter.

If you can, sit in nature, near a tree, in a meadow, by a waterfall, etc. If you can't, imagine yourself sitting in the calm, rejuvenating energy of a natural setting.

Open the Winged Disk Meditation connecting to your source energy as bright, coherent light that you inhale through your Crown Chakra and down into your Heart Chakra.

When your Heart Chakra feels full of light, extend your left hand and turn it palm up. Then place your right hand over your heart chakra.

On an inhalation, invite all parts of yourself to come home. You don't need to know what they are. Imagine your left palm is magnetized, drawing the pieces of yourself back to you, transporting them along your arm and into your heart. Feel free to move your left hand in a dance around you as you collect the different parts of returning self.

As you exhale, send energy from your right hand into your heart, welcoming yourself home. Feel love for all returning parts including the shadow parts you didn't want to own.

Continue this cycle, nurturing and strengthening your returning parts with your breath. Notice your Hara-line becoming brighter and stronger. See the shining light of your core as you integrate the light of your totality.

When you're finished, place both hands over your heart. Connect to your source and feel deep love and gratitude for all parts of self and all parts of the Universe. Know that you belong, right here, doing exactly what you're doing to contribute to the whole.

Return to present-time, everyday awareness with a new sense of completeness.

Close the Winged Disk activation and return to present-time, everyday awareness wtih a new sense of completeness.

Ground, center, and shelter.

Learning to Shelter and using Discharging and Recharging practices allows us to thrive as Empaths and take our place in the evolution underway. Remember: we are all Empaths of varying degrees and are all developing our skills, consciously or not. Every one of us is meant for these times.

Conclusion

Completing the Circle

"The significant problems we face today cannot be solved at the same level of thinking we were at when we created them."

—Albert Einstein

Accepting our place as a spiritual being cocreating this reality is the essence of the transformation we are living—the paradigm shift underway. Many different prophecies have foretold the times we're now in. The Mayan prophecies say this is the ending of an Age, or World. In the creation stories as told in the Mayan *Popul Vuh,* previous Ages ended as humans either could not or would not worship the gods. What does it mean to worship the gods? Perhaps it's a metaphor for acknowledging the god force within. Worshiping the gods may be as simple as honoring the divine within all, the plants, animals, Earth, and all the unseen realities. Maybe it means putting spirituality first in our choices and actions. What would it mean in our life and choices if we did?

In this moment we are creating the direction of the future. What that direction will be depends on the awareness with which we make our choices. How each of us behaves in the trials of this transition will determine the future; what we do depends on what we hold precious, how much we care, and what we believe about reality.

It's time for each of us to define what we believe and what we treasure, then align our actions accordingly. When conflict and fear seem to prevail, react with thoughtfulness, calmness, and love. Practice living without conflict. Choose to transform anxious, fear-filled, and angry thoughts. Most importantly, we're being asked to reidentify ourselves, to shift out of the old, be our true selves, and align with the frequency of the new paradigm.

When embracing the new, there's always a moment of fear as we wonder how. How do I become the new me? Energetically, it is the moment we disengage our energy fibers from their attachments and float free. Then we create a vision, send our fibers to attach to it, and let self be pulled forward. The secret is to vision a compelling future.

Shifting Identity

Technology is based on laws of nature. How can it be otherwise? The algorithms used in social media are designed to respond to every click we make. Every click returns to us what we are interested in. Eventually, the social media feed we are on gives us a perfect reflection of what we already believe. It hooks into our wounds, fears, dreams, and desires and feeds back our thoughts and attitudes, solidifying our identity. This is an exact replica of how we manifest the world around us. Our attitudes, thoughts, and beliefs create a vibration that acts the same as clicking a social-media link. The vibration attracts our next experience that exactly matches what we vibrate with. Then we act as though this externalization of our internal state is the ultimate reality.

In fact, the ultimate reality is reflected through the hologram and the awareness that we are one. What happens to one of us impacts all of us. We're being socially engineered into polarized camps where we project our greatest fears and dislikes onto the other half of humanity. This is an old, outmoded strategy. It only works if we buy into believing there is an us and them, someone to hate and demonize.

In the book *The Game of Life and How to Play It*, author Florence Scovel Shinn proposes that all our mistakes are not failures; they're avenues of learning and growth, not our weakness, but part of our wholeness. She says that if even one person holds another in a vision of wholeness, that person cannot fail.[1] As long as one person sees all of our so-called mistakes, all of the places we fell short, all of the hurt we caused, as part of the process of becoming, we cannot fail.

How do you see the people around you: your parents, children, partners, friends? Is the first thought of them of their failures, or how they've let you down? Or, can you be the one person who sees them in the wholeness of their path—as people with divine essence, working to resolve issues and grow?

This is what's required of us now, that through energy awareness we shift our identity and see that we are one and we are whole. The Tibetan lamas and tribes of the Sierra Nevada in Colombia care for the planet and provide us room to grow because they know this. Nature knows this. Earth has never let us go. We are the most nascent species on the planet and all of nature seeks our evolution. The NDEs of Dannion Brinkley and others illustrate that we are made of spirit and do not die. Life is an exquisite opportunity. Let's not waste it hating.

We are all one. How many times has this been said and by how many spiritual traditions? And if each of us really believed it, what would change if we treated others as if they were ourselves? To paraphrase Machaelle Small Wright, how would the world change if we behaved as if the God in all life mattered?

Here is the bottom line: we are in this together, and in the transition underway, none of us makes it unless all of us do. Choose love. Move beyond the duality of good and bad and of us and them. Enjoy life, follow your heart, and engage the path and language of energy. Be your whole self. In this life, you get to be you.

Appendix A

Origin of the Meditations

My fascination with subtle energy began as a child when my pet rabbit died in my arms. I watched the light leave his eyes and felt him suddenly become much heavier. I was confused by this; if something left, shouldn't he be lighter?

Convinced there was a deeper reality than what I could see and feel, I began looking for confirmation. My parents were intelligent, professional people with open minds who studied the Edgar Cayce material and encouraged curiosity. Consequently, there were many books around the house for me to browse. When I was thirteen, I read Edgar Cayce's book *Auras: An Essay on the Meaning of Colors* and for the next several years spent many cross-eyed hours trying to see auras. I never did, at least not that way.

I felt my first aura when I was in my late teens. I was reading and petting my cat, Lamar, when I noticed a strong resistance against my hand each time my hand approached her body as I stroked her. The resistance felt like two north poles of a magnet being pushed together. Until then, I didn't realize that auras could be felt. I explored the resistance and was able to define a border around her body. Lamar responded to my feeling her aura exactly as if I were petting her fur. She rotated her head to expose her ears and rolled to expose her belly as my hand passed over. I knew that she could feel my ministrations clearly and that we were interacting on a level satisfactory to us both.

This event opened me to the kinesthetic experience of energy. It also launched my career into massage therapy and energy bodywork. As I became more proficient at feeling and moving energy, I began to see in my mind's eye what my hands were feeling.

The patterns in this book were discerned over a period of thirty years. I didn't receive this information passively; I went searching for it. I didn't find this information because I'm a good human being. Exploring these patterns and the practices in this book, however, is helping me become a better human being.

Each of us is capable of discovering truth. No one is more special than any one else; we're all equipped with everything needed. I offer these activations and practices to others with respect, from one person walking her path to another. I fully expect that each person who works with these will modify them for their own use.

The decision to write a book featuring the energy activations came about during a forty-day mantra meditation exercise in August 2005. About halfway through, I finished the daily repetition of the mantra and sat in the vibrant silence of the after-time. My body pulsated and my energy field felt brilliantly clear. In the empty space behind my eyes, I saw the book take form and present itself in a complete version, chapters laid out with topics and content. I flipped through the pages and realized I was being inspired to put everything I had ever learned about energy into a book. It seemed impossible. Yet, I said yes.

All of the energy practices in this book have been experienced first-hand. I don't write about anything I haven't learned through personal experience. I would love to hear about your experiences. Feel free to contact me through my website *explorationsinenergy.com*.

Look forward to hearing from you.

—Synthia

The Spiral Pillar of Light

I was introduced to the basics of this pattern in a session with Barbara Marciniak and the group she channels called the Pleiadians, also known as the P's. Barbara opened the session by calling on the Pillar of Light to access the P's and to provide protection. I began to work with this meditation on a regular basis, observing how it impacted the aura and activated higher connection. This slightly different version offers a gentler and, for me, more expanded experience.

Professionally, I use the Spiral Pillar of Light in my bodywork sessions and to clear and cleanse my treatment room and energy tools. Personally, I use this to deepen my meditation practice, to clear my personal space, and for grounding during stressful encounters.

I love this pattern's ability to contain my own harmful projections when I'm out of balance, ensuring I don't harm or drain another person.

Like you, I work each day to clear my field and take responsibility for what I transmit and project. Sometimes I fail, and when I do, I return to these practices.

Earth and Sky

The first time I felt this flow I was doing a simple conscious breathing exercise when I became aware of the movement of energy between heaven and earth. I saw the image of a tree with my body as the trunk, and the energy entering and leaving my Crown and Base Chakras, forming branches above my head and roots below my feet. The more grounded I became in Earth, the more expanded I became in the sky. I felt I was a bridge between Earth and sky, as Indigenous people describe.

This perception changed being centered, grounded, and energetically aware, from being a matter of personal growth to that of contributing to a greater system. I saw how the actions of each of us impact the quality for all life. I have since seen this meditation in various forms in different practices, proof we all have access to universal energy information.

Circle of Life

Circle of Life is based on the Great Central Channel meridian of Chinese medicine. The Central Channel is composed of two paired channels or meridians. The front or yin meridian, named the Conception Vessel, flows down the center front of the body and under the torso. It changes into the Governing Vessel and rises up the spine and over the top of the head. Together, the two make a continuous circuit. The Great Central Channel is the first set of meridians to develop in the embryo. It interacts with the chakras and feeds all other meridians. When it gives rise to other channels, it rises as described in the pattern, up the Hari-line, dividing the body in half.

I first learned to meditate with this channel during the study of Jin Shin Do Bodymind Acupressure and later saw it as a Taoist meditation called the microcosmic orbit. The traditional meditation focuses on accumulating chi in the Hara that is then sent along the pathway of the Governing and Conception Vessels.

The variations in this book focus on the coccyx as the collecting place of chi rather than the Hara, an adaptation to alleviate the effects of premature Kundalini energy rising. People were presenting in treatment with energy accumulating in the sacrum causing vibration, heat, and agitation. In session, I asked for insight into how to relieve the symptoms and saw this coccyx variation. The alteration changed the focus from accumulating energy to distributing it, easing the physical discomfort of awakening Kundalini while using the excess energy to help in the clearing process.

The second variation uses the inner channel of the traditional Central Channel in which both Governing and Central channels flow up the center of the body and create a fountain of energy at the crown.

Chakra Clarity

This is the second traditional meditation. Meditating with the chakras is often used to access blocks and limitations, as well as clarify developmental issues. This practice supports spiritual evolution. It's used here as a tool for self-exploration and the development of visioning skills to access imagery and metaphor to communicate with the subconscious mind. The information stored in the deeper layers of the subconscious mind directs our responses to daily stimuli and perceived limitations in life. When we learn the language of imagery, we can begin to discover the unconscious script we live by. The process of accessing imagery can be applied to all meditative practice.

Chakra Fibers

When I was a college student at Michigan State University, every Saturday at 7 a.m., a wonderful man provided two hours of free yoga in the student union. One day, toward the end of the session, I entered a deeply relaxed state with my eyes semi-open and with a soft gaze and my mind quieted of random thoughts. I became aware, in a detached sort of way, that I was gazing at the instructor's aura. Although there was a field of silver blue around him, what was more striking was the energy streaming off him in fibers or filaments of light. It actually looked and acted like flames and was unlike any light I had ever seen. It clearly contained consciousness, was alive, and was interactive with the surroundings.

I connected what I saw to the fibers described by Carlos Castaneda, who teaches that the chakra fibers are anchors into reality and sensors to explore. Since that experience, I've seen the living light filaments in several different circumstances. Kinesthetically, it is the most prominent aspect I feel in the energy field. This activation challenges us to pay attention to how attached we are to dogmatic or habitual ways of being and thinking, and how free and available we are for inspiration.

My first direct experience of how the fibers connect in love relationships happened when I first met my husband. Our chakras linked together with a distinct popping sound as each one connected. Since then, I've worked extensively with love connections between people and can attest to the fact that the fibers are damaged with violent treatment.

Weaving the Nadis

This activation was revealed in 2002 when a client came for treatment after a severe car accident. Her car had spun many circles and the woman was knocked unconscious. As I worked on her energy field, I felt with my hands and saw in my mind's eye the pathway of the Nadis. They appeared as shoelaces, tying her energy structures in alignment. In her case, the laces on the right side were too loose with too much of the lace pooled on that side. The left side was too tight, restricting the energy flow. I had the image of her car spinning and the centrifugal force pulling the right side of her Nadis to the outside. I ran my hands along the pathway as described in the activation pattern until the right and left sides were even.

After this session, I began to meditate with the pattern and found that evenness along this pathway prepared the body for Kundalini rising. The pattern helped resolve issues in the chakras, creating a gentle suction along the Nadis and inviting Kundalini. When Kundalini rises organically as the result of clear pathways, it is a powerful, yet gentle expansion. Serenity is the keyword for this activation. It's calm, gently flowing water, soothing the body-mind and healing the spirit.

Five-Hearts Open

This activation opened during a session in 1999. I was providing a simple relaxation/rejuvenation massage and was flowing along in a free-form state of mind when I noticed my Hara-line light up as rays of energy entered my Crown Chakra, then descended the Hara-line into my heart. The energy built in my heart until it became almost uncomfortable, then streamed down into my hands and feet. My sense of self extended out to meet the world at a different level. As I massaged this person's body, the energy from my hands extended beneath her skin, meeting an inner plane of energy. I simultaneously massaged her skin as well as a deeper plane of energy with my energy extension. My feet were experiencing the same expansion: physically on the ground and energetically connected to a deeper, inner plane of Earth energy.

For the rest of the day, I walked as though lifted from the energy of Earth with knees high, stepping deeply, and building charge. My hands and heart touched into the essence of what was around me. I saw the image of an Egyptian relief with the people walking with knees high and hands raised with palms outward, giving me a new understanding of the phrase *walk like an Egyptian*. I find this activation initiates itself when needed with clients. I activate it myself when I want to charge my system from the heart of Earth.

Queen Nefertiti's Headdress

I saw this activation pattern in 2003 during a session with a client coming for depression. Although this person was very beautiful and extremely talented, liked and respected by everyone, she was caught in old patterns of low self-esteem and an inability to manifest joy. Her belief system and identity were formed through a severe childhood illness.

We'd worked together for many years; in this session we were both open for something new. When I asked for inspiration, the headdress appeared in her energy field, the striations of the headdress interacting with the aura. She used her breath to pull energy through the cone. I felt the vibration in my body as the layers in her aura changed frequency. Negative thoughts and beliefs stood out in relief against her vibrating field until the thought-forms burst like bubbles, followed by a feeling of lightness for her.

The activation needs to be used on a regular basis. Like taking a daily shower, it's needed more on some days than others.

Winged Disk

I've been drawn to the symbol of the winged disk my entire life. I find the symbol hidden in objects all around me. It appears at milestone moments, a synchronistic reminder to stay true to myself. This activation came in meditation. The symbol simply descended from the sky until the disk was located over my heart and my arms became the wings. While profoundly energizing, it's essentially a gentle, nurturing flow, ministering to the aches, pains, and exhaustion of the heart and soul.

Celtic Cross

This was actually the first activation I received. I was living in Canada, at the end of a period working with Greenpeace, visiting a friend in

Montréal. My friend had just ended a relationship with a deeply disturbed man. She lived in an apartment over a shop, and the stairs were strewn nightly with debris. Apparently, the man was engaged in an ongoing battle of revenge, littering her space, painting obscenities on the stairway walls in red paint, and psychically attacking her in her sleep.

The first night I was there, I was exhausted and fell deeply asleep. In the early hours, I woke with a deep sense of dread. Opening my eyes, I was assailed by the image of a man's face, enlarged and enraged, filling the entire ceiling. His eyes bore into me, emanating anger and hatred. I felt his jealousy as the room seemed to spin. Completely unprepared to deal with a psychic attack, I didn't know what to do and simply asked for help. I immediately saw the Celtic Cross, as described in the meditation, form around both myself, my friend, and the entire apartment. The attack quickly ended and there were no further assaults during the rest of the visit.

Since then, I learned that Dion Fortune, an early 1900s metaphysician from London, taught that the circle surrounded by four satellites was the symbol for the "psychic police," the forces that uphold spiritual law. That certainly fit my experience. Ten years later, when I met my husband I learned that this pattern played a significant role in his life. Colin is a crop circle researcher who coauthored the first book on the subject published in 1989 and has been in the forefront of investigation since 1983. This pattern of a circle surrounded by four satellites appeared as a crop circle in the late 1980s and played a critical role in his research. Colin named the formation the Celtic Cross, and I have kept the name for this meditation.

Mystic Triangle

My first contact with this activation was in the mid-1980s. I tried to spend time each day at sunrise and sunset facing the sun, expressing appreciation and gratitude for all that each day brought. During the practice, I would bring my hands together over my third eye and make a triangle using the two index fingers and thumbs. I felt this drew in sunlight to my third eye. It was grounding, energizing, and somehow deeply familiar.

The advancement of this activation happened in the fall of 1993, a month or more after Colin and I were married. We were sound asleep when we were both awakened shortly after 3 a.m. Colin suddenly sat up and appeared to be filled with light, which expanded him like a balloon. Lying there, I felt unable to move, as though I were turned off.

While filled with light, Colin received information about triangles in the landscape between sacred sites and crop circles, a major part of his research. He reports receiving understanding about how to access Earth energy. After a few minutes, the light left him and he deflated. He attempted to move to the side table to write the experience down but, as the light left him, it poured into me, expanding me. I began to see triangles in the human body focused on the palms of the hands and the third eye. After about five minutes, the light simply went out and I deflated as well. We wrote down the information, observing the similarities with no idea what to do with it.

We understood how to use this information after an event in March 2006 when we used triangulations to create a communication portal as described in the meditation. What kind of portal is created depends on your intention and on the level of awareness you bring to the practice.

Pyramid Purification

This activation came in summer 2006. Throughout the years, Colin and I have been deeply touched by the commitment of some cultures to stabilize Earth in times of crises. The Tibetan lamas and the tribes in the Sierra Nevada in Colombia are two examples that inspired us. We opened our nightly meditation in an attitude of service. One night, we were joined by two energy beings. Neither of us knew if we were meeting with the light body of living people, with people who were passed over, or with spiritual guides. The four of us were positioned in a square that became a four-sided pyramid. Each sat in a corner of the pyramid in cross-legged position as described in the meditation. Our job was to hold the construct while Spirit worked.

As we sat in this configuration, shadows and vapors began to be drawn into the base of the pyramid and were fed to the violet flame. The energy became brilliant, living light that was beamed out through the apex. We were witnessing the calling home of negative thought-forms and the returning to the light of pain, humiliation, sadness, and all the emotions that led us to destructive actions. It was humbling and a little frightening.

The Living Matrix

This is the newest of the meditations. It arrived in 2010 while I was working with an exceptional client. This client is working to manifest her spiritual matrix in all aspects of her life. As she lay on the table, I saw the twenty light filaments entering her fingers and toes. I started to tell her what I saw, but before I could say more than three words, she told me the same information from the perspective of how it felt in her body. We went back and forth, sharing in the description of The Living Matrix as it came into being in her body. Afterward, we both felt connected, uplifted, and in harmony with a higher order of affairs.

The next time I saw this pattern was in my regular long-distance meditation with Johanna Sayre. As we met in the etheric and settled into our meditation, the pattern activated in my body. I saw Johanna and myself floating in white clouds within a matrix of crisscrossed lines of force. It felt like being in the crossing point in dimensional fishnet stockings. We were side by side, linked together along with others, lines of force going to the level above and connecting all of us to our guides, and lines of force going below to the people we guided. It was a profound awareness of the manner in which we interconnect.

Dancing with the Elements

This moving meditation is dedicated to my first energy mentor, Louisa Poole. She taught me how to be free and to move forward fearlessly, even when terrified. She taught me how to extend my energy senses to meet the world. This meditation is modified from a weekend spent with her at Killam's Point in Branford, Connecticut, where we danced with the Devas and fairies of Earth.

Pineal Self-Activation

Colleen Behan originally taught me how to activate the pineal gland in a Lightworkers course. Later, at a conference in Malta, I told a room full of people that I was available to perform the activation on anyone who wanted it. Of course, everyone did. It was exhausting, and to avoid this problem again, I opened to find other ways. I saw the pattern here for self-activation. To take part in Colleen's activation course, visit *thespiritoflight.org*.

Appendix B

Resources

Books

Spirituality, Consciousness, and Science

Andrews, Colin, and Stephen J. Spignesi. *Crop Circles: Signs of Contact* (New Page Books, 2003).

Andrews, Synthia, and Colin Andrews. *The Complete Idiot's Guide to the Akashic Record* (Alpha Books, Penguin, 2010).

Andrews, Synthia, and Colin Andrews. *The Complete Idiot's Guide to 2012* (Alpha Books, Penguin, 2008).

Andrews, Synthia, and Bobbi Dempsey. *Acupressure and Reflexology for Dummies* (Wiley, 2007).

Becker, Dr. Robert, and Gary Seldon. *The Body Electric* (Quill Press, 1985).

Bodanis, David. *E=mc²: A Biography of the World's Most Famous Equation* (The Berkley Publishing Group, 2000).

Braden, Gregg. *The Divine Matrix* (Hay House, 2008).

Brinkley, Dannion, and Kathryn Brinkley. *Secrets of the Light: Lessons from Heaven* (HarperOne, 2009).

Brinkley, Dannion, with Paul Perry. *Saved by the Light: The True Story of a Man Who Died Twice and the Profound Revelations He Received* (HarperOne, reprinted 2008).

Castaneda, Carlos. *The Teachings of Don Juan: A Yaqui Way of Knowledge*, 3rd Ed. (University of California Press, 2008).

Chopra, Deepak. *The Seven Spiritual Laws of Success: A Practical Guide to the Fulfillment of Your Dreams* (Amber-Allen Publishing, 1994).

Dychtwald, Ken. *Bodymind* (Tarcher Putman, 1986).

Ereira, Alan. *The Elder Brothers* (Knopf, 1992).

Ereira, Alan. *The Elder Brothers' Warning* (Tairona Heritage Trust, 2009).

Emoto, Masaru. *Messages from Water*, Vol. 1 (Hado Publishing, 1999).

Hay, Louise. *You Can Heal Your Life*, 2nd ed. (Hay House, 1984).

Hurtak, J. J. *An Introduction to The Keys of Enoch*, 4th ed. (Academy for Future Science, 1997).

Jenny, Hans. *Cymatics: A Study of Wave Phenomena and Vibration,* 3rd ed. (Macromedia Press, 2001).

Kafatos, Menas, and Robert Nadeau. *The Conscious Universe: Parts and Wholes in Physical Reality* (Springer, 1999).

Kenyon, Tom. *Brain States* (World Tree Press, 2001).

Keyes, Ken. *Handbook to Higher Consciousness* (Eden Grove Editions, 1997).

Lovelock, James. *Gaia: A New Look at Life on Earth* (Oxford University Press, 2000).

Marciniak, Barbara. *Earth: Pleiadian Keys to the Living Library* (Bear and Company, 1994).

Marciniak, Barbara. *Family of Light: Pleiadian Tales and Lessons in Living* (Bear and Company, 1998).

Marciniak, Barbara. *Path of Empowerment: Pleiadian Wisdom for a World in Chaos* (New World Library, 2004).

Marciniak, Barbara, and Tera Thomas. *Bringers of the Dawn: Teachings from the Pleiadians* (Bear and Company, 1992).

McTaggart, Lynne. *The Field: The Quest for the Secret Force of the Universe* (HarperPerennial, 2002).

McTaggart, Lynne. *The Intention Experiment: Using Your Thoughts to Change Your Life and the World* (Free Press, 2008).

Melchizedek, Drunvalo. *The Ancient Secret of the Flower of Life,* Vol. 1 and 2 (Light Technology Publishing, 2000).

Mitchell, Dr. Edgar. *The Way of the Explorer,* rev. ed. (New Page Books, 2008).

Oschman, Dr. James L. *Energy Medicine: The Scientific Basis* (Churchill Livingston Publishing, 2000).

Pert, Dr. Candace. *Molecules of Emotion: The Science behind Mind-Body Medicine* (Simon & Schuster, 1999).

Radin, Dean. *The Conscious Universe* (HarperEdge, 1997).

Radin, Dean. *Entangled Minds: Extrasensory Experiences in a Quantum Reality* (Paraview Pocket Books, 2006).

Sheldrake, Rupert. *A New Science of Life* (Park Street Press, 1995).

Sheldrake, Rupert. *The Presence of the Past: Morphic Resonance and the Habits of Nature* (Park Street Press, 1995).

Shinn, Florence Scovel. *The Game of Life and How to Play It* (DeVorss & Company, 1978).

Talbot, Michael. *The Holographic Universe* (HarperCollins, 1991).

Targ, Russell. *Mind-Reach: Scientists Look at Psychic Abilities* (Hampton Roads Publishing, 2005).

Targ, Russell, and Jane Katra. *Miracles of Mind: Exploring Nonlocal Consciousness and Spiritual Healing* (New World Library, 1998).

Tipping, Colin C. *Radical Forgiveness: Making Room for the Miracle* (Quest Publishing & Distribution, 2002).

Tolle, Eckhart. *A New Earth: Awakening to Your Life's Purpose* (Plume Books, 2005).

Wilbur, Ken. *A Theory of Everything* (Shambhala, 2001).

Williams, Paul. *Das Energi* (Entwhistle Books, 1982).

Williams, Paul. *Remember Your Essence* (Entwhistle Books, 1999).

Wright, Machaelle Small. *Behaving as if the God in All Life Mattered,* 3rd Ed. (Perelandra, Ltd., 1997).

Wright, Machaelle Small. *Perelandra Garden Workbook: A Complete Guide to Gardening with Nature Intelligences* (Perelandra, 1993).

Young-Sowers, Meredith. *Agartha: A Journey to the Stars,* reprint (New World Library, 2006).

Young-Sowers, Meredith. *Spirit Heals: Awakening a Woman's Inner Knowing for Self-Healing,* 1st ed. (New World Library, 2007).

Young-Sowers, Meredith. *Wisdom Bowls: Overcoming Fear and Coming Home to Your Authentic Self* (New World Library, 2006).

Mayan

Calleman, Carl Johan. *The Mayan Calendar and the Transformation of Consciousness* (Inner Traditions, 2004).

Freidel, David, Linda Schele, and Joy Parker. *Maya Cosmos: Three Thousand Years on the Shaman's Path* (Perennial, 2001).

Jenkins, John Major. *Maya Cosmogenesis 2012* (Bear and Company, 1998).

Stray, Geoff. *Catastrophe or Ecstasy: Beyond 2012* (Vital Signs Publishing, 2005).

Remote Viewing

Buchanan, Lyn. *The Seventh Sense: The Secrets of Remote Viewing as Told by a "Psychic Spy" for the U.S. Military* (Pocket, 2003).

McMoneagle, Joseph. *Remote Viewing Secrets* (Hampton Roads Publishing, 2000).

Morehouse, David. *Remote Viewing: The Complete User's Manual for Coordinate Remote Viewing* (Sounds True, 2007).

Targ, Russell. *Limitless Mind: A Guide to Remote Viewing and Transformation of Consciousness* (New World Library, 2004).

Sacred Geometry

Melchizedek, Drunvalo. *The Ancient Secret of the Flower of Life,* Vol. 1 (Knight Technology Publications, 1999).

Michell, John. *The New View over Atlantis* (Thames and Hudson, 2001).

Pogačnik, Marko. *Sacred Geography: Geomancy: Co-creating the Earth Cosmos* (Lindisfarne Books, 2008).

Schneider, Michael. *A Beginner's Guide to Constructing the Universe: The Mathematical Archetypes of Nature, Art, and Science* (HarperPerennial, 1995).

Stewart, Malcolm. *Patterns of Eternity: Sacred Geometry and the Starcut Diagram* (Floris Books, 2010).

Subtle Energy and Energy Structures

Brennan, Barbara. *Hands of Light* (Bantam Books, 1988).

Brennan, Barbara. *Light Emerging: The Journey of Personal Healing* (Bantam Books, 1993).

Gerber, Richard, *Vibrational Medicine: The #1 Handbook of Subtle-Energy Therapies* (Bear & Company, 2001).

Judith, Anodea, and Selene Vega. *The Sevenfold Journey: Reclaiming Mind, Body and Spirit through the Chakras* (Crossing Press, 1993).

Myss, Caroline. *Anatomy of the Spirit: The Seven Stages of Power and Healing* (Three Rivers Press, 1997).

Pond, David. *Chakras for Beginners: A Guide to Balancing Your Chakra Energies* (Llewellyn, 1999).

Shumsky, Susan G., and Dannion Brinkley, *Exploring Auras: Cleansing and Strengthening Your Energy Field* (New Page Books, 2005).

Teeguarden, Iona Marsaa. *The Joy of Feeling: Bodymind Acupressure,* 2nd ed. (Japan Publications, 1987).

Websites

Training Centers

Astral projection: *www.monroeinstitute.org*

Energy awareness training: *www.explorationsinenergy.com*

Jin Shin Do Bodymind Acupressure: *www.jinshindo.org*

Pineal gland and cranial temple activation: *www.thespiritoflight.org*

Remote viewing: *www.virtualviewing.org*

Nature Cocreation and Flower Essence

Findhorn: *www.findhorn.org*

Flower Essences: *www.earthlightessences.com*

Perelandra: *www.perelandra-ltd.com*

A Place Called Hope, Inc.: *www.aplacecalledhoperaptors.com*

Consciousness Research, Teaching, and Products

The Academy for Future Science: *affs.org*

Dannion Brinkley: *www.facebook.com/DannnionBrinkley*

Circles Phenomenon Research: *www.colinandrews.net*

Edgar Cayce's Association for Research and Enlightenment: *www.edgarcayce.org*

Greater Reality: *www.greaterreality.com*

Healing Rhythms—Wild Divine: *www.unyte.com*

Inspiration: *www.creativethinkingwith.com*

The Institute for Consciousness Research: *www.icrcanada.org*

Institute of Noetic Sciences: *www.noetic.org*

Intentional Peace Experiment: *www.lynnemctaggart.com*
The Life of Gandhi: *www.mkgandhi.org*
Lucid Dreaming: *www.lucidity.com* and *www.world-of-lucid-dreaming.com*
Drunvalo Melchizedek: *www.drunvalo.net*
The Monroe Institute: *www.monroeinstitute.org*
Paradigm Research Group: *www.paradigmresearchgroup.org*
The Pleiadians, channeled by Barbara Marciniak: *www.pleiadians.com*
Prosperity: *www.abundance-and-happiness.com*, "Inspiration for Just About Everyone"
Remote Viewing Training: *www.corepotentials.ca/remote-viewing*
The Society of the Inner Light: *www.innerlight.org.uk*

Notes

Chapter 1

1. "First 3D Map of the Universe's Dark Matter Scaffolding," The European Space Agency, January 7, 2007, *www.esahubble.org*.

Chapter 2

1. Jonathan Haidt and James Morris, "Finding the Self in Self-Transcendent Emotions," *Proceedings of the National Academy of Sciences of the United States of America* 106, 19 (May 2009): 7687–7688.

Chapter 5

1. "Parallel Universes and the Many-Worlds Theory," *Universe Today,* accessed April 7, 2022, *www.universetoday.com*.
2. "Quantum Physics: David Bohm," *Space and Motion,* accessed May 4, 2022, *www.spaceandmotion.com*.

Chapter 6

1. David Bodanis, $E = mc^2$: *A Biography of the World's Most Famous Equation* (New York: Berkley Books, 2000).
2. Britannica, s.v. "Photon," accessed April 7, 2022, *www.britannica.com*.
3. Hans Jenny, *Cymatics: Bringing Matter to Life with Sound,* *www.youtube.com*.
4. Masaru Emoto, *The Hidden Messages in Water* (New York: Atria Books, 2011).

Chapter 7

1. Ronald E. Matthews, MS, "Harold Burr's Biofields: Measuring the Electromagnetics of Life," *Subtle Energies & Energy Medicine* 18, 2 (2007): 55–61.

2. Caroline Myss, *Anatomy of the Spirit: The Seven Stages of Power and Healing* (New York: Three Rivers Press, 1997).
3. Carlos Castaneda, *The Teachings of Don Juan: A Yaqui Way of Knowledge,* 3rd ed. (Berkeley: University of California Press, 2008).
4. Candace Pert, *Molecules of Emotion: The Science behind Mind-Body Medicine* (New York: Simon & Schuster, 1999).
5. Barbara Brennan, *Light Emerging: The Journey of Personal Healing* (New York: Bantam Books, 1993).
6. Barbara Marciniak, *Earth: Pleiadian Keys to the Living Library* (Rochester, VT: Bear and Company, 1995).

Chapter 8

1. Menas Kafatos and Robert Nadeau, *The Conscious Universe: Part and Whole in Modern Physical Theory* (New York: Springer-Verlag, 1999).
2. "First 3D Map of the Universe's Dark Matter Scaffolding," The European Space Agency, January 7, 2007, *www.esahubble.org*
3. Michael Talbot, *The Holographic Universe* (New York: HarperCollins, 1991).
4. Global Coherence Research | HeartMath Institute, *www.heartmath.org.*
5. Marie Jones and Larry Flaxman, *The Resonance Key* (Franklin Lakes, NJ: The Career Press, 2009).
6. Panagopoulos, Dimitris J., "Polarization: A Key Difference between Man-Made and Natural Electromagnetic Fields, in Regard to Biological Activity," *Scientific Reports,* 5 (October 2015).
7. James Lovelock, *Gaia: A New Look at Life on Earth* (Oxford, UK: Oxford University Press, 2000).
8. Bruce Cathie, *The Energy Grid: Harmonic 695: The Pulse of the Universe, The Investigation into the World Energy Grid* (Kempton, IL: Adventures Unlimited Press, 1997).
9. Ibid.
10. Rupert Sheldrake, *A New Science of Life: The Hypothesis of Morphic Resonance* (Rochester, VT: Park Street Press, 1995).
11. Lynne McTaggart. *The Intention Experiment: Using Your Thoughts to Change Your Life and the World* (New York: Atria Books: Reprint edition, 2008).
12. Tim Wallace-Murphy, *Hidden Wisdom: Secrets of the Western Esoteric Tradition* (New York: The Disinformation Company, 2010).
13. Maud Worcester Makemson, *The Book of the Jaguar Priest: A Translation of the Book of Chilam Balam of Tizimin* (New York: Henry Schuman, 1951).
14. *Planetary, weareplanetary.com.*
15. Alfred Watkins, *Old Straight Track: Its Mounds, Beacons, Moats, Sites and Mark Stones* (London, UK: Abacus Books, 1972).

16. Drunvalo Melchizedek, *The Ancient Secret of the Flower of Life,* Vol. 1 and Vol. 2 (Flagstaff, AZ: Light Technology Pub., 2000).

Chapter 9

1. Ken Dychtwald, *Bodymind* (New York: Tarcher Putman, 1986).
2. Candace Pert, *Molecules of Emotion: The Science Behind Mind-Body Medicine* (New York: Simon & Schuster, 1999).

Chapter 11

1. Dean Radin, *Entangled Minds: Extrasensory Experiences in a Quantum Reality* (New York: Paraview Pocket Books, 2006) pp. 164–169.
2. N. E. Thing Enterprises, *Magic Eye* (Kansas City, MO: Andrews and McMeel, 1993).

Chapter 14

1. Lynne McTaggart, *The Power of Eight: Harnessing the Miraculous Energies of a Small Group to Heal Others, Your Life, and the World* (New York: Simon and Schuster, 2018).

Chapter 16

1. Barbara Brennan, *Light Emerging: The Journey of Personal Healing* (New York: Bantam Books, 1993).

Chapter 17

1. Lynne McTaggart, *The Field: The Quest for the Secret Force of the Universe,* updated edition (New York: Harper Paperbacks, 2008) and Lynne McTaggart, *The Intention Experiment: Using Your Thoughts to Change Your Life and the World* (New York: Free Press, 2008).

Chapter 18

1. Heenam Yoon, Sang Ho Choi, et al., "Human Heart Rhythms Synchronize While Co-Sleeping," *Front Physiol.* 10, 190 (March 2019).
2. Michael Talbot, *The Holographic Universe,* (New York: HarperCollins, 1991).
3. Ibid., p. 53.
4. Dean Radin, *Entangled Minds: Extrasensory Experiences in a Quantum Reality* (New York: Paraview Pocket Books, 2006).
5. Ibid.

6. H. E. Puthoff, "CIA-Initiated Remote Viewing Program at Stanford Research Institute," *Journal of Scientific Exploration* 10, 1 (March 1996): 63–76.
7. Carlos Castaneda, *The Teachings of Don Juan: A Yaqui Way of Knowledge,* 3rd ed. (Berkeley: University of California Press, 2008).

Chapter 19

1. Chittaranjan Andrade and Rajiv Radhakrishnan, "Prayer and Healing: A Medical and Scientific Perspective on Randomized Controlled Trials," *Indian J Psychiatry* 51, 4 (Oct–Dec 2009): 247–253.
2. Matt Neason, "The Power of Visualization," *Sports Psychology Today,* accessed April 7, 2022, *www.sportspsychologytoday.com.*
3. Norman Doidge, MD, *The Brain That Changes Itself: Stories of Personal Triumph from the Frontiers of Brain Science* (New York: Penguin Publishing Group, 2007).
4. Dr. Robert Becker and Gary Seldon, *The Body Electric* (New York: Quill Press, 1985).
5. Dr. Richard Gerber, *Vibrational Medicine,* 3rd ed. (Rochester, VT: Bear & Company, 2001).
6. Dr. Franz Lutz and Hans Andeweg, *Resonance Therapy in Eight Steps* (Cappenberg, Germany: Institute for Resonance Therapy, 1995).
7. Dr. Ian Stevenson, *Children Who Remember Previous Lives: A Question of Reincarnation* (Jefferson, NC: McFarland & Company, 2000).
8. Renée Weber, *Dialogues with Scientists and Sages: The Search for Unity* (New York: Penguin [Non-Classics], 1990).
9. Dannion Brinkley and Paul Perry, *Saved by the Light: The True Story of a Man Who Died Twice and the Profound Revelations He Received* (San Francisco: HarperOne, 2008).

Chapter 20

1. David Freidel and Linda Schele, *A Forest of Kings: The Untold Story of the Ancient Maya* (New York: HarperPerennial, 1992).
2. John Major Jenkins, *Maya Cosmogenesis 2012: The True Meaning of the Maya Calendar End-Date* (Rochester, VT: Bear & Company, 1998).
3. Maud Worcester Makemson, *The Book of the Jaguar Priest: A Translation of the Book of Chilam Balam of Tizimin* (New York: Henry Schuman, 1951).
4. Dr. Robert Becker and Gary Seldon, *The Body Electric: Electromagnetism and the Foundation of Life* (New York: Quill Press, 1985).
5. Paramahansa Yogananda, *Autobiography of a Yogi* (Los Angeles: Self-Realization Fellowship, 2006).
6. Dr. Rick Strassman, *DMT: The Spirit Molecule* (Rochester, VT: Park Street Press, 2000).

7. Sidney B. Lang, et al., "Piezoelectricity in the Human Pineal Gland," *Bioelectrochemistry and Bioenergetics* 41, 2 (December 1996): pp. 191–195.

8. R. Krstić, "Pineal Calcification: Its Mechanism and Significance," *Journal of Trans, Supplementum 21* (1986): 415–32.

9. I. Galliani, E. Falcieri, et al., "A Preliminary Study of Human Pineal Gland Concretions: Structural and Chemical Analysis," *Bollettino della Societa Italiana di Biologia Sperimentale* 66, 7 (July 1990): 615–22.

10. Simon Baconnier, Sidney B. Lang, et al., "Calcite Microcrystals in the Pineal Gland of the Human Brain: First Physical and Chemical Studies," *Bioelectromagnetics* 23, 7 (October 2002): 488–95.

11. N. A. Belyavskaya, "Biological Effects Due to Weak Magnetic Field on Plants," *Advances in Space Research* 34, 7 (2004): 1566–74.

12. Renée Weber, *Dialogues with Scientists and Sages: The Search for Unity* (New York: Penguin [Non-Classics], 1990).

13. Ben Best, "Chapter 9—The Amygdala and the Emotions," *www.benbest. com.*

14. M. A. Persinger and K. Makarec, "The Feeling of a Presence and Verbal Meaningfulness in Context of Temporal Lobe Function: Factor Analytic Verification of the Muses?" *Brain and Cognition* 20, 2 (November 1992): 217–26.

15. Gary E. R. Schwartz and Linda G. S. Russek, "Registration of Actual and Intended Eye Gaze: Correlation with Spiritual Beliefs and Experiences," *Journal of Scientific Exploration* 13, 2 (1999): 213–29.

Chapter 21

1. Judith Orloff, *The Empath's Survival Guide* (Louisville, CO: Sounds True, 2017) Kindle Edition, p. 7.

2. Elaine Aron, *The Highly Sensitive Person, www.hsperson.com.*

3. Rollin McCraty, et al., "The Coherent Heart: Heart-Brain Interactions, Psychophysiological Coherence, and the Emergence of System-Wide Order," *Integral Review* 5, 2 (December 2009).

4. Lindsay M. Oberman, Jaime A. Pineda, et al., "The Human Mirror Neuron System: A Link between Action Observation and Social Skills," *Social Cognitive and Affective Neuroscience* 2, 1 (March 2007).

5. Alison C. Holland, Garret O'Connell, et al., "Facial Mimicry, Empathy, and Emotion Recognition: A Meta-Analysis of Correlations," *Cognition and Emotion.* 35, 1 (February 2021): 150–168. Epub September 13, 2020.

6. *The Brain with David Eagleman.* 2015. Episode 5, "Mirroring Others." Aired November 11, 2015, on PBS.

Conclusion

1. Florence Scovel Shinn, *The Game of Life and How to Play It* (Camarillo, CA: DeVorss & Company, 1978).

Index of Meditations

Index

guidance, 7
gut feelings, 98–99

H
Hara, 75, 111
Hara-line, 72, 84
Hartmann grid, 89
healing, body, 203–219
  awareness and, 207–208
  balancing chi and, 212–213
  conditions for, 205–206
  death and dying, 217–218
  energy field scanning and, 208–210
  energy structures, repairing, 213–215
  events and situations, 219
  flow and, 207
  information for guiding, 206
  old trauma, 215–217
  overview of, 203–204
  science in, 204–205
  through correspondence, 210–212
  vitality and, 206
healing, relationship, 176–179
  exercise, 177–178
Heart Chakra, 76–77
Highly Sensitive Persons (HSP), 237. *see also* Empaths
holograms, 59–62
  described, 59
  dimensions within, 60–61
  making of, 59–60
  meditations and, 62
  for seeing energy, 122–123
  singularity consciousness and, 61
holographic consciousness, ESP and, 192
Holographic Universe, The (Talbot), 62
hooks, 131–132
  exercise for removing, 135
human energy systems, 69–85. *see also* aura; chakras
  aura and, 70–72
  chakras and, 69–70, 72–73
  described, 69
  evolutionary structures, 82
  Hara-line and, 84
  higher-dimensional chakras and aura layers, 84–85
  interacting, 69–70
  Kundalini and, 83–84

layers of aura and chakras, 73–79, 80
  meditations for clearing aura and chakras, 79
  meridians and, 81–82
  Nadis and, 82
Hundredth Monkey Effect, 89

I
identity shifting, 250–251
illness, 105
imagination, 183–184
imbalance in relationships, 170–172
inner garden exercise, 150
inner knowing, 100
inner resources, developing. *see also individual headings*
  energy protection, 125–139
  overview of, 107
  personal power, 109–115
  subtle energy, 117–123
inner vision, 100
Institute of Resonance Therapy (IRT), 205
intention, 183–184
Intention Experiment, The (McTaggart), 90, 187
intuition, 98–99, 191

J
Jenkins, John Major, 223
Jenny, Hans, 65
Jones, Marie, 87
journals, 16

K
karma, transmuting, 163
karmic backlash, 138
  exercise for overcoming, 138–139
Ketheric/Causal Layer of aura, 79
kinesthetic sensations, 98
k'ul energy flows, 222
Kundalini, 74, 83–84
  resonance and, 226
  rising, energy disruption and, 128

L
ley lines, 88, 91
  connecting with, exercise, 152–153
Light Emerging: The Journey of Personal

About the Author

Synthia Andrews is a naturopathic doctor with a thirty-five-year career as a massage therapist and energy intuitive. Her work specializes in the underlying emotional and spiritual components of health and healing. She was on faculty for fifteen years at the Connecticut Center for Massage Therapy, taught in the Kripalu Yoga Institutes, School of Bodywork, and is an authorized teacher of the Jin Shin Do Foundation. For the past thirty years, she's joined her husband, research-author Colin Andrews, in the study of consciousness and spirituality.

She is coauthor of *Acupressure and Reflexology for Dummies* (Wiley, 2007), *The Complete Idiot's Guide to 2012* (Alpha Books, Penguin, 2008), and *The Complete Idiot's Guide to the Akashic Record* (Alpha Books, Penguin, 2010). She is author of *The Path of Emotions* (New Page Books, 2013), *The Path of Presence* (New Page Books, 2016), and *The Complete Idiot's Guide to Self-Hypnosis* (Alpha Books, Penguin, 2014).

Currently, Synthia's focus is on teaching private classes in Energy Awareness and Healing. She can be reached at *www.andrewshealing arts.com* and *www.explorationsinenergy.com*.